Eric and Sam introduce people from cities around the world who implement both the first and last sermons of Jesus, and have found that this kingdom he inaugurated brings both personal salvation and public transformation, with hope for people and places. This book is a terrific gift.

—Dr. Raymond Bakke, Chancellor, Bakke Graduate University of Ministry

This book allows you not only to see examples of churches around the world engaging their cities but also to synthesize their commonalities in a way that is transferable. My hope is that the fruit of this book will be an engaged church announcing the kingdom in clear, simple, and profound ways in the heart of our communities.

—Dr. Rick McKinley, Lead Pastor, Imago Dei Community

This book reminds us that with a kingdom-sized gospel, love for the city, and the humility to partner with others, God can use any church to bring deeper *shalom* to its community.

—Dr. Amy L. Sherman, Director, Sagamore Institute's Center on Faith in Communities

Eric and Sam offer theory that is transferable to every city, along with practices from their own experiences. I commend this book to every pastor and community leader who is committed to their city.

—Jim Herrington, Executive Director, Mission Houston

This book provides a construct for how to think about cities as well as a map for the church to take the gospel, in its fullness, to every sector of the city.

—Rev. S. Douglas Birdsall, USA Executive Chairman, the Lausanne Movement

This book helps us understand what it means to follow Jesus and to see our cities transformed. The authors' research is exceptional and thorough. Their concepts are proven by the stories they put forth. Read it, study it, reflect on it ... then practice it.

—Dr. Bob Roberts, Lead Pastor, NorthWood Church

This book is timely, with rich material to stimulate conversation, build conviction, and ignite the church to transform the cities of our world. I will read and reread this one.

—Carol Davis, Director, LeafLine Initiatives

Eric and Sam combine their theological insight, practical experience, and creative strategies for city transformation. I pray that passion will ignite the hearts of Christians around the globe to initiate and give themselves for city transformation.

— MARK VISVASAM, Chennai Transformation
Network, Chennai, India

I've waited a lifetime for this. I want to give this book to those whose toe is out the door and now need guidance in taking the next steps. We will make this book a text for training churches to transform their cities.

— KIT DANLEY, Founder and President,
Neighborhood Ministries

This book is a roadmap for city transformation. Read it, follow it, and your city will be changed for good.

— JIM TOMBERLIN, Church Consultant and Strategist,
Multi-Site Solutions

This primer on city ministry equips readers for a more strategic, kingdom-centered approach. If more Christians followed Jesus down this path of love, we would see seeds of transformation blossom — within our churches as well as our cities.

— HEIDI UNRUH, Congregations, Community
Outreach and Leadership Development Project

This book is a primer for taking the whole gospel to the whole city. It is a must-read guidebook for those engaged in kingdom transformation.

— KEVIN PALAU, President, Luis Palau Association

This book inspires us to build Christian community and position the church to move with God. It will quickly become required reading for anyone who desires to do serious kingdom damage!

— BILL YACCINO, Executive Director, Christ Together

This book is a great tool for missional leaders who are trying to figure out how to make a kingdom impact on the city.

— GREG LILLESTRAND, US Director, Communities in
the City, Campus Crusade for Christ

Eric and Sam helped us to develop an all-embracing and down-to-earth strategy to transform our city. I highly recommend their book to all who want to see their cities transformed by God's love and their own loving actions.

— KERSTIN HACK, Director, Down to Earth Media,
Berlin

Eric and Sam have written the book we've been waiting for. Their analysis provides new insight, and their assessment a clear perspective on how to love our communities for and with and to Christ.

— PHIL MIGLIORATTI, Mission America Coalition/
Loving Our Communities to Christ

Anyone serious about Jesus' mission will be wonderfully enriched, stretched, and encouraged by this book.

— DAN KIMBALL, Author, *They Like Jesus but Not the Church*

This book provides a better understanding of the *shalom* of Jeremiah 29:7, in reference to seeking the peace and prosperity and welfare of the whole city!

— LARRY E. CHRISTENSEN, Executive City Director,
New York, Campus Crusade for Christ

Eric and Sam are extraordinary guides for those who want to see real city transformation.

— AGUSTIN GARDUÑO, National Director, Leader
Impact Group, Mexico

This book provides the foundation of truth for "integral" urban mission.

— VIJU ABRAHAM, Association for Christian
Thoughtfulness (ACT), Mumbai, India

Eric and Sam took years off our learning curve by helping us see what needed doing and giving us the language to clearly articulate our mission.

— HOWARD WEBB, aka "Higgins," Coordinator, Love
Your Neighbour Network, New Zealand

Eric and Sam have written a masterpiece grounded in their experience in local situations and in their interaction with leaders of city movements nationally and internationally. This book has theological and sociological depth that will equip you for the work of societal transformation.

— DR. GLENN BARTH, President, GoodCities

This book is a well-written, comprehensive, inspirational, and practical theology of changing cities. I highly recommend it to senior pastors and others who want to make a difference in their cities and regions, and who need real-life ideas to make it happen.

— DR. GARY KINNAMAN, Author, Former Senior Pastor

Eric and Sam present theological and biblical insight for transforming a city. They share useful ideas and methods to engage the city whilst transforming it. It gives the reader a thorough understanding of the why and how-to of city transformation.

—RICHARD RAJOO, Marketplace Leadership Centre, Malaysia

Authentic and practical, yet grounded in good social theory and biblical truth, this book provides applicable principles, not cookie-cutter answers. Don't just read it; dive into it and stay a while.

—DON R. SIMMONS, PhD, Distinguished Lecturer, California State University, Fresno

This book is a great combination of principles and history, as well as stories of kingdom impact. It is a must-read for anyone who really wants to impact their city. Enjoy!

—CHIP SWENEY, Metro Outreach Pastor, Perimeter Church

We learned a lot from Eric and Sam's experience and implemented it in the vision and practice of our network. This book puts it all into written letters—comprehensible and workable. "Go and do likewise" . . . and multiply!

—AXEL NEHLSEN, Director, Together for Berlin

Read this book and get ready to see the raw power of God at work transforming lives. Maybe even your own.

—BARBARA J. ELLIOTT, Author, *Street Saints: Renewing America's Cities*

As the church recalibrates toward its missional beauty, practitioners will lead the way. In this book, you'll learn from proven leaders, and you might even save decades of frustration by taking four hours to read every page.

—HUGH HALTER, Coauthor, *The Tangible Kingdom* and *AND*

TO TRANSFORM
A CITY

FOREWORD BY REGGIE McNEAL

TO TRANSFORM A CITY

WHOLE CHURCH
WHOLE GOSPEL
WHOLE CITY

ERIC SWANSON   SAM WILLIAMS

ZONDERVAN®

ZONDERVAN.com/
AUTHORTRACKER
follow your favorite authors

ZONDERVAN

To Transform a City
Copyright © 2010 by Eric Swanson and Sam Williams

This title is also available as a Zondervan ebook. Visit www.zondervan.com/ebooks.

This title is also available in a Zondervan audio edition. Visit www.zondervan.fm.

Requests for information should be addressed to:

Zondervan, *Grand Rapids, Michigan 49530*

Library of Congress Cataloging-in-Publication Data

Swanson, Eric, 1950 –
    To transform a city : whole church, whole Gospel, whole city / Eric Swanson and Sam Williams.
        p. cm.
    Includes bibliographical references (p. 209).
    ISBN 978-0-310-32586-4 (hardcover, jacketed) 1. City churches. 2. Cities and towns —
Religious aspects — Christianity. 3. Communities — Religious aspects — Christianity. I.
Williams, Sam, 1943 –. II. Title.
    BV637.S93 2010
    266.00973'091732 — dc22   2010010795

Published in association with the literary agency of Mark Sweeney & Associates, Bonita Springs, Florida 34135

Cover design: Tammy Johnson
Cover photography: Fotosearch
Interior design: Matthew VanZomeren

Printed in the United States of America

---

13 14 15 /DCI/ 23 22 21 20 19 18 17 16 15 14 13 12 11 10 9 8 7 6 5

To Scott Beck,
who launched us into the adventure
of cities with two simple words:
"Love Boulder"

CONTENTS

FOREWORD

Jesus loved parties. For good reason. His Father has a penchant for them. Jesus once said that angels are having parties in heaven all the time; then he told a story about a wayward son's return home that included a party, just so we could understand the Father's love for parties. In another parable, Jesus has servants of the King relentlessly issuing invitations until the banquet hall gets filled, so determined is the Lord of the banquet to have a party. Jesus himself went to parties often. Sometimes he was a celebrated guest, sometimes not (though Simon the Pharisee's slight couldn't cancel the celebration). Jesus performed his first miracle at a party and promised his disciples that the Father is planning a honkin' good time when we all get to heaven.

If we claim to be Jesus' followers, then we need to pick up on this part of his missional methodology. It's time for the church to call a party! A special kind of party. Not a party where people are invited to come in. Rather it's a street party. The church is not the honoree; the community is. It's a party where the church acts as host and servant, just like Jesus did at his last earthly party with his disciples. It's not a party to build up the church. It's a party to strengthen the community.

So why aren't we addressing and sending out invitations? Why do we instead occupy ourselves with "doing church" and watering down Jesus' promise of abundant life as something reserved for people who busy themselves with church activity? Why do we often act more like the older brother who seemed allergic to parties? Why do we hoard our resources for ourselves, putting out midnight buffets on the cruise ship for already-sated club members?

It's time for the church to call a party!

I think the answer lies in the church's self-understanding. For centuries, we have seen the church as a *what*, something outside ourselves. It is a building on the corner of Third and Main. It is an organization we belong to, we support, we serve and pray for. We "go to church" and invite others to do the same. We hire people to run it. In exchange, we expect *it* to provide *us* (as something differentiated from *it*) a program of spiritual growth. In the past few years, we have focused lots of attention on making the church "successful," as measured by its organizational growth and health.

Seeing the church as a *what* has resulted in a church-centric approach to our understanding of mission. That has in turn created our perspective on how the church fits into our culture (see fig. 1).

In figure 1 the various components, or "domains," of our culture are pictured as silos. This compartmentalization of society is a signature development of the modern world and its increasing complexity. The church's response to this world was to build its own silo. We developed a full-blown parallel church culture complete with media, entertainment, education, recreation, you name it. Our methodology for constructing our silo was attractional marketing with a con-sumer/customer-service orientation. We thought that if we built better churches, we would have better people and communities.

The results of this approach have been stunningly poor. With annual receipts of over $100 billion in the United States for all religious causes, we do indeed have the best churches humanity can build. We have Six Flags Over Jesus. How-ever, our communities aren't any better. Nor are people who show up every week to support the church. When asked, they "reveal" that they are not a bit happy with their spiritual development, and their lifestyles typically don't reflect anything distinctively Jesus-like. On top of all of this, an increasing number of people in our culture simply want nothing to do with this organized institutional religious activity we call church. Simply put, church as a *what* isn't cutting it!

In the New Testament, the church is not a *what*; it's a *who*. Jesus is identified as the head not of a corporation but of a body. He is not a senior partner in a corporation; he is a spouse in a marriage. In other words, the church is *people*. Missional followers of Jesus see *themselves* as the church. I am the church if I

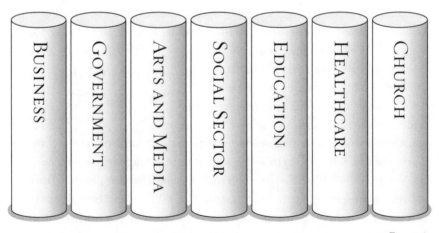

Figure 1

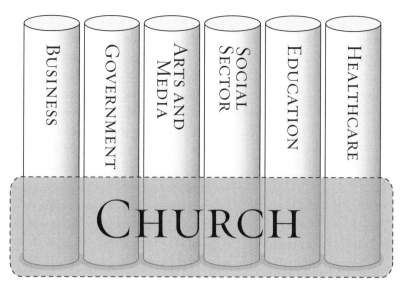

Figure 2

am united with Christ; so are you. I am not *all* the church and neither are you, but we *are* the church nonetheless. This means that *everywhere* you and I are, the church is present. We are as much the church on Monday at work as we are anytime we gather with other followers of Jesus for designated church stuff. You and I, as the continuing incarnation of Jesus in the world, are supposedly acting as salt and light in our worlds.

This means that church as a *who* sees its relationship with culture very differently. Take a look at figure 2.

The missional church sees itself as the *people of God* (a *who*) already deployed across all domains of culture. These life-place assignments have been made by a God who desires to plant the incarnational presence of his Son everywhere, because God so loves *the world*, not just the church. Whereas "doing church" builds the church silo (a *what*) in our first diagram, "being church" (as a *who*) in this diagram releases the church to impact the world—right where God's people already are.

Clearly, this church is what the New Testament has in mind. As this book points out, there is no reference in the New Testament to church that is smaller than a city. Only church as a *what* can have us talking about "a" church in town. The biblical notion of church as a *who* would lead us into a discussion of "the" church in town. Competing *what*s can't think like this; only *who*s can.

> In the New Testament, the church is not a *what*; it's a *who*.

Church as *who* fulfills the covenant that God first made with Abraham when God created a people to partner with him in his redemptive mission in the world. That covenant indicates that we have been blessed to bless. Simply put, we are the blessing people. That is both our distinct privilege and our distinct responsibility. In our blessing of the world, we live out the passion that God has to bless all people so that they know this about him and are drawn to him. It means that the church does not have a mission; the mission has a church. The mission is God's. It is redemptive, addressing everything that sin marred across the entire bandwidth of the human condition. It is a mission being played out in the world beyond just God's people. In this biblical understanding of the church, we grasp that the church is not the point; the mission is the point. We have been created to be boots-on-the-ground partners.

> The condition of our communities is the scorecard on how well the church is doing at being the people of God.

On a macro scale, this view of church means that every community should be better if the church gets the mission right. The scorecard can no longer be about how well our individual congregations are doing. The condition of our communities is the scorecard on how well the church is doing at being the people of God.

That's where this book comes in. Eric Swanson and Sam Williams are the two best party planners I know in helping you pull off a kingdom fest fit for a city. With decades of experience between them, and dozens of engagements with cities around the globe, they bring a rich portfolio of insight and expertise for how the church can practice being the church through serving the city. I can't imagine trying this without their guidance.

For those of you yearning to see this festival break out, Eric and Sam have provided the party tools you need. They have finally put down their best party tips in *To Transform a City*, from ideas on how to inspire those you lead to get in a festive mood (theological and biblical insight) to advice on how to word the invitation (guidelines for practicing collaboration) to hints on what to do when the party gets going (methodologies for service).

So ... what are you waiting for? Call the party!

—Reggie McNeal
Missional Leadership Specialist, Leadership Network
Author, *The Present Future* and *Missional Renaissance*

ACKNOWLEDGMENTS

We are so grateful for our wives and life partners, Eric's Liz and Sam's Nancy, who have stood by us, encouraging us to take the biggest bite of what God has put before us. We could not imagine doing what we do without your love and encouragement. Thanks for the long tether that always draws us home.

We'd also like to thank our friend Krista Petty from Backyard Impact and Ryan Pazdur, Ben Irwin, Brian Phipps, and the team at Zondervan for their passion, thoroughness, and attention to detail in giving editorial oversight to this project.

Eric is especially grateful to Bob Buford, Tom Wilson, Dave Travis, Reggie McNeal, Gary Dungan, and his friends and fellow laborers at Leadership Network.

INTRODUCTION

In the fall of 1998, my (Eric's) friend and soon-to-be employer Scott Beck called together a small group of friends and Christian leaders from Boulder, Colorado, to fast every Thursday and then meet at his house at 7:00 p.m. for a couple of hours of prayer followed by dinner at Denny's. Scott was a very successful entrepreneur in his early forties and was divesting himself of some of his larger business engagements at this time in his life. Forever generous and giving, he was looking for new ways to bless others as a result of being blessed. As we gathered, our prayers began focusing on our own community. We prayed for the city leaders of Boulder by name, using the local newspaper to guide us. We asked God for direction and guidance and talked about impacting our city. We brainstormed about clever billboard campaigns, evangelistic efforts, athletic ministries, dinners for city leaders ... but nothing with a sense of authenticity seemed to resonate with us. After a couple of months of concerted prayer, Scott said he had gotten from the Lord what we were fasting and praying for. "It's just two words." We all waited in anticipation. "This is what the Lord is saying: 'Love Boulder!'" That was it. When we asked him for clarification, all he could say was, "Love Boulder!" That was our direction. It was not about reaching Boulder, converting Boulder, changing Boulder; it was about *loving* Boulder. It was a simple message but something that guided our steps into the future.

FEEBLE ATTEMPTS OF LOVE

How do we love a city? Sometimes we are held captive by our past experience and we can only envision a future that consists of doing more of or doing better what we have done in the past. As a group of pastors and Christian leaders, we were becoming familiar with the concept of "one church in the city," so together we sponsored two full-color, full-page ads at Christmas and Easter, sponsored by "the church in Boulder, meeting in the following locations ..." They were totally lame, cost several thousand dollars, and no one came to church because of them, but honestly it was the best thing that white, middle-aged evangelicals could do to express love for the city—we took out an ad in the paper!

In the spring of 1999, we held our first four-day pastors' prayer retreat at St. Malo's Retreat Center near Estes Park. I had picked up the idea from a friend from Toowoomba, Australia (go figure!). His counsel led us to contact International Renewal Ministries (IRM) out of Portland, Oregon. Our first prayer retreat was a great time of reconciliation, fellowship, and corporate and personal prayer, but we still had no idea of how we could love Boulder.

To figure that out, we had to build the plane as we were flying it. Having access to some financial resources, we sought to strengthen marriages in our community through marriage conferences. This was a step in the right direction but not yet what we were looking for. In the spring of 2000, Scott hired Sam specifically to work with pastors of Boulder County. Scott had heard Sam speak at a men's retreat and drove him to the airport, pumping him with questions, and liked what he heard. In addition to successfully leading and planting churches, Sam had experienced transformational ministry in Marin County, which you'll learn about later in the book. Sam and I had been close friends for over thirty years, and my wife, Liz, and I were delighted when he and Nancy moved to Boulder. However, we were still uncertain what shape "Love Boulder" would take.

BREAKTHROUGH

At our fourth pastors' prayer retreat, we had a breakthrough in our approach to the city that helped shape the theology of what we were experiencing with the city officials. (More about that later.) We devoted one evening to praying for the city. Pastors were praying the usual militant prayers to "take our city for God" and "bring down the stronghold" and for the church to be triumphant in the city and resume its rightful place in the city. But something didn't sit right. After breakfast the next morning, as we gathered for prayer, one leader spoke up. "I don't know what it is, but when you get a bunch of male pastors in the room praying, sometimes what happens is more an expression of male testosterone than the Holy Spirit. I don't think our prayers last night reflect the heart of Jesus for the city. He wept over the city and wanted to gather the city to himself." He then turned to Jeremiah 29:7 and read, "[S]eek the peace and prosperity of the city to which I have carried you into exile. Pray to the LORD for it, because if it prospers, you too will prosper." Wow! After some discussion, we decided that everything we did toward the city would be an expression of love for the city. We

> We would seek the welfare of the city ... and that changed everything!

would not condemn the city; we would look for ways to bless the city. If Jeremiah's tribe could seek the peace and prosperity of Babylon, the city of their captors, we could do the same for Boulder. We would seek the welfare of the city … and that changed everything! We were discovering what it meant to love Boulder.

THE MAGIC BUS TOUR

As we talked about loving our city, one pastor said, "I don't know how to love the city, because I don't know the city. If I needed to show someone where the homeless shelter was, I wouldn't know where to take him." Other pastors nodded in agreement. So we organized what came to be known as The Magic Bus Tour. Sam set up appointments with the executive directors of the eight largest human-services agencies in Boulder — the shelter for the homeless, the food bank, the home for runaway youth, and so on. Riding in a rented minibus, the pastors spent the day visiting each of the eight agencies, ending at the Boulder County AIDS project. At each agency, the staff told what they did and how churches could help them. At the AIDS project, the pastors ended up praying for the staff and volunteers of this difficult "ministry," and one of the pastors of one of our most theologically conservative churches ended up volunteering there, taking meals to homebound patients and coordinating other volunteers to serve.

LITTLE ROCK

After reading Robert Lewis's *The Church of Irresistible Influence*,[1] we decided to rent a larger bus and took thirty-five pastors and parachurch leaders to Fellowship Bible Church in Little Rock, Arkansas, to be part of the Church of Irresistible Influence conference. Why we decided to take a bus and stop at every Cracker Barrel restaurant between Boulder and Little Rock is now beyond us. It was a grueling twenty-hour ride each way, it was all but impossible to sleep, and the greasy food gave us indigestion, but the fellowship and camaraderie were priceless. We all experienced what a church could be in relationship to the community.

Leaders went back intent on discovering how we could be good news to our community. Believing that we don't need to duplicate human services, churches began forming partnerships with human-services agencies, with the firm conviction that we can partner with any organization that is morally positive and spiritually neutral. The director of one human-services agency said to leaders of my own church, "I never thought an organization like ours would be partnering with an organization like yours." Churches lined up to house the homeless one night of the week during the seven coldest months of the year. Schools were adopted with the understanding that the church would be there, not just actively helping but also acting as a safety net for kids who needed a backpack, winter coat, or pair of shoes. This happened organically. Decisions were not made, nor were assignments given, by fiat from the top down. Individuals and churches began gravitating toward areas of highest need. Articles about the church began appearing on the front page of the newspaper, enthusiastically embracing and lauding what God's people were doing in "letting their light shine." Instead of the pastors writing copy and buying space to tell the community about church (remember our lame ads?), because Christians were simply loving and serving, others were writing the articles ... and it was all free! Momentum was starting to grow. Love Boulder was sprouting wings.

In that same spirit, we sponsored a series of pastors' luncheons where we invited city officials to give us insight as to what loving a city might look like. At a minimum, we could love Boulder by loving these officials who served our city. One pastor had done a great job building relationships with the leaders of our city, and it seemed that when he asked leaders to join us for lunch ... they showed up. We brought in the mayor, the editor of the newspaper, the chief of the fire department, the chief of police, the city manager, the city planner, the heads of our two school districts, the university president, the district attorney, and so on. We asked each of them to tell us what they did, their vision for a healthy city, and three impossible things they needed to accomplish that no person could do for them. These three things became prayer requests for these officials, and we ended our times praying for these leaders and enthusiastically blessing them, regardless of their religious persuasion. We told them, "This is what pastors do; we pray for people." Some cool things began to happen. After being prayed for, one leader said, "This was one of the greatest days of my life." Another official said, "I know people pray for me, but in my whole life I've never heard anyone pray for me." Our district attorney asked if she could come back to be with the pastors a second time after all three of her "impossible requests" were amazingly fulfilled — a conviction on a tough case, reconciliation with her daughter, and even she herself getting married! She now had three more requests. Some of our city leaders were coming to faith, and we were beginning to understand the power of love.

Kingdom Assignments

In the fall of 2002, we (Sam and Eric) attended a Generous Giving conference in Southern California. During the conference, we heard Denny and Leesa Bellesi speak on what they called "kingdom assignments." When we heard the concept, we knew what to do. It would be our next step in loving Boulder. We returned to Boulder and told the pastors what we had seen and heard. Two churches took us up on the offer to fund a kingdom assignment. We'll tell one church's story here.

In June of 2003, inspired by the Bellesis' book *The Kingdom Assignment*,[2] senior pastor Tom Shirk of Calvary Bible Church preached on the parable of the talents and then handed out crisp hundred-dollar bills to 110 people and asked them to multiply this money for the kingdom and give the money to something God cares about. In three months the money had been leveraged into over fifty thousand dollars and given to plant churches, to support Sudanese refugees, and to aid the Boulder County Safe House, Boulder Shelter for the Homeless, and a myriad of other kingdom causes.

But more kingdom assignments were coming. In September 2003, Tom preached on Luke 12:16–34 on the dangers of loving possessions. He followed the message by challenging families and individuals to sell a "treasure" between September and Thanksgiving and bring the proceeds back to Calvary. Two hundred people responded by holding garage sales and by selling timeshares, big-screen TVs, and even a Rolex watch. By November these two hundred people brought in well over eighty thousand dollars, which was given to three human-services agencies in town that serve the poor and to two churches as seed money to begin their own kingdom assignments.

Momentum was growing. Four hundred people from Calvary signed up for Kingdom Assignment III in January of 2004. Their assignment was to give ninety minutes over the next ninety days to serve "the least of these" (Matt. 25:31–46) in a tangible way. To facilitate engagement, Calvary invited thirty-five human-services agencies and ministries to Calvary for a community service fair. Kingdom Assignment III was followed that Easter with a fourth kingdom assignment designed to bring the message of Easter to those outside the church.

In June of 2004, for the first time in Calvary Bible Church's 115-year history, Tom asked the community not to come to church on Sunday but instead to go to the community. Seven hundred people, representing 90 percent of the families who attend Calvary, worked all day Saturday and three hours on Sunday morning painting, landscaping, cleaning, and refurbishing the three schools as part of "KA5 — Extreme Makeover: Boulder Valley Schools Edition." They painted forty classrooms and dozens of hallways. They scraped a pound of gum from the underside of desks, tables, and railings. Working in intergenerational teams, they washed windows and trimmed bushes and restriped the parking lots. Artists from Calvary painted two huge murals at the elementary school. They cleaned the dust from every pipe and vent. As the work drew to a close, some folks went room by room, offering up prayers of blessing and thanks for the teachers, staff, and students of each room (Jer. 29:7). They wrote three hundred personal letters of appreciation to the teachers and staff of the schools. In all, they gave over six thousand hours of work and three thousand dollars' worth of paint and materials to bless these three schools. The work project was followed by a worship and celebration service held in the auditorium of the high school they cleaned. The entire weekend culminated in a barbecue and community blood drive in the parking lot of the high school. In 2004, Calvary Bible Church received the Colorado Governor's Award for the Volunteer Organization of the Year as recognition of its commitment to the community.

Momentum Continues

Since 2004, in addition to the ongoing engagements by individual churches, a growing number of churches have come together for an annual weekend of community service called ShareFest (a name borrowed from the Nehemiah Group in Little Rock). This past year, for instance, over thirty-five hundred people from thirty-five churches worked on fifty different sites around Boulder County and north Denver. Families and businesspeople, government officials, teachers and pastors all pitch in to make a sustainable difference in the community. The financial impact on schools and organizations was valued at over six hundred thousand dollars.

We like to say, "As difficult as it is to learn to surf, it's still far easier to catch a wave than to cause a wave," and churches engaging their cities with deeds and words of love is a wave God is causing. We are the first to admit that we are rookies — rhinestone urban missionaries who can't hold a candle to the labor others in the city have done and are so faithfully doing. We both live in suburbia. But we also believe that "when the tinder is dry, any spark will do." And if God is using us to spark something that is on his heart, we readily want to play that role.

> "As difficult as it is to learn to surf, it's still far easier to catch a wave than to cause a wave."

Who This Book Is For

For the past several years, we have been engaging with city leaders in cities large and small in the United States and around the world. Broadly speaking, this book is for anyone who has an interest in cities and for those who want to have a part in what God is doing in and through the city. Since 2007, more people live in cities than in rural areas—and that is a trend that will never reverse. To effectively serve God's purposes in the future, we must come to *understand* the city.

This book is for those who want to live missionally. That's an important concept to grasp, especially for the times we live in today. Our understanding of the church is shifting from seeing it as a place where the many send the few ("Lord, thank you for raising up that dear, sacrificial family to faithfully work in Guatemala") to seeing it as a place where the few equip and send the many (Eph. 4:11–12). Missional thinking embraces the belief that God intends for every one of his children to be living on mission, partnering with him in his redemptive mission in the world.

This book is also for the "city reachers." We purposefully shy away from that term in this book, since there are very few cities that really want to be "reached." But you know who you are—a select group of people with an overenlarged heart and the capacity to embrace a vision for ministry larger than a single church. You think about the kingdom. You think about the broken. You think about who needs to be at the table. Though often misunderstood and underappreciated (and always underfunded), you have the call of God on your life. We want to encourage you: don't give up! Cities are the future of the church, and God has positioned you where you are for such a time as this.

How This Book Is Laid Out

In the midst of writing this book, we watched the United States engage in a heated presidential race. Inevitably the question "Who is more qualified?" regularly came up. Isn't it interesting that although our founding fathers, when determining the qualifications for president, could have included things like the number of years of executive, legislative, or judicial experience, they instead specified only three qualifications: the person has to be a natural-born citizen, has to be at least thirty-five years of age, and must have resided in the United States for fourteen years. That's it! The founders assumed that succeeding generations could figure out the specifics. In the same way, we aren't going to lay out too many specifics that may or may not apply to your particular situation. We are assuming that you are qualified for that task and can figure out the painful specificities at the local level. Because we want to wrap ourselves around big *ideas* as well as a big *ideal*, you will find that this is not really a tactical or how-to book, though we do try to give examples and suggest effective tactics to illustrate what we are saying. We are intentionally writing this book at the strategic level, talking about the whole city, in the hope that this book will lead to local application of the vision we present.

We write to help you understand how to *think* about cities. We write about the importance of cities and what it looks like for cities to be transformed. Because cities are far larger than churches, we are writing about the kingdom and how the whole church can bring the whole gospel — in word and deed — to the whole city. Can you think of anything more exciting than that? At the end of each chapter, we have done our best to formulate and include questions that will lead you to reflect and challenge you to think. These will also serve as good questions to talk about with a larger team of people who love your city. We believe that cities can and will be transformed, but it will take a change in thinking ... not in degree but in kind.

> We believe that cities can and will be transformed, but it will take a change in thinking ... not in degree but in kind.

We've also included some diagrams in the book. Feel free to copy them and adapt them to your setting. We believe that visually illustrating a concept helps us to discover new relationships between ideas, to learn what is missing and how to serve God's purposes more effectively. We encourage you to draw your own circles and quadrants and arrows and vectors to help you see and understand the task in front of us. Share what you are learning with others. Help spread the message!

OUR MISSION

For the past few years, we have adopted this mission for our lives: "To change the world by engaging the church worldwide in the needs and dreams of their communities so as to bring about spiritual and societal transformation." This mission statement is not something we want to leave written in a notebook or engraved on a plaque on the wall. We want it to be written on our hearts in such a way that we are able to say yes or no appropriately when opportunities arise.

Finally, we invite you to join us as a co-laborer in this mission. The word translated as "fellow worker" (used some thirteen times in the New Testament) is the Greek word *synergos*, from which comes the English word *synergy*. We like to think of synergy as the force that allows us to play off of and

> "To change the world by engaging the church worldwide in the needs and dreams of their communities so as to bring about spiritual and societal transformation."

maximize our individual strengths. None of us, as individuals, can ever be as smart as all of us working together. When synergy occurs, we are able to exceed our individual potential: 1+1=>2. As co-laborers, we not only accomplish more, but we also become better people in the process of sharing the load. That's what this book is about. Will you join us in the work as we seek to better understand what God is doing in and through the cities of this world?

CHAPTER ONE

THE IMPORTANCE OF CITIES

The city dweller becomes someone else because of the city. And the city can become something else because of God's presence and the results in the life of a man who has met God. And so a complex cacophony raises its blaring voice, and only God can see and make harmony of it.

—Jacques Ellul, *The Meaning of the City*

On Wednesday, May 23, 2007, Shao Zhong, clutching a black plastic bag filled with all his possessions, shuffled off the train onto the platform of Beijing's West Railway station. He was from a small rural village in the Shaanxi province and had arrived at the city to work in a factory with several others from his village. Shao Zhong was moving to the city that day and was one of over three hundred thousand passengers arriving at the station. But unbeknownst to him, his arrival at that moment signaled a historic event. Shao's arrival in Beijing that morning tipped the global demographic scales from a rural to an urban majority. There are now, scattered around the globe, more people living in cities than in the rural areas of the world. Most important, this is an irreversible trend. For the rest of human history, the earth's population will be more urban than rural.[3] We believe that this historic shift has huge implications for the mission of the church as we seek to transform our communities.

WHAT IS A CITY?

As we begin to think about cities and their transformation, it is helpful to begin by defining exactly what we mean by a *city*. Is a city different than a town or a village or a hamlet?[4] Is a city defined by the size of the population, its place and geography, or its function ... or some combination of all three? In the early years after the founding of the United States, Americans were quick to confer the title of *city* on almost any small settlement. In 1871, for example, the city we know today as Boulder, Colorado, was incorporated under the great name of Boulder City—but it was really nothing more than a small mining settlement. The same was true for "cities" like Dodge City, Kansas; Silver City, Nevada; and hundreds of other small towns across the United States that added the impressive-sounding surname. Defining a city is not as easy as one might think. All cities are not defined equally, regardless of what they are named.

In his beautifully illustrated book *The City Shaped*, Spiro Kostof refers to two popular definitions for the term *city*: "Two sensible definitions, both from 1938, would allow us a good starting point. For L. Wirth, a city is a 'restively large, dense,' and permanent settlement of socially heterogeneous individuals.' For Mumford, a city is a 'point of maximum concentration for the power and culture of a community.'"[5]

Words like *dense, permanent*, and *heterogeneous* are helpful terms to get us started. Clearly, cities involve a certain concentration of people in a limited geographic area. Richard Sennett defines a city as "a human settlement in which strangers are likely to meet."[6] He goes on to suggest that "for this definition to hold true, the settlement has to have a large, heterogeneous population, the population has to be packed together rather densely; market exchanges among the population must make this dense, diverse mass interact."[7] In other words, at the most basic level, cities are groups of people densely packed together. But size and density of the population don't really capture the full picture of a city, so we'd like to consider a more practical, simple definition for the purposes of this book.

A WORKING DEFINITION

Rather than working our way through ever more complex sociological definitions, we'd prefer to start with a minimalist definition for a city that goes beyond mere matters of size and population density. In the spring of 2008, I (Eric) attended a three-day conference in New York City called Q, sponsored by the Fermi Project,[8] and listened to Tim Keller speak on cities. Tim is the founding pastor of Redeemer Presbyterian Church in Manhattan—an influential church that has helped to plant over ninety churches in New York City. He is also one of the clearest-thinking emerging voices on cities. Keller defined a city that day as "a walkable, shared, mixed-use, diverse area. It is a place of commerce, residence, culture, and politics." We like that definition because it defines a city by utility and function rather than the size of the population. It is a definition that is both scalable and culturally transferable. Each of the words in the definition was chosen carefully and crafted to express the unique and inherent function of any city: *walkable, shared, mixed-use, diverse, a place of, commerce, residence, culture, politics.* This is a definition that works for Mexico City (provided you are willing to walk for a long, long time) and Mumbai, India, as well as San Diego, California, and Boulder, Colorado. We've found that it's a definition that works for just about any "city" you find yourself in. Occasionally we'll also use the term *community* in this book in a way that is interchangeable with the word *city*, but in either case we are referring to the place where you live, work, play, and interact with others in the ways that Keller has defined for us.

> "A city is a walkable, shared, mixed-use, diverse area. It is a place of commerce, residence, culture, and politics" (Tim Keller).

WHAT GOOD CITIES NEED

In defining cities, it will also be important for us to think about what cities have needed in order to thrive and grow throughout different stages of human history. Joel Kotkin, writing in his book *The City: A Global History*, provides some insight for us. He writes, "Since the earliest origins, urban areas have performed three separate critical functions—the creation of sacred space, the provision of basic security, and the host for a commercial market. Cities have possessed these characteristics to greater or lesser degrees. Generally speaking, a glaring weakness in these three aspects of urbanity has undermined life and led to their eventual decline."[9]

Kotkin suggests that there are three critical functions—sacred space, security, and a commercial market—that every city must provide for its people. Church leaders who want to engage in holistic, kingdom-minded ministry in and to the city must learn to recognize and engage deeply in all three spheres. We'll address this more in later chapters, but at this point it is important to recognize these key, critical functions of every city.

WHAT MAKES A MODERN CITY?

Cities have been around for thousands of years, but modern cities have developed and grown over the last several decades as they have benefited from technological innovations and scientific developments. In particular, three transforming innovations have been essential in creating the booming, modern cities of our world.[10] The first innovation that makes possible the modern city is the passenger elevator, first put into service in 1857 in New York City. The elevator allows millions of people to live in vertical space rather than simply spreading out horizontally. The elevator brought significant economic shifts to building construction by altering the values of the different floors. Before the invention of the elevator, the cheapest rent was usually found on the highest floors. After all, who would ever want to climb twenty flights of stairs lugging a pound of cheese, a bag of flour, and a half gallon of milk? But after the installation of elevators, the upper floors went for the premium prices, as they had the best views and were farther away from the street noise and the traffic.

The second great innovation that makes possible the modern city is the steel-framed building (1884–85). This innovation, now found in countries all over the world, allows for the construction of buildings that soar well over one hundred stories high. In cities like Hong Kong, Dubai, and Shanghai, where the cost of labor is cheaper than the cost of materials, skyscrapers not only are functional in design but also are themselves works of art. The tallest buildings of the twentieth century were the Petronas Twin Towers of Kuala Lumpur, each tower standing over twelve hundred feet high. But these are not just functional buildings. The towers combine stainless steel with glass, melding beauty and functionality to give the dwellers the most prestigious address in Malaysia. Standing next to one of the towers on a recent trip, we were astounded by the quality of the craftsmanship and the artistry of the buildings. They are truly breathtaking.

The third great innovation that allows modern cities to thrive (and survive) is air-conditioning. First made economically feasible in 1902, when it was installed in the New York Stock Exchange building, air-conditioning is what makes it possible for significant work to be accomplished indoors, even in the sweltering heat of summer in the tropical and subtropical areas of the world (or in your home office, for that matter). When people are asked to rank the greatest inventions of the twentieth century, air-conditioning is always near the top of the list.

NEW URBANISM

Not all of the developments in modern cities have been positive, and more recent movements are offering a corrective alternative to the mistakes of the past. In response to the rise of modern cities characterized by isolated high-rise buildings, many urban planners today are advocating smaller, mixed-use, walkable urban spaces. These are the spaces that are driving much of the revitalization of urban living. More and more families and individuals are eschewing the sterility of the suburbs and returning to redesigned urban centers where they can experience the vitality of city life. Writing on behalf of this new urban movement, Eric Jacobsen defines the new urbanism as "a movement of architects, builders, city planners, and lay persons that advocates development based upon principles of historic downtowns and traditional neighborhoods."[11] If you look around your city (in the United States), you will probably find that when an old shopping mall is torn down, it is usually replaced by buildings and structures built on the architectural values of this new urbanism. The new community that emerges consists of local businesses, eating establishments, entertainment areas, affordable housing, and common space all designed so that (in theory) people can live, work, learn, and play in this new urban community.

THREE CITY MODELS

Even with our working definition of a city, we should also note that not all cities were designed or settled with the same purpose or function in mind. Canadian-American architect Kevin Lynch suggests there have always been distinct ways of thinking about the design and layout of cities. He proposes three conceptual city models.[12] The first model is what he calls the "cosmic" model of cities. These are cities whose spatial layout reflects the symbolic representation of a belief system. As an example, ancient Chinese capital cities were laid out in perfect squares, with their twelve gates representing the months of the year. Roman cities were laid out according to the equinox and solar axis. A city's high places were typically reserved for temples of worship. Lynch notes that a city doesn't need to be ancient to be designed with cosmic and symbolic significance. Washington, D.C., planned at the end of the eighteenth century, was designed so that there was physical separation between the three branches of government (executive, legislative, and judicial), represented by three different edifices. The spatial layout of the city reflects the separation of governmental powers.

The second model that Lynch describes is what he calls the "practical" city. These cities are "imagined as a kind of machine, chiefly a machine for commerce. Such cities are pragmatic and functional; they grow according to material needs, as new parts are added and as old parts are altered. Their urban form derives from simply the addition of undifferentiated parts; they have … no wider significance."[13]

This definition is not meant to suggest that practical cities are in any way inferior to cosmic cities — they simply have a different organizing structure. New York City, for example, with its planned gridded layout of city blocks, is a practical city. Although it is beautiful, it was built and designed, as a port city, primarily for commerce.

The third model for a city is what Lynch calls an "organic" city: "As the name suggests, this is the city considered as a kind of organism: cohesive, balanced, and indivisible. Medieval towns are organic—their layouts look natural rather than man-made." The streets of organic towns tend to meander; they are of differing widths and are rarely straight. Over the decades, neighborhoods and boroughs are added and joined together in the labyrinth of the organic city. London is a good example of an organic city.

Six Reasons We Need to Engage with Cities

Cities and urban areas also have a different role in shaping culture than do rural areas. While rural areas do have an effect on the culture of a nation or people group, there are at least six reasons why we need to engage at a deeper level with cities.

1. Cities have a transforming effect on people.
2. Cities form a creative center.
3. Cities create fertile ground for thinking and receptivity.
4. Cities can help people live more efficiently and productively.
5. Cities are valued by God.
6. The early Christian movement was primarily urban.

1. Cities Have a Transforming Effect on People

While rural areas tend to have a conserving effect on the culture, city living changes who people are and how they see themselves. Tim Keller tells us why this is true: "The city puts you in proximity to people who think differently than you do, so *you* must think differently."[14]

A popular American song written in 1918 after America's entry into WWI was titled "How Ya Gonna Keep 'Em Down on the Farm (After They've Seen Paree)?" The lyrics to the second stanza go like this:

> How ya gonna keep 'em down on the farm
> After they've seen Paree?
> How ya gonna keep 'em away from Broadway,
> Jazzin' around and paintin' the town?
> How ya gonna keep 'em away from harm?
> That's the mystery!
> They'll never want to see a rake or plow
> And who the deuce can parlez-vous a cow?
> How ya gonna keep 'em down on the farm
> After they've seen Paree?

This song struck a chord with the American people because it reflected the inherent attraction of the city. After all, who would want to move back to the country after experiencing Paris or New York? The songwriters knew that something happens to people who have been to the city. They learn to adapt to a new way of life. This type of personal transformation was only negligibly possible in rural areas. Yale historian Wayne Meeks notes that the cities, in contrast to the conservative villages, were defined as places of change: "The conservatism of villages [is] their 'central characteristic.' 'They and their population hovered so barely above subsistence level that no one dared risk a change.' If some extraordinary circumstance should compel a villager to seek change—a lucky inheritance, a religious vision, or even, rarely, the accumulation of a little real money through frugality, shrewdness, and hard work—it must be in the city that he would work out his new life."[15]

> City living changes who people are and how they see themselves.

People came to the cities to seek their fortune and find a new life, and for this reason cities needed the attention and focus of the church. In 1893, Scottish evangelist and writer Henry Drummond, writing an address on cities, admonished his readers, "To make cities—that is what we are here for. To make good cities—that is for the present hour the main work of Christianity. For the city is strategic. It makes the towns; the towns make the villages; the villages make the country. He who makes the city makes the world. After all, though men make cities, *it is the cities which make men*" (emphasis ours).[16]

Drummond goes on to say that the city actually has a greater transformational effect on one's spiritual formation than the church itself. "[T]he church with all its splendid equipment, the cloister with all its holy opportunity, are not the final instruments for fitting men for Heaven. The city, in many of its functions, is a greater church than the church. It is amid the whirr of its machinery and in the discipline of its life that the souls of men are really made. How great its opportunity is, we are few of us aware."[17]

For good or for evil, it is the city that shapes and transforms the lives of people.

2. Cities Form a Creative Center

Connections, conversations, and transactions take place in the city at a far greater rate than they do in rural areas. Lewis Mumford notes, "The unique office of the city is to increase the variety, velocity, extent, and continuity of human intercourse."[18] It is the exchange of things and thoughts that creates something that never previously existed. In his book *The City: A Global History,* Joel Kotkin observes, "Cities compress and unleash the creative urges of humanity. From the earliest beginnings, when only a tiny fraction of humans lived in cities, they have been the places that generated most of mankind's art, religion, culture, commerce, and technology. This evolution occurred most portentously in a handful of cities whose influence then spread to other centers through conquest, commerce, religion, and, more recently, mass telecommunications."[19]

There is far more connectivity in the city — financial transactions, knowledge transference, media production — that provides the seedbed for social change. This isn't a new reality. Even Socrates once said, "The country places and the trees don't teach me anything, and the people in the city do."[20] Nobel Prize–winning economist Robert Lucas asks the question, "What can people be paying Manhattan or downtown Chicago rents for, if not to be around other people?"[21] People are attracted to cities because they are magnets for talent and ambition. Even though people can live and work from nearly any location in our globalized, digital, and virtual world,

- three-quarters of the nation's entertainers and performers work in Los Angeles;
- Washington, D.C., is home to 78 percent of all political scientists;
- more than half of all fashion designers work in New York;
- more than a third of all petroleum engineering jobs are in Houston.[22]

Cities attract the people who shape the thinking and the values of a nation. Tim Keller writes, "People who live in large urban cultural centers, occupying jobs in the arts, business, academia, publishing, the helping professions, and the media, tend to have a disproportionate impact on how things are done in our culture.... I am continually astonished at how the people I live with and know affect what everyone else in the country sees on the screen, in print, in art, and in business.... The people who live in cities in the greatest numbers tend to see their values expressed in the culture."[23]

To bring real change to a society, one must strategically start in the city. Keller distinguishes what he calls "tactical evangelism" from strategic kingdom influence: "If you want to win lawyers, go to the country. If you want to alter the legal system, go to cities."[24] There is a difference between reaching individuals and changing an entire culture, and cities are the strategic means to bring about societal change.

Viju Abraham from Mumbai, India, shares our commitment to working in the city. For nearly three years, Viju was part of a Global Learning Community that we hosted in Colorado, consisting of city leaders from fourteen cities around the world. As a young man in India, Viju was captivated by the importance of cities after studying the book of Acts. He reached a life-changing moment when he reread Acts 19:8 – 10: "[Paul] entered the synagogue [in Ephesus] and continued speaking out boldly for three months, reasoning and persuading them about the kingdom of God. But when some were becoming hardened and disobedient, speaking evil of the Way before the people, he withdrew from them and took away the disciples, reasoning daily in the school of Tyrannus. This took place for two years, so that all who lived in Asia heard the word of the Lord, both Jews and Greeks" (NASB).

> "If you want to win lawyers, go to the country. If you want to alter the legal system, go to cities" (Tim Keller).

What stunned Viju as he read this passage was that while Paul concentrated his ministry on one city — Ephesus — an entire region was reached with the good news! The city, as the locus of commerce and social interaction, was the God-ordained vehicle for impacting the entire region. If you transform a city, you will transform the province. One city really *can* make a difference.

3. Cities Create Fertile Ground for Thinking and Receptivity

The city also creates a seedbed for creative thinking, providing access to new ideas and new ways of dealing with problems and challenges. In his book *The City in History*, Lewis Mumford recognizes the role that cities serve in unleashing the creative forces of individuals. He writes, "If there is likely to be one person of exceptional ability in every generation, in, say, ten thousand people, a group of only one thousand may have to wait many generations before it has the advantage of a superior mind; and that mind, by its very isolation, may lack the stimulus from other minds that will help it to find itself. But a hundred thousand people, in Sumer or Babylon, in Jerusalem or Athens, in Baghdad or Benares, might produce at least fifty exceptional minds in a single lifetime; and these minds, by the very closeness of urban communication, would be open to a far greater variety of challenges and suggestions than if they appeared in a smaller community."[25]

We do want to note here that not all cities are equal in their influence. New York and Los Angeles collectively shape the expressions and content of traditional media more than most other cities of the world combined (with the possible exception of Mumbai).[26] We've heard it said that the Los Angeles – produced television show *Baywatch* has been shown in 140 countries and watched by billions of people (not that you've ever seen this show, of course). That's quite a reach. The financial cities of the world like London, New York, Singapore, Hong Kong, and Frankfurt, though they may not have the largest population, have the greatest influence on the world economy. In the 1940s, journalist A. H. Raskin remarked that "in a single afternoon in a single Manhattan skyscraper, decisions would be made that would determine what movies would be played in South Africa, whether or not children in a New Mexican mining town would have a school, or how much Brazilian coffee growers would receive for their crop."[27] In the last sixty years, the importance of cities has only further increased. When we think strategically about the future of the church, we cannot even begin to entertain the idea of transforming our communities without recognizing and understanding the powerful impact of the cities of the world. A kingdom-minded Chinese businessman showed us that he understood the growing influence of cities when he said to us, "If the twenty-first century is China's century, and all cities in China are influenced by Beijing, then Beijing must be the most important place to leverage our influence."

4. Cities Can Help People Live More Efficiently and Productively

Healthy cities have resources. Cities have spare parts to repair what is broken. Cities create within themselves, through supply and demand of scale, the organic abilities to thrive. Regarding efficiency (getting the maximum results from the minimum of resources and effort), Geoffrey B. West, president of the Santa Fe Institute, discovered two interesting facts about the attraction of cities. First, "[a] doubling of population [in cities] requires less than a doubling of certain resources. The material infrastructure that is analogous to biological transport networks — gas stations, lengths of electric cable, miles of road surface — consistently exhibits sublinear scaling with population. Second, [a] doubling of population is accompanied by more than a doubling of creative and economic output. We call this phenomenon 'superlinear' scaling: by almost any measure, the larger a city's population, the greater the innovation and wealth creation *per person*."[28]

More people can have a sustainable existence in the city, at a cheaper cost, than in rural areas. And once they come together, their creative and economic output supersedes their numerical size. All over the world, we can observe people moving to the cities, and those who govern often encourage them to do so.[29] China's solution to rural poverty is not a program of social welfare to support those in rural areas. Instead they invite the rural poor to join the booming economy of the city.

Environmentally, "urban living is kinder to the planet, and Manhattan [New York City] is perhaps the greenest place in the U.S. A Manhattanite's carbon footprint is 30 percent smaller than the average American's."[30] Surprisingly, it takes fewer natural resources to sustain life in the city than it does when people live "off the land": growing their own food, cutting and burning their own wood, and seeking to sustain themselves as individuals.

5. Cities Are Valued by God

Ray Bakke notes that the word *city* is cited some 1,250 times in the Bible — 160 times in the New Testament (*polis* in Greek) and 1,090 times in the Old Testament (*ir* in Hebrew).[31] Cities are strategic to God in the working out of his plans. Consider how often God addresses specific cities by name — Jerusalem, Babylon, Tyre — warning them, chastising them, loving them, and lauding them. Paul's letters in the New Testament are addressed to *cities* — "To the church at Rome," Philippi, Ephesus, and other cities of Asia Minor. Though there were many house "churches" in each of those cities, Paul wrote to them as one church, addressing his teaching to the broader context of the city and not just to individual congregations. Reading through the Gospels, we find only two times when it is recorded that Jesus wept: once over the death of his friend Lazarus, and a second time over the city of Jerusalem. The spiritual condition of the city moved the heart of Jesus. He himself was born in a village but died in a city. The story of the Bible begins in a garden and ends in a city. In many ways that we may not fully understand or grasp, cities are irrevocably tied to the eternal plans of God.

6. The Early Christian Movement Was Primarily Urban

Sociologist Rodney Stark tells us that "[t]he original meaning of the word *pagan* (*paganus*) was 'rural person,' or more colloquially 'country hick.' It came to have religious meaning because after Christianity had triumphed in the cities, most of the rural people remained unconverted."[32] He goes on to say, "All ambitious missionary movements are, or soon become, urban. If the goal is to 'make disciples of all nations,' missionaries need to go where there are many potential converts, which is precisely what Paul did. His missionary journeys took him to major cities, such as Antioch, Corinth, and Athens, with only occasional visits to smaller communities such as Iconium and Laodicia.... Any study of how Christians converted the empire is really a story of how they Christianized the cities."[33]

Christianity, in the early years, was primarily an urban movement. Even as he anticipated the end of his life, Paul was still plotting, planning, and praying how he might get to Rome — the most powerful center of influence in the known world (Rom. 1:11 – 15). Today we see that same concern among major denominations, parachurch organizations, and church-planting groups as they turn their attention to the cities of the world.

Global Movements

There are at least two great, global movements in the world today that the church must recognize and understand: *urbanization* and *immigration*. Urbanization is the movement of people from rural areas to cities, and it is having a profound impact on our world. Tim Keller writes, "Cities are growing in the 'Third World' at an enormous rate and are regenerating in the U.S. and Europe. In the U.S. even smaller cities have seen a renaissance of their downtown cores, as professionals, immigrants, international business leaders, empty-nest baby-boomers, artists, and the 'young and hip' move back in.[34] The coming world 'order 'will be a global, multi-cultural, and urban order."[35]

> Paul was plotting, planning, and praying how he might get to Rome — the most powerful center of influence in the known world.

Fueled by a desire for better jobs, people are coming to the cities of the world looking for better opportunities. With the move toward a capital-driven economy in the past few years, China has seen between 90 million and 300 million people move from the hinterland into its bourgeoning cities. These are numbers that "even at the low end match the entire workforce of the United States."[36] To put things in perspective, this is now the largest migration in human history.[37] To accommodate the unprecedented size of this migration—a movement that is fueling China's factories—China is now building new cities from scratch. "China has between 100 and 160 cities with populations of 1 million or more (America, by contrast, has nine)."[38]

Today there are more than 400 cities with populations over one million, and "[by] 2015 there will be more than 225 cities in Africa, 903 in Asia and 225 in Latin America ... [that] will have more than 1 million people."[39] In light of these statistics, urban missiologist Ray Bakke makes this astute observation: "Missions is no longer across the ocean and geographically distant; it is across the street and is culturally distant, in our cities and in cities on all six continents. In reality we have moved from a world of about 200 nations to a new world of some 400 world-class cities."[40] Greg Lillestrand, Director of Community Ministries for

Campus Crusade for Christ, astutely observes, "I believe the missional challenge of the twenty-first century is the city. It is the new '10/40' window of this generation, and fundamentally it is a different challenge than impacting the unreached in the remote places of the world."[41]

IMPLICATIONS FOR THE CHURCH

The implications that these changes have for the church are mind-boggling. Evangelistic strategies that have historically been quite effective in rural areas are ineffective with city dwellers. Philip Jenkins writes, "In 1900, all the world's largest cities were located in either Europe or North America.... Today, only three of the world's ten largest urban areas can be found in traditionally advanced countries, namely Tokyo, New York City, and Los Angeles.... Currently, 80 percent of the world's largest urban conglomerations are located in either Asia or Latin America."[42] God has localized the Great Commission by bringing the nations to the cities of the world. The ends of the earth have, in large measure, come to the cities.

THE SECOND GLOBAL MOVEMENT

The second great, global movement is immigration, the movement between nations. People from the south are moving to the north all over the globe. This migration is once again fueled by the abundance of jobs and the shortage of workers in the global north. Jenkins notes that "western Europe has between 10 million and 20 million illegal immigrants from Africa and Asia, over and above the legally settled communities."[43] With its declining population, "the French government argued

> God has localized the Great Commission by bringing the nations to the cities of the world.

that Europe would have no alternative but to admit 75 million immigrants over the coming half-century" to fill jobs and pay for social services for existing and aging residents.[44]

Even as the United States tightens its borders, America bulges with immigrants. The "ends of the earth" have now settled in our "Jerusalems" — our hometowns and cities — and present unique opportunities for engagement with people of different cultures. Within the boroughs of New York "is a Dominican city of 500,000, a West Indian city of 800,000, a Haitian city of 200,000 in Queens, two Chinatowns of over 100,000, 80,000 Greeks, 200,000 Jews,

40,000 Hindus, 150,000 Arabs and Middle Easterners."[45] Nearly every community in the United States has experienced an influx of immigrants from Latin America, Asia, eastern Europe, and Africa. With immigration, the tension between assimilation and maintaining cultural identity has fueled debates in school districts and boardrooms. With the addition of these diverse cultures come new norms that require new levels of diversity and tolerance. Whether we use the metaphor of a melting pot or a tossed salad, the blending of cultures in America is here to stay. The real question is whether the church will welcome these immigrants or ignore and despise them.

We've shared a number of statistics and facts with you, but the reality of these changes was personally illustrated to us a few years ago in our Global Leadership Community. We had a breakout time with the gathered leaders of fourteen cities where we asked them to independently identify the three greatest problems their cities faced. As they reported back to the group, we were amazed to discover that nearly every city, from Berlin to Beijing, Auckland to Atlanta, identified immigration as one of its most pressing issues. Cities are looking for wisdom in addressing this issue—how will the church respond to the growing immigration crisis/opportunity?

HISTORICAL RESPONSE OF THE CHURCH

It can be helpful to remember that the current influx of immigrants into the United States is not without precedent. In the 1800s, millions of immigrants flocked to America's shores and settled in her swelling cities, and this growth led to numerous problems. "The massive crowding, illnesses, and social problems created by the influx of largely unskilled, illiterate, foreign-speaking individuals was unparalleled in our history. In New York City, two-thirds of the population lived in tenements in 1890."[46] But immigration was also seen by church leaders as an invitation to ministry. This ministry often took the form of settlement houses where churches created, financed, and staffed outreach programs to help the most marginalized inhabitants of the inner cities. These churches formed Bible classes, established kindergartens, and organized industrial schools, clubs, loan banks, job bureaus, dispensaries, reading rooms, and other programs that laid the groundwork for later social reforms.[47] The church reinvented itself to meet the needs of these immigrants. Beryl Hugen writes, "These churches viewed themselves as 'institutions' that ministered seven days a week to the physical and spiritual wants of all the people within their reach. [They] sponsored clinics, free Saturday night concerts, self-supporting restaurants and lodging houses, wood wards for the unemployed, 'fresh air work' for women and children, and … there was a marked emphasis on practical education. Institutional churches sponsored libraries and literary societies and carried on kindergartens, trade schools, and community colleges."[48]

In the face of the challenges brought by immigration, the church simply responded to the needs of the generation with wisdom and compassion.

WHERE DO WE GO FROM HERE?

So how should the church respond to the movement of immigrants today? Do churches see these changes as new avenues of ministry or as problems? Consider what a difference it would make if every immigrant or refugee family was befriended by a local church. What if the first contact that every immigrant had in a new city was with a loving group of Christ followers who welcomed them, took them around the city, taught them how to use public transportation, and showed them where the thrift stores were and where the ESL (English as a second language) classes were meeting. Do you think that would make a difference?

Participants in our Global Leadership Community shared with us how the leaders of the largest church in their Asian city went to the government officials and simply asked them how they could best serve the city. The city officials said that they needed help in dealing with Muslim immigrants for the first thirty days after their arrival. The church responded by renting an apartment building that could house several families. In the first few months, seven Muslims embraced "Isa" (the Muslim name for Jesus) as Lord, and they now serve as leaders in this innovative ministry to immigrants.

THE PROBLEM MAY BE THE SOLUTION

Psalm 107 is sometimes referred to as a "city psalm." Consider what the psalmist writes in these verses in light of what we have been talking about.

> Some wandered in desert wastelands,
>   finding no way to a city where they could settle.
> They were hungry and thirsty,
>   and their lives ebbed away.
> Then they cried out to the LORD in their trouble,
>   and he delivered them from their distress.
> He led them by a straight way
>   to a city where they could settle.
>
> —Psalm 107:4–7

We believe that God is intentionally bringing the peoples of the world into the cities. What first appears to be a problem, the influx of immigrants to the cities, may actually be a part of God's plan of redemption. Consider what the apostle Paul says in Acts 17:26–27: "From one man he made every nation of men, that they should inhabit the whole earth; and he determined the times set for them and *the exact places where they should live.* God did this so that men would seek him and perhaps reach out for him and find him, though he is not far from each one of us" (emphasis ours).

> The story line of the Bible may begin in a garden, but it ends in a city.

What if—just maybe—it was God's plan that at this time in history, he would bring the peoples of the world into the cities of the world so that they would seek and find him? The story line of the Bible may begin in a garden, but we should remember that it ends in a city. Will the church embrace this urban identity and respond to these societal changes? Can the cities and communities of the world be transformed by the power of God?

For Reflection and Discussion

1. Describe the size and influence of your city. What is it known for? What are its centers of influence? What do you like about your city?
2. Is your city a better or worse place to live than it was five years ago? Why?
3. How would you describe the differences (family, friendships, work and leisure, etc.) between city and rural life in the area where you live?
4. In what ways do you think ministry in a city might differ from ministry in a more rural area?
5. Where, in your city, might unique opportunities for ministry be disguised as "problems"?
6. What are some practical ways your church could minister to the people who are moving into your city, the newcomers and immigrants?

CHAPTER TWO

CITY AND COMMUNITY TRANSFORMATION

Those who would transform a nation or the world cannot do so by breeding and captaining discontent or by demonstrating the reasonableness and desirability of the intended changes or by coercing people into a new way of life. They must know how to kindle and fan an extravagant hope.

—Eric Hoffer, *The True Believer*

At the beginning of each season, the head basketball coach of a large, well-known U.S. university calls the team together for the first meeting of the year. As the rookies enter the meeting room, they expect to see chalkboards, diagrams, depth charts, and scouting reports—but something is amiss. They walk into a room set up with tables graced with fine linen and adorned with bone china and an array of silverware and crystal glasses. The players are invited to have a seat around the tables, and a well-coiffed, punctilious woman teaches them how to place a linen napkin on one's lap and how to ask for the salt, as well as the purpose of the multiple pieces of silverware and crystal. Then the players practice what they have learned over a well-prepared meal. The coach then explains why he wants the players to learn their table manners: "After a team wins the Division I National Championship, they are invited to the White House for dinner with the president. And I want to be sure all of you know what to do when you get there." This is what it means to "begin with the end in mind." Granted, this team has yet to win a national crown, but we believe the point is still there. As we consider city transformation, what exactly is the end we have in mind? What would it look like for our city to be transformed?

What Is Transformation?

First, let's start by thinking about the term *transform*. The dictionary gives two primary definitions of the word.

1. To change the form or appearance
2. To change in condition, nature, or character[49]

For our purposes, we want to emphasize *both* definitions. In other words, community transformation not only changes the outward appearance of a community but also alters the very character or nature of the community. It may be helpful to consider the distinction between transforming and reforming. *Reform* means "to make better ... to improve by removing faults or abuses."[50] It involves a change brought about by the removal of problems and errors. As individuals, we can reform our lives and make better choices by avoiding certain things, but only God can bring about lasting transformation by doing something new that changes the character of a person or a community. The first thing we need to understand about community transformation is that it is the work of God. James McGregor Burns also helps to clarify this distinction by pointing out the differences between simply changing or modifying something that already exists and real, authentic transformation: "To change is to substitute one thing for another, to give and take, to exchange places, to pass from one place to another.... But to transform something cuts much more profoundly. It is to cause a metamorphosis in form or structure, a change in the very condition or nature of a thing, a change into another substance. It is a radical change in outward form or inner character, as when a frog is transformed into a prince or a carriage maker into an auto factory."[51]

> Only God can transform by changing the nature and character of a person or a community.

Transformation changes the outward appearance, but it also creates something new — changing the very nature and character of the community.

Community Transformation

Community transformation is an expression that is frequently thrown around and can mean different things to different people. Consider just a few of the definitions we've heard from church leaders around the world:

- "When a community is transformed, growing numbers of converts function as mature disciples in the city, and the social, political, and economic fabric of the entire community begins to change." — Steve Capper, executive director of Mission Houston

- "B community where justice, mercy, faithfulness, and hope pervade every city system, and the church of Jesus Christ is actively engaged in making this possible." — Jon Sharpe, founder of The Center for Global Urban Leadership[52]
- "A deeply rooted change in people's spiritual, social, economic, physical, behavioral, and political conditions growing out of an encounter with the triune God and resulting in their growing enjoyment of wholeness of life under the will and ordinances of God." — Gary Edmonds, Breakthrough Partners[53]
- "The process whereby individuals, peoples and the city as a whole increasingly and dramatically become more like God's intention for them." — Jack Dennison, founder of CitiReach International[54]
- "A process by which the whole church takes the whole gospel to the whole city so that the power, the peace and the presence of God is experienced by every means possible through an effective witnessing community in every neighborhood, people groups and all spheres of society." — The Chennai Transformation Network in South India[55]

As we define community transformation, it is important that we recognize that this type of transformation involves the conversion of individuals, but it goes beyond that. Bob Moffitt, founder and president of Harvest Foundation, has worked in various countries throughout the developing world. He writes, "I define biblical transformation as the process of restoration to God's intentions of all that was broken when humanity rebelled against God at the Fall. It is not the same as spiritual conversion, though it begins there. It is God's work. He calls his people to participate with him in it. This ongoing process will not be fully completed until Christ returns."[56]

Those involved in God's process of community transformation will see lives changed and people converted to Christ, but these are not the same thing as a community transformed by the power of the gospel. Individual transformation is a partner to community transformation — not a substitute for it.

SPIRITUAL AND SOCIETAL TRANSFORMATION

For the past few years, both of us have embraced a mission statement that defines our life goal: "To change the world by engaging the church worldwide in the needs and dreams of their communities so as to bring about spiritual and societal transformation." The phrase *spiritual transformation* reflects our desire to help people love God with all of their mind, heart, soul, and strength. We use the phrase *societal transformation* to refer to the work of helping people learn to love their neighbors as themselves (Matt. 22:37–39).

To further simplify things, we might say that spiritual transformation begins as believers begin to match their own attitudes and thoughts with the heart that God has for their community. This happens when we begin to value what God values; we start to care about the people he cares about and begin working where he is at work around us. We know from the Scriptures that God cares about the poor and the needy, the widows, aliens, and orphans, so this is often a great place to begin our focus. Whenever a Christian shows that he or she is "merciful as [his or her heavenly] Father is merciful" (Luke 6:36), it is evident that genuine spiritual transformation is taking place—Christ followers are reflecting the compassionate heart of God.

> *Spiritual transformation comes from helping people love God with all of their mind, heart, soul, and strength. Societal transformation comes from helping people love their neighbors as themselves.*

Wherever the gospel has gone, this spiritual transformation is reflected in a wake of societal impact. Orphanages are started, universities and hospitals are founded, the hungry are fed, the homeless are sheltered, and those dying of AIDS are comforted. People come to know Christ in powerful ways. Churches that make a difference in the life of the community are started. Francis Schaeffer has pointed out that "[e]very single revival that has ever been a real revival, whether it was the great awakening before the American Revolution; whether it was the great revivals of Scandinavia; whether it was Wesley or Whitefield; wherever you have found a great revival, it's always had three parts. First, it has called for the individual to accept Christ as Savior.... Then, it has called upon the Christians to bow their hearts to God and really let the Holy Spirit have His place in fullness in their life. But there has always been, in every revival, a third element. It has always brought *social change*."[57]

Schaeffer, like many others, recognized that authentic spiritual transformation and societal transformation go hand in hand. Jim Wallace, the president and executive director of Sojourners, goes as far as to say that "[s]piritual activity isn't called revival until it changes something, not just in people's inner lives but in society."[58] Having a single focus on individual conversion is never sufficient. It fails to reflect the visible presence of Jesus to the community.

Societal transformation is what often follows authentic spiritual transformation in a community. It's what happens when the *secular society* begins caring about the needs of the community just as much as the church does. In our community of Boulder, for example, nearly every compassionate human-services agency (Boulder Shelter for the Homeless, the Emergency Family Assistance Association, Boulder Day Care Nursery, etc.) was started by a local church and eventually adopted by our community. Every hospital in your community that bears the name *Saint* (Saint Joseph's, Saint Luke's) is a witness to a time when the community, to some extent, chose to adopt the values of the Christian community and experienced a degree of transformation. In some cases, the church has chosen to hand these institutions over to the community; nevertheless, even these small evidences of societal impact are for the better. When the secular society begins to care about and value the things that the church cares about, this cycle of societal transformation is complete. Indirectly, through the witness of the church, the culture begins to value the things that God values.

Dr. Martin Luther King Jr. is a shining example of this type of transformation. Dr. King had a dream that reflected the heart of God, a dream for racial equality that mirrored God's heart for justice. As he stood on the steps of the Lincoln Memorial in August of 1964, what began as a spiritual issue—a call for the church to live out its calling—sparked a societal transformation that led to concrete changes, as evidenced by the Civil Rights Act of 1964, the Voting Rights Act of 1965, and the Fair Housing Act of 1968. Real community transformation occurs when the "dreams" of those who follow Christ are translated into values and laws that reflect the kingdom of God. How difficult is this type of transformation? To transmit knowledge through the spoken and written word is relatively easy. To create an alternative story of *what could be* that affects attitudes is more difficult and more time-consuming. As people begin to live out the new vision, their behavior is different. When the new values and behavior are adopted by greater society for the greater collective good, real transformation has occurred. Figure 3 helps us to visualize this process.[59]

INDIVIDUAL TRANSFORMATION

To aid us in considering both the limits and possibilities for community transformation, it is helpful to begin by considering the process of personal transformation. Personal transformation is similar, in many respects, to the biblical truth of our personal salvation in Christ. Various aspects of our salvation are reflected in

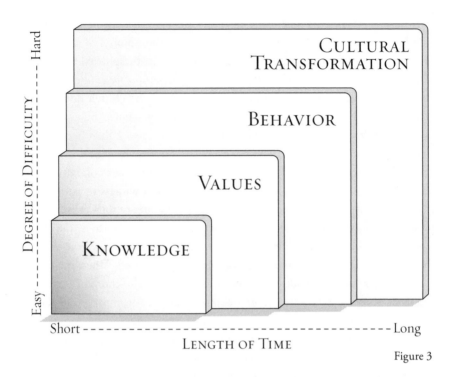

Figure 3

the truth of our salvation: I have been saved (Eph. 2:8), I am being saved (Phil. 2:12), and one day I will be saved (1 Peter 1:5). In a similar way, we can say that as a follower of Christ, I have been transformed—this is transformation *past*. But in addition to the past, every Christian is also encouraged to continue the transformation process through the renewing of their mind—"Do not conform any longer to the pattern of this world, but *be transformed* by the renewing of your mind" (Rom. 12:2, emphasis ours). There is an ongoing process of transformation that each and every Christian is engaged in. The apostle Paul reminds us that "[w]e ... are being transformed into his likeness with ever-increasing glory" (2 Cor. 3:18). In other words, in addition to the reality of my past changes, I am being transformed today—this is transformation *present*. And along with this ongoing process, there is the truth that one day the transformation process will be complete: "The Lord Jesus Christ ... *will transform* our lowly bodies so that they will be like his glorious body" (Phil. 3:20–21, emphasis ours). This is transformation *future*. I can say without any contradiction that I have been transformed, I am being transformed, and one day I will be completely transformed. Personal transformation is a process.

The common element that unites all three phases of my transformation is my relationship with Jesus Christ. He is the one who began the transformation process, he is the one who continues it, and one day he will bring it to completion when I see him face-to-face. "[W]e know that when he appears, we shall be like him, for we shall see him as he is" (1 John 3:2).

COMMUNITY TRANSFORMATION

What if that same understanding of my personal transformation in Christ were applied to the idea of *community* transformation? Might cities be transformed in the same way that you and I are changed? There is an interesting parable Jesus tells in Matthew 13:33 about the kingdom: "The kingdom of heaven is like yeast [leaven] that a woman took and mixed into a large amount of flour until it worked all through the dough." If you have ever baked bread, you know that yeast is the critical ingredient that makes dough rise and serves as the difference between fresh, soft bread and a tortilla or flatbread. The magical difference is that the yeast cells begin to multiply when they are placed in the warm dough. Although a package of yeast may appear harmless and inert, when it is blended into the mixture, it becomes a catalyst that causes dough to rise so it can be baked into tasty, soft bread. As the yeast is worked into the dough and the yeast cells begin to multiply, they influence every bit of the dough, making the entire dough rise. Churches that choose to involve themselves in the life of their community through acts of love and service take on the characteristics of yeast. Though the acts of love may appear to have little effect at times, the seeds of transformation are being planted, regardless of whether the community recognizes them. The key to changing a community is not the *speed* at which it happens; it's the fact of the church's involvement in the community that makes the critical difference. The presence of the yeast will always cause the dough to rise. Externally focused churches that engage their communities with good works and good news will see their communities transformed into something new.[60]

> An externally focused church that is present and involved in a community begins the process of changing that community.

Similar to the way that the presence of Christ in our life begins the personal transformation process, so too an externally focused church that is present and involved in a community begins the process of changing that community. And just as it takes the thorough penetration of the yeast to transform flour, water, and sugar into bread, it takes the church penetrating every domain of the community to transform the community. Light illuminates, salt preserves, but it is the leaven that transforms.

Figure 4

The Process of Transformation

Unpacking the process of transformation may be the most important thing you will take away from this book. Figure 4 is a simple diagram that shows this process.

Community transformation begins with and is led by people who themselves are being transformed. We should never underestimate how important an individual believer with a changed heart can be and how much impact he or she can have upon the world. Jeremiah 5:1 reminds us that it takes only one person to affect the outcome of a city. The highest level of transformation (that with the most measurable change) occurs at the lowest and most basic level—that of the individual follower of Christ. This individual transformation occurs when a person comes to know Jesus Christ in a personal way and begins to live under his lordship: "If anyone is in Christ, he is a new creation; the old has gone, the new has come!" (2 Cor. 5:17). Conversion is the prerequisite to transformation. Several decades ago, Walter Rauschenbusch wrote, "We can conceive of a state of society in which plenty would reign, but where universal opulence would only breed universal pride and wantonness. Personal rebirth and social rebirth are inseparably necessary. The social order cannot be saved without regenerate men."[61]

Personal transformation happens through a personal encounter with Jesus. The apostle Paul reminded his readers of the 180 degree changes in lifestyle that should result from an encounter with Jesus when he penned his words to the believers at Ephesus: "He who has been stealing must steal no longer, *but must work, doing something useful with his own hands, that he may have something to share with those in need*" (Eph. 4:28, emphasis ours). Thieves are transformed into generous givers. Paul continues, "Get rid of all bitterness, rage and anger, brawling and slander, along with every form of malice. *Be kind and compassionate to one another, forgiving each other, just as in Christ God forgave you*" (4:31–32, emphasis ours). Malicious, angry people, prone to fighting, become agents of God's grace and forgiveness. "Do not get drunk on wine, which leads to debauchery. *Instead, be filled with the Spirit*" (5:18, emphasis ours). Alcoholics and addicts are changed into Spirit-filled people. The Spirit of God changed lives in the city of Ephesus, and he is changing lives in our cities today.

Service Transforms Individuals

It's also important to remember that serving others changes and transforms the very people who are serving. When we speak at seminars across the country, one of our key points is that while people can *learn* through good preaching, personal Bible study, and healthy small groups, most people don't *grow* past a certain point if they are not involved in serving others. Although we are saved by grace through faith and not by our good works (Eph. 2:8–9), we are saved so that we are free to do the good works that God has prepared in advance for us to do (Eph. 2:10). In fact, every helpful resource that God has given us—leaders to prepare us (Eph. 4:11–12), God's Word to equip us (2 Tim. 3:16–17), the body of Christ to encourage us (Heb. 10:24), spiritual gifts to empower us (1 Peter 4:10)—points to the same goal of actually *doing* something.[62]

Churches Must Be Transformed before Transforming Others

The need for transformation in our cities and communities is great, but the area over which pastors and church leaders typically have the most influence (and the area perhaps in most desperate need of change) is the church itself.[63] In 2 Chronicles 7:14, God reminds his people that it is through the repentant hearts of the people who are *called by his name* that he will bring healing to the land. Sadly, while many Christian leaders are fairly adroit at pointing out the changes needed in other domains of society (media, education, entertainment, family, etc.), they can be blind to the need for change in their own churches. Christian leaders, unable to motivate their church members to follow God's precepts, still vocally demand that secular society live by them. But what a different message we would convey to the world if the church showed the world an alternative story of a truly transformed life, infused with kingdom values lived out through missional actions. The latest research shows us that although 84 percent of young people say they personally know a Christian, a mere 15 percent think the lifestyle of those Christ followers is any different from the norm.[64]

Richard McBrien, professor of theology at Notre Dame, suggests that we seek a more balanced role for religion in pluralistic America. His insights are helpful to church leaders contemplating their own role in the transformation of society, particularly his emphasis on the priority the church should give to seeking moral conformity among its own membership. "First, every religious community may demand conformity to its beliefs on the part of its own members. Second, no group in a pluralist society may demand that government legislate a moral conviction for which support in society at large is lacking. Third, any group, including any church, has the right to work toward a change in society's standards through persuasion and argument. Finally, no group may legitimately impose its religious or moral convictions on others through the use of force, coercion, or violence."[65]

> Christian leaders, unable to motivate their church members to follow God's precepts, still vocally demand that secular society live by them.

McBrien's words are a helpful reminder that individual transformation does not come about through force, threats, and shame. Christian leaders may often mistakenly focus their judgment on those outside the church, asking them to adhere to Christian moral standards, while ignoring the behavior of the very people in their domain of influence — fellow church members. For example, consider the hot-button topic of gay marriage, a topic we suspect will be an issue of contention for many years. If church leaders are serious in their belief that marriage is sacred, that Christ should make a difference in our marriages, that God really does hate divorce (Mal. 2:16) and the effect that divorce has on children, one would think that most churches would be working harder to reduce or eliminate divorce among Christ followers and strengthen healthy marriages. Yet sadly, according to George Barna's research, "born-again" Christians in the United States have a higher divorce rate (27 percent) than the general population (25 percent). Even atheists and agnostics have a much lower divorce rate (21 percent) than believers.[66] Where is our "street cred" when we preach about having healthy families yet fail to hold our own families together? Consider the transforming effect it could have on American society if Christians alone stopped divorcing one another! The divorce rate in the United States would plummet precipitously. (Incidentally, the United States has the highest divorce rate of any country in the world.) Doesn't it make sense for church leaders to realign their focus by confronting the moral failures within our own church family? Keep in mind that we do not see this as an either-or issue. Believers can work hard at upholding family values in the broader culture *and* work on reducing divorce among God's people.

This same principle can also be applied to the tragedy of abortion and the church's belief in the sanctity of human life. Sadly, there are approximately 1.25

million legal abortions performed each year in the United States. Even sadder, 70 percent of girls and women who have abortions indicate they are (at least nominally) Christian (43 percent Protestant and 27 percent Catholic).[67] What effect would it have on our society if today all Christian women would refrain from having an abortion? More than 875,000 babies would be saved. If we took out the nominal Christians from that statistic and merely encouraged all women who claim to be born again to stop having abortions, 250,000 babies would be spared.[68] Our point is this: how can we expect (or in some cases demand) others to adopt the values and ethics of Christians when we as Christ followers so easily flout them? Rich Nathan, lead pastor at Vineyard Church in Columbus, Ohio, writes, "People need and deserve straight talk from Christians.... But first let's make sure that in our communication we're targeting our greatest firepower toward those who are presently inside the church, while showing maximum patience and grace toward those outside the church."[69]

Putting our hope in politicians to appoint judges who will uphold conservative Christian values is merely a stopgap measure at best. Until the confirmation of Sonia Sotomayor in August 2009, of the nine U.S. Supreme Court justices, all but two (Ginsburg and Breyer) were appointed by Republican presidents after *Roe v. Wade* was passed in 1973. We believe that followers of Christ should be engaged and responsible citizens and that we have a biblical responsibility to work toward efforts we believe have moral significance, but we should be aware that we do not place our ultimate hope for a spiritual kingdom in the hand of any government or earthly leader. We would do well to remember the words of Edward Gibbon in *The Rise and Fall of the Roman Empire*: "In Roman society all religions were to the people equally true, to the philosophers equally false, and to the government equally useful."[70] Governments are necessary, but they lack the power to bring real and lasting change. If God is going to use his church to bring that transformation to our communities, then it is the church itself that needs to be transformed.

> How can we expect (or in some cases demand) others to adopt the values and ethics of Christians when we as Christ followers so easily flout them?

A Different Approach

Cal Thomas is a conservative American columnist whose writings appear in over 550 newspapers and who is heard on over 300 radio stations. He wrote the following piece of helpful advice following the 2008 presidential elections.

Too many conservative Evangelicals have put too much faith in the power of government to transform culture. The futility inherent in such misplaced faith can be demonstrated by asking these activists a simple question: Does the secular left, when it holds power, persuade conservatives to live by their standards? Of course they do not. Why, then, would conservative Evangelicals expect people who do not share their worldview and view of God to accept their beliefs when they control government? Too many conservative Evangelicals mistake political power for influence. Politicians who struggle with imposing a moral code on themselves are unlikely to succeed in their attempts to impose it on others. What is the answer, then, for conservative Evangelicals who are rightly concerned about the corrosion of culture, the indifference to the value of human life and the living arrangements of same- and opposite-sex couples? If results are what conservative Evangelicals want, they already have a model. It is contained in the life and commands of Jesus of Nazareth. Suppose millions of conservative Evangelicals engaged in an old and proven type of radical behavior. Suppose they followed the admonition of Jesus to "love your enemies, pray for those who persecute you, feed the hungry, clothe the naked, visit those in prison and care for widows and orphans," not as ends, as so many liberals do by using government, but as a means of demonstrating God's love for the whole person in order that people might seek Him? Such a strategy could be more "transformational" than electing a new president, even the first president of color.[71]

How radical would it be if the church simply lived like Jesus?

WEST AFRICA

Ben Ecklu, who lives in Ghana, West Africa, and serves as Campus Crusade's director of affairs for West Africa, says, "If Christians are sixty to seventy percent of the population of Ghana, then we must own sixty to seventy percent of our country's problems. If just the Christians did things differently—like not dumping their trash in the streets—the city would change drastically … just like that!" The people of West Africa long to experience a different church. Speaking in the voice of the non-Christians and Muslims of West Africa, Ben says, "I want to see, taste, and smell Christianity. I want to see Christianity walking around."[72]

Recently a friend of ours, who had been listening to some of the stories we were sharing about what God was doing in our community, wrote a glowing report of what God was doing in Boulder and emailed it to his network of friends. His story attempted to say that Boulder was a changed community because of specific acts of giving, kindness, engagement, and service that some of the churches had been involved in. But the truth is that Boulder itself has changed very little! If there is a story of change in our community, it is a story of a changing church—a church that is seeking to live out the gospel that Jesus lived and taught. Little by little, we are being changed, becoming more like Christ as we engage in meeting the needs and fulfilling the dreams of our community. In many places, churches have been absent from the life of their community for so long that at best we can say we still have a long way to go.

> "If Christians are sixty to seventy percent of the population of Ghana, then we must own sixty to seventy percent of our country's problems" (Ben Ecklu).

Counselors and psychiatrists (and those who spoof them) will always remind us, "The only person you can change is yourself." That's equally true for the church as we consider our relationship with and our influence in the community. We can't really change the community; only God can do that. But as we depend upon God's grace, we work out our salvation, experiencing individual transformation—and from there we are free to love our community. We can serve the city, love the city, and bless the city—but only God has the power to transform the city.

The Process of Community Transformation

A great picture of these three phases of transformation (individual, church, and community) can be seen in Isaiah 61:1–6. This is a very simple passage that should be in the toolbox of every believer who thinks about and is working toward community transformation. In these six verses, we learn how transformation happens. If you are in a position to have your Bible in front of you as you read this next section, you will see for yourself the unfolding of this amazing process.

1. *Transformation begins with one person who is yielded to the Spirit of God.* "The Spirit of the Sovereign Lord is on me, because the Lord has anointed me to preach good news to the poor" (v. 1). The empowering presence of God's Spirit is where all transformation begins. In many ways, Isaiah himself serves as a great example of this. We read in Isaiah 6:8 that when the Lord was looking for a willing, available person, Isaiah

responded, "Here am I. Send me!" The critical mass to transform a community begins with just one person who is yielded to the Spirit of God.

2. *Transformation comes through proclamation and demonstration of the gospel.* As you read the rest of verse 1 and into verse 3, Isaiah describes how his message will come—through *both* a verbal message *and* a lifestyle of love and compassion. Look at the words Isaiah uses. He is "proclaim[ing]" a message, while at the same time he is "bind[ing] up the brokenhearted," "releas[ing] from darkness ... the prisoners," "comfort[ing] all who mourn," and "provid[ing] for those who grieve." The gospel flies on wings of good news and good deeds. Transformation is the result of both "compassionate deeds and passionate proclamation of the gospel."[73] We need both of these and must be careful that we avoid neglecting either one. The works verify the words and the words clarify the deeds.

3. *Transformation begins as people are transformed.* A wonderful exchange occurs when people yield their lives to Jesus Christ. Look at verse 3. They receive "a crown of beauty *instead of* ashes, the oil of gladness *instead of* mourning, ... a garment of praise *instead of* a spirit of despair" (emphasis ours). Isn't that an incredible exchange? But wait, there's even more. "They [the formerly despairing, ash-covered mourners] will be called oaks of righteousness, a planting of the Lord for the display of his splendor." The small acorns grow into large oak trees. The children grow up and become strong leaders. When people are genuinely transformed by the power of God, it is the splendor of God that is displayed to the world, and God's splendor is best seen in changed lives. In her book *Restorers of Hope*, Amy Sherman sheds additional light on the reason why restored lives have power and impact. She writes, "The most basic reason why the 'restorers' are effective is that they lead people to Jesus Christ—the source of salvation and the power for self-transformation. Restorers emphasize a reformation of the heart and a renewal of the mind. The spiritual growth they encourage is directed and specific. It is centered on Jesus and the Bible."[74]

4. *Transformed people want to transform their communities.* Verse 4 is quite instructive. "They [these oaks of righteousness] will rebuild the ancient ruins and restore the places long devastated; they will renew the ruined cities that have been devastated for generations." When people are transformed by God's Spirit, they are compelled to act in response. They challenge the status quo. Though things may have been destroyed for generations, they rebuild, restore, and renew.

5. *Transformation occurs when the work is taken over by others.* "Aliens will shepherd your flocks; foreigners will work your fields and vineyards" (v. 5). Who are the aliens and foreigners? Crop circles and abductions aside, one of the best tests of the sustainability of your work is whether it can be transferred to others. If you were to leave your community for a year and then return, what would you find? Would the work you started have continued? Perhaps the best thing that can happen is seeing a group of "foreigners" and "aliens" (strangers to you) take over your flock and your field. They become the community builders, taking over and continuing the work that you began.

> The highest compliment a city transformer can receive is to be known as a priest or a minister of God's grace to the community.

6. *Transformation is recognized by how the city identifies your role.* "And you will be called priests of the LORD, you will be named ministers of our God" (v. 6). In this generation, the most important ministerial titles will not be those conferred by a seminary or ordination board — they will come from those in the community. What began with a single, visionary individual has now culminated in a transformed community. The highest compliment a city transformer can receive is to be known as a priest or a minister of God's grace to the community.

Recently I (Eric) was in Thailand teaching a weeklong class (appropriately called To Transform a City) to expatriate Christian leaders living in East Asia. After I unpacked this sixth point of Isaiah 61, somebody in the class said, "That's what happened to Travis!" I turned to Travis Todd and asked to hear the full story. He explained that in August 2005, he and his wife, Sonya, along with their two daughters, were in the States for a furlough after serving for seven years with Campus Crusade for Christ in East Asia. On August 29, Hurricane Katrina hit Travis's hometown of Pass Christian, Mississippi (the city has a population of 6,500, and its name is pronounced "Pass Christy-Ann"). The only thing left of his childhood home was the foundation and a bathtub, and unfortunately, the rest of the town didn't fare much better. Travis organized a massive effort to rebuild, renew, and restore this broken city. Utilizing more than twelve thousand Campus Crusade–affiliated students, the community of Pass Christian began the process of healing and recovery. As a result of Travis's work through the extensive involvement of Campus Crusade and the aid and relief they provided to the community, the city bestowed on him the following honor: "Be it resolved by the Mayor and Board of Aldermen of the city of Pass Christian as follows: The Governing authorities do hereby proclaim April 26, 2006, as 'TRAVIS TODD DAY' and urge all citizens to commend him for his invaluable efforts and leadership, for which the City will be eternally grateful."[75]

The city effectively named Travis their minister and priest, the one who had restored the "ancient" ruins of Pass Christian.

You may already know this, but in Luke chapter 4, when Jesus entered the synagogue in his hometown, the scroll of Isaiah was handed to him. Jesus knew exactly where to turn. His text for the day would be Isaiah 61 — proclaiming and comforting, telling good news and being good news. This is the passage Jesus used to define and describe his own ministry of healing and restoration. "Today this scripture is fulfilled in your hearing," he spoke after reading it aloud (Luke 4:21). If we want to be his followers, walking in his footsteps, then it may be a good first step to spend some time meditating and reflecting on the passage that captured his own heart — Isaiah chapter 61.

WHAT A HEALTHY COMMUNITY LOOKS LIKE

Have you ever asked yourself, "If God were to build a city from the ground up, what would it look like?" Amazingly, there are actually passages of Scripture that describe such a city. When God envisions the New Jerusalem in Isaiah 65:17 – 25, he outlines the elements that must be in place for a healthy, whole community where his *shalom* (peace and wholeness) is present. The city to be built by God is a place where

- there is joy (v. 19);
- there is an absence of weeping and crying (v. 19);
- there is no infant mortality (v. 20);
- people live out their full lives (v. 20);
- people will build houses and live in them (vv. 21 – 22);
- people will sow and reap (vv. 21 – 22);
- there is fulfilling and meaningful work (v. 22);
- there is confidence that the next generation will face a better life (v. 23);
- people experience the blessing of God (v. 23);
- there is intergenerational family support with family structures intact (v. 23);
- there are rapid answers to prayer (v. 24);
- there is an absence of violence (v. 25).

Zechariah 8:4–5 also gives us a postcard scene from the city of God: "[M]en and women of ripe old age will sit in the streets of Jerusalem, each with cane in hand because of his age. The city streets will be filled with boys and girls playing there." Doesn't that describe the community you'd want to live in, a place of wisdom, laughter, and joy?

Perhaps the greatest desire that God has for the city, though, is that it would be reconciled back to him. Jesus' words give us a glimpse of God's heart for the brokenness of a city that tries to live without his presence and guidance: "O Jerusalem, Jerusalem,... how often I have longed to gather your children together, as a hen gathers her chicks under her wings, but you were not willing" (Matt. 23:37). God longs for people of the city to be reconciled to him through a relationship with his Son, Jesus.

What does God desire for the broken people of the city? Nearly every community is filled with widows, orphans, immigrants, and those who are hungry and thirsty, strangers to one another, sick, or imprisoned. God cares about each of these people, and he wants his redeemed people to do the same. A healthy community is one where "the least of these" (Matt. 25:31–46) are cared for with the same love that we would offer to Jesus himself, were he in need of our care.

In 1990, the Population Fund Report on cities defined its strategies for livable urban areas. Gathering data from the world's largest one hundred metropolitan areas, researchers employed a thirteen-page questionnaire to determine the factors that define quality of life in these one hundred cities. Ten parameters were chosen to determine the *livability* of these cities. Based on these criteria, an urban living standard score was calculated. Though they are far from comprehensive, these parameters provide a helpful scorecard, highlighting the various ways that a community can be transformed:

1. Public safety (based on local police estimates of homicides per 100,000 people)
2. Food costs (representing the percentage of household income spent on food)
3. Living space (being the number of housing units and the average number of persons per room)
4. Housing standards (being the percentage of homes with access to water and electricity)
5. Communication (the number of reliable sources of telecommunications per 100 people)
6. Education (based on the percentage of children, aged 14–17, in secondary schools)

7. Public health (based on infant deaths per 1,000 live births)
8. Peace and quiet (based on a subjective scale for ambient noise)
9. Traffic flow (being the average miles per hour during rush hour)
10. Clean air (based on a one-hour concentration in ozone levels)[76]

By overlaying these contemporary community standards on the biblical vision of Isaiah 65, we can begin to get a sense of God's heart for community transformation. Where, among this list of stated standards for good city life, are there opportunities for the church to be involved in community transformation?

Ultimate and Ulterior Motives

Community transformation is not about "Christendom" — placing Christianity or the church at the center of society or trying to reestablish the church as the center of the community.[77] It is more like the kingdom leaven (Matt. 13:33) that is worked into all parts of society and lived out in such a way that people in every sector and every domain of society can know someone who truly follows Jesus. Conversion is our *ultimate* motive but not our *ulterior* motive in loving and serving others. "Ultimate motive" means that we absolutely want every person on earth to be in a right relationship with God through Jesus, in the same way that God does not desire any to perish but all to come to repentance (2 Peter 3:9; 1 Tim. 2:3–4). But "ulterior motive" means that we do acts of love and service toward others *so that* they become Christians (which could signify that if they don't become Christians, we stop loving and serving). It is important to remember that we don't engage in the needs, dreams, and pains of our communities so that they will become Christians; rather we engage the community because we *are* Christians. We don't serve *to convert*, but we serve because we *have been converted*. We contend that the most fertile ground for evangelistic conversations is a servant-rich environment. Ron Sider puts it this way: "Our social concern dare not be a gimmick designed to bribe people to become Christians. Social action has its own independent validity. We do it because the Creator wants everyone to enjoy the good creation. At the same time, when our genuine compassion also has an evangelistic dimension, we rejoice. Again and again, that is exactly what happens when we truly care for the needy and stand with the oppressed who seek justice."[78]

> Conversion is our *ultimate* motive but not our *ulterior* motive in loving and serving others.

We recognize that selfless service does not always lead to salvation. Jesus cured ten lepers of their hideous disease, but only one made the "God connection" and returned to give thanks (Luke 17:11–19). But that didn't stop Jesus from healing them. The number of good deeds we do is not always proportionate to the number of conversions we see. Jesus did most of his miracles in cities where there was the least repentance (Matt. 11:20–24), but that didn't keep him from healing and blessing.

TRANSFORMATION DOWN UNDER

In October 2005, we were invited to New Zealand to meet with groups of pastors and leaders and speak with them about community transformation. (It was a tough assignment, but somebody had to do it.) After landing in Auckland and grabbing a Ponsonby meat pie, we were whisked by our host, Higgins, down to the city of Christchurch on the South Island. After our presentation to the leaders of Spreydon Baptist Church on the topic of being an externally focused church, we took the second hour to learn all about the church's ministry. One by one, the church staff shared their passion for ministry with us. This is a church that for several years has been engaged in various externally focused efforts to serve their community. They began by first discovering the needs in their community. At that time, the greatest area of need for the people there was addressing the problem of consumer debt. Many of the people had found themselves trapped with high-interest consumer loans (credit card debt, etc.) and felt that they might never be able to escape the bondage of debt. As the leaders of the church considered how to best address this need, they noticed something else. Many of the believers had money sitting idly in the bank, earning a mere 1 percent to 2 percent interest, money that could be used for kingdom purposes. So the leaders of Spreydon Baptist started a bank by pooling money from believers who wanted their savings put to good and godly use. Contributors would "invest" between one hundred dollars and one hundred thousand dollars, and the church trained one hundred and thirty "budget counselors" to offer training, encouragement, and support. Then they simply invited people in their community to apply for 0 percent interest loans to help them pay off consumer debt. The recipients of the loans meet weekly with the budget counselors, who soon become life counselors addressing spiritual as well as material concerns. In the five years that the program had been running, the church had paid down $2.6 million in debt for the people of Christchurch—and they have had a 98 percent payback rate! This is a church that is setting captives free from the bondage of financial debt. This is a church that has discovered how to become good news to their city.

In addition to running the debt program, Spreydon Baptist teaches English to recent immigrants, they have after-school and holiday care for children, they work in the arts community, and during the week they have a worship service made up mostly of folks with mental illness. Their efforts to help the children of their city through after-school and holiday programs have spread to other churches as well. Today around 10 percent of the children's centers in the city are located in churches.

The influence of these efforts has not gone unnoticed, and government officials have communicated that they want all future children's programs to be influenced by these kingdom-minded Christians. What Spreydon Baptist has done is simply transformational. All of their ministries begin with one question: "What are the needs of the community?" Recently the city council approached Spreydon Baptist and asked them two questions: "Do you realize that you are the largest supplier of human services in the city? How can we help you more?"

City transformation begins with a transformed church that engages the needs of the city with works *and* words of love—good deeds and good news. We are to live seeking "the peace and prosperity of the city" that God has placed us in. We are to "pray to the Lord for it, because if it prospers, [we] too will prosper" (Jer. 29:7). Robert Linthicum writes, "The essential task of the church is to work for its society's *shalom*—to work for the full and total transformation of all the people, forces and structures with the love of God."[79] And one day, when the kingdom of this world becomes the kingdom of our Lord (Rev. 11:15), the city will finally be fully transformed. Since complete transformation is not entirely possibly until that final day, we should remember that city transformation (like personal conformity to Christ) is more like the North Star than the North Pole—a direction to pursue rather than a destination we arrive at.

> City transformation begins with a transformed church that engages the needs of the city with works *and* words of love — good deeds and good news.

What Community Transformation Is Not

In addition to defining community transformation, we need to address what community transformation *is not*. First, community transformation does not mean that everything will be perfect in the city. The test of transformation is not whether we can leave our doors unlocked at night. It does not mean that everyone agrees on everything and there is a unanimous consensus of opinions. In Matthew 13, Jesus unfolds a series of parables that are instructive for understanding the kingdom of God. In one of these, the parable of the weeds (Matt. 13:24–30, 36–43), he gives us some principles that relate to the idea of community transformation. Jesus teaches his disciples that the kingdom of heaven is like a man who sowed good seed in his field. But while everyone was sleeping (or not paying attention), an enemy came and sowed weeds among the wheat and then went away. When the crop sprouted, the servants went to the master and asked whether they should pull up the weeds. The master said, "No.... Let both grow together until the harvest" (vv. 29–30). As Jesus explains the meaning of the parable to his followers, he explicitly tells them that it is not until his return that "[the angels] will weed out of his kingdom everything that causes sin and all who do evil" (v. 41). Until that time, the sons of the kingdom and the sons of the Evil One will continue to grow side by side. In other words, while evil can be restrained in our communities, it will not be eradicated until God finishes the work he started. Until that time, we work toward what Steve Garber, director of the Washington Institute for Faith, Vocation and Culture, calls "proximate justice." "Proximate justice realizes that something is better than nothing. It allows us to make peace with *some* justice, *some* mercy, all the while realizing that it will only be in the new heaven and new earth that we find all our longings finally fulfilled, that we will see all of God's demands finally met. It is only then and there we will see all of the conditions for human flourishing finally in place, socially, economically, and politically."[80]

We work toward the possibility of proximate justice—of *something* rather than nothing—knowing ahead of time that it will never be *everything* on this side of the restoration. In many ways, this is a positive thing, since most of us would actually rather live in a country that allows free (and sometimes unedifying) speech than in a country where *all* the commands of God are made into civil law and where the use of unwholesome words (Eph. 4:29) is a misdemeanor.

Second, community transformation is not *once and for all*. New energies must constantly be invested into a community to maintain the fruit of previous efforts. We can gain some insight from the laws of science as we consider this principle. Those with chess-club-sized brains tell us the law of entropy means that "energy spontaneously tends to flow only from being concentrated in one place to becoming diffused or dispersed and spread out."[81] Entropy explains why a hot pan, taken off the stove, takes on the temperature of the room rather than the other way around. Entropy explains why things rust and decay. It explains why batteries wear down and why air escapes from a punctured tire. Entropy explains why objects roll downhill rather than uphill. Every building, every program, every community is wearing down. Sadly, these things don't just renew themselves.

There are two key factors that can interrupt the law of entropy. The first is when new energies are invested into the community: some communities seem to maintain their charm (or even get better) with the passing years. The people of the community continue to seek the good of their city and invest their time and effort into revitalizing it. Buildings are repainted, lawns are mowed, and weeds are pulled.

> The transformations that happen in a community can easily reverse themselves without new bonded relationships between people and entities in the community or without sustained input of energy and resources.

The second factor that interrupts the natural tendency toward entropy is the strength of the chemical bonds in an object. This explains why mountains don't quickly flatten out and an overhanging rock doesn't just fall from a cliff. Entropy is slowed down and prevented by the strength of the chemical bonds between the molecules that make up the rock. In the same way, the entropy of a community can be hindered or blocked by the strength of the social bonds in the community. When people are connected to one another, when the church is connected and partnering with others who care about the community — schools, human-services agencies, the business community, and government agencies — the bonds between those in the community are stronger than the law of entropy. The stronger the social bonds, the stronger the community; the weaker the bonds, the weaker and more prone to decay is the community. The transformations that happen in a community can easily reverse themselves without new bonded relationships between people and entities in the community or without sustained input of energy and resources.

CHURCHES CAN AND MUST MAKE A DIFFERENCE IN A COMMUNITY

As will be noted in chapter 3, God's people have historically been his hands, feet, and voice in the world. Cities, communities, and cultures have been transformed and revitalized as churches have sought to follow Jesus, making his presence known. Sociologist Rodney Stark summarizes the urban impact of the early church in the first few centuries.

Christianity served as a revitalization movement that arose in response to the misery, chaos, fear and brutality of life in the urban Greco-Roman world … by providing new norms and new kinds of social relationships able to cope with many urgent problems. To cities filled with the homeless and impoverished, Christianity offered charity as well as hope. To cities filled with newcomers and strangers, Christianity offered an immediate basis for attachment. To cities filled with orphans and widows, Christianity provided a new and expanded sense of family. To cities torn by violent ethnic strife, Christianity offered a new basis for social solidarity. And to cities faced with epidemics, fire, and earthquakes, Christianity offered effective nursing services…. For what they brought was not simply an urban movement, but a new culture capable of making life in Greco-Roman cities tolerable.[82]

If the church is missing from the conversation of a community, the community will languish.

CHANGING CULTURE

Austrian philosopher and priest Ivan Illich was once asked, What is the most revolutionary way to change society? Is it through violent revolution or gradual reform? Illich gave a careful answer. "Neither," he said. "If you want to change society, then you must tell an alternative story."[83]

In his book *Culture Making,* Andy Crouch describes how he makes chili con carne, complete with chopped onions, green peppers, and tomatoes. Chili is something that he and his wife thoroughly enjoy during the colder months of the year. But when the chili is set on the table, his children protest because they don't like green peppers and chopped tomatoes. Being nonindulgent parents, Andy and his wife have decided that that's just too bad. This is the way they like their chili, and sooner or later the kids will also *learn* to like it. And if they don't, they can make their own chili any way they want when they move out of the home. For now, this is what chili in the Crouch household looks like. Still, there is one exception to this rule that Andy is willing to consider.

There is one thing our children could do, though, that could have a decisive effect on our family's culture of the table. If I come home on a Tuesday night … and find dinner already simmering on the stove, even if it's not chili, I will likely be delighted…. Consider this a parable of cultural change, illustrating this fundamental rule: The only way to change culture is to create more of it…. Cultural change will only happen when something new displaces, to some extent, existing culture in a very tangible way…. No matter how much we may protest — condemning the cultural goods on offer — unless we offer an alternative, the show will go on.[84]

Andy's point is simple: were his children to make their dinner, he'd be willing to forego his plans to eat chili that night. While *changing* something about a particular culture may not always yield results, perhaps the better option is to start by *creating* something new. As the church, we have the opportunity to influence and transform our communities and our culture—not by being a critic of the culture, not by merely creating a vision of a different culture, but by embodying the change we would like to see and actually living out the kingdom message of Jesus. Lasting cultural change will happen only as believers create a more attractive and compelling picture of what life can be—living out what it means to put others above ourselves, valuing servanthood above power, doing acts of justice, loving mercy, and walking humbly with God.

> Cultural change will happen only as believers create a more attractive and compelling picture of what life can be.

Ubiquitous and Local

Because the church is always local in its presence in a community, we believe that the local church is in the best position to make a sustained and positive kingdom difference in the world. Some have argued that the church is the best distribution system for human services in the world. Could it be that the social forces shaping our culture today are providing new opportunities for the church to make an impact through our service and ministry in the community?

For Reflection and Discussion

1. What does community transformation assume about the way the world is?
2. What does community transformation assume about the way the world should be?
3. How would you define "community transformation" in your city?
4. If your community were transformed, how could you tell? What would be different? (A helpful exercise is to write a newspaper article as if it were written ten years from now. Start with a headline, then include faux interviews with various leaders: "Our city back then was ..." "We decided to work together because ..." "Our catalyst to change was ..." "Today things are so different. For example ...")
5. What is an area of your city where you could create culture? What might that look like? Why, do you think, would it be attractive to others?

CHAPTER THREE

UNDERSTANDING THE KINGDOM

> Why here is the most radical proposal ever presented to the mind
> of man, the proposal to replace the present world order with God's
> order, the Kingdom of God.
>
> — H. G. Wells

I n January of 2005, we (Eric and Sam) hosted our first Global Leadership Community, at Lost Antler Ranch outside of Estes Park, Colorado. This Leadership Community gathered every six months for nearly three years over a five-day period during which we prayed, talked, ate, Nordic-walked, and fished together. The group was composed of two leaders from each of fourteen cities around the world — Oslo, Berlin, Mexico City, San Salvador, Mumbai, Beijing, Auckland, and seven cities in the United States. Previous to 2005, we (Eric and Sam) had been traveling to different cities around the world and telling city leaders in each location what God was doing in the other cites we had been to. "Well, in Berlin they ...," "In Beijing the house church leaders are ...," "In Boulder a group of pastors is ..." The response had been somewhat predictable, sort of like the reaction you get when you tell someone, "You should have been here last week!" They had listened politely but weren't really able to connect with our experiences secondhand. So over breakfast one morning the thought had occurred to us, "Instead of traveling to each of these cities, what if we brought all of these city leaders to Colorado to meet together?" On the back of a baklava-stained napkin at a restaurant outside Athens, we outlined four qualifications for the leaders in this group:

1. The leader had to be the *go-to person* for city transformation in that city, the person who could connect and convene other key leaders in the

city. A second person could be a key pastor or business, foundation, or nonprofit leader in the city.

2. The leader had to be a *practitioner*, not just a thought leader. There would be room for thought leaders as resource people, but our key leaders had to be actively doing something in the city.

3. The leader had to be *committed to multiplying* the process in his or her own setting.

4. We had to *like hanging out* with that person. Our rationale was, "If I like you and I like this other person, chances are you are going to like each other." Studies show that every group has a limited amount of energy, which can be expended either on making the relationships work or on the mission itself. We wanted the energy to go toward the mission. We realize that not all groups can do this, but since we had the choice, we chose to organize in this manner. Later we found our justifying verse — Mark 3:13: "Jesus ... called to him those he wanted." But our theory proved true. For the most part, these folks got along fabulously, kept in touch, and visited each other between the gatherings, even tearing up when the Leadership Community finally came to an end.

It was an impressive and talented group — the leader of the largest house church network in Beijing, the leaders of the largest city transformation initiative in Europe, our friend Higgins from New Zealand. Each leader came to the group with his passion for cities and a passion for living. Jan Sirevaag from Oslo taught many of us how to use walking sticks for Nordic walking. "When I turned fifty, I told my wife, Gudveig, 'I'm fifty, fat, and finished!' Then I started Nordic walking and lost thirty kilos. Now I'll be sixty, svelte, and sexy!" He kept us entertained with his witty aphorisms. We even had a name for our city transformation effort. We called it Metromucil (after the popular orange-flavored laxative), and our theme was "city *movements* everywhere." We had yellow hats made up with an orange logo matching the distinctive Metamucil label. I guess that shows our age! For each gathering, we brought in an outside resource person who would speak two or three times on a topic of common interest and then act as a "consultant in residence" for the remainder of the week.

Each morning we started with a devotional. One bluebird morning in June we asked Layo Lieva from San Salvador to lead us in the Word. Layo has been in ministry in El Salvador for over thirty years and has the long view of doing ministry in one country. He understands the theology of *place*. He told us how, when he was a student and his country was a mere 3 to 5 percent professing evangelicals, he and his friends would dream of what their country could be like if just one-third of the people in El Salvador knew Christ.[85] "What if...?" grew legs as they began strategizing about how to best reach their country. That morning, Layo had some good news to share with us. After thirty years of ministry, between 32 percent and 38 percent of El Salvadorans were now believers. Moreover, every man, woman, and child had (statistically speaking) been evangelized at least three times in the past fifteen years. Conversions in the country have led to new church-planting efforts, and in El Salvador today there is one evangelical church for every seven hundred El Salvadorans. (The Saturation Church Planting folks suggest that having at least one culturally relevant and geographically accessible church for every thousand people means that a country is "saturated.") In fact, one of the largest churches in the world is located in this tiny country in Central America. Elim Church in San Salvador is a cell-based church with an attendance of 147,000 people who meet in cell groups all over the city. The name of Jesus is frequently lifted up in public media. El Salvador boasts five Christian newspapers, five Christian television stations, and nineteen Christian radio stations. There is now an association of Christian high schools, and there are four Christian universities. There are two evangelical hospitals and numerous Christian mayors and government officials. People even fly in to meet and pray with the country's president on a weekly basis. There are annual "Jesus Marches" replete with banners and bands. Layo noted that there is now "a festival of Christian work." As we listened, we sat there smiling at the good news Layo was sharing with us—it was like an answer to his prayers! But Layo wasn't smiling. He concluded his glowing report with these words: "Our country has never been worse off!" We were shocked. Worse off? How could that be?

Layo went on to tell us that despite these outward signs of religious growth and the apparent penetration of Christianity into the social institutions of the country, the mental and moral infrastructure of the country had been destroyed. Nine people a day died by violent crimes. Drug use was out of control. Thirty-five percent of people were unemployed. Gangs were prolific and violent. One study showed that 32 percent of gang members came from evangelical homes. The most common complaint to the police was "evangelical noise"—preachers who drive through the streets blaring their message from speakers mounted atop their cars. Why the disconnect? What went wrong? Layo gave us his personal assessment: "We settled for conversion rather than transformation. We don't need to do better; we need to do it different. I'm not sure if we need any more church plants, if they are like the ones we have now. What we need is a different kind of church."

Let's think of El Salvador as a laboratory for ministry methodology. If we were to get everything we wanted, all that we were working toward right now—

saturation evangelism, church planting, Christians elected into office, Christian schools established, and a Christian voice in media—what would happen? Would our cities truly be transformed? Darrow Miller's insights help explain why places like El Salvador may be *converted* but not transformed: "Evangelizing and planting churches is essential to, but not adequate for, Kingdom transformation. They are means to an end—not ends in themselves.... Being converted doesn't automatically entail a complete shift in beliefs.... Here is precisely where many missionary efforts have failed. Too often, their vision ends with numbers of conversions, numbers of churches planted, or the size of church growth. When this is the case, there is little motivation for discipleship. There is little or no vision to see these precious new churches operate as engines of Kingdom transformation."[86]

> "We settled for conversion rather than transformation" (Layo Lieva).

Perhaps change will come not from doing things better but from doing them differently.

THE KINGDOM AS A STARTING POINT

Thinking about transformation is best done in the context of the kingdom of God. Leading from any other point of view will lead us to a less-than-biblical view of the world, its problems, the solution, and ultimate redemption. Tim Keller writes, "The Biblical teaching on the kingdom is that: a) the world was created good, and b) everything is fallen and tainted because we lost the ruling power of God through sin, and c) everything will be restored by the final return of the King. Every 'world-view' has to answer the question: 'what is wrong with life and how can it be fixed?' ... Only the Christian world-view locates the problem with the world not in any one part of the world or in any one group of people but in Sin itself. And it locates the solution in God's grace and the coming of the kingdom."[87]

As we think of defining the kingdom, it can be helpful to begin by defining what the kingdom is not. We are struck by the thinking of Pastor Greg Boyd, who reminds us that the kingdom of God is not to be confused with our political movements: "For some evangelicals, the kingdom of God is largely about, if not centered on, 'taking America back for God,' voting for the Christian candidate, outlawing abortion, outlawing gay marriage, winning the culture war, defending political freedom at home and abroad, keeping the phrase 'under God' in the Pledge of Allegiance, fighting for prayer in the public schools and at public events, and fighting to display the Ten Commandments in government buildings."[88]

As worthy as these endeavors might be, they themselves are not what the kingdom is about. So what, exactly, is the kingdom?

A Personal Journey

A few years ago, I (Eric) found myself repeatedly referring to the kingdom in my conversations, while hoping like crazy that no one would ask me what I actually meant when I talked about it. The truth is that I had never really studied what the Bible teaches on this topic. My theological training and my background had led me to believe that the kingdom of God was a future reality and that we were now living in the age of the church. Whenever I would read the New Testament and see the word *kingdom*, I would mentally substitute the word *church* (to make it applicable) or, if that didn't make sense, I'd just dismiss it as something God would do in the distant future. I decided that I needed a better handle on the kingdom, so I printed out all 152 verses in the New Testament (NIV) that included the word *kingdom* or *kingdoms* and did my best to read them every day for a month. Was I ever surprised at what I discovered!

Why Did John the Baptist Get Such a Huge Response?

The first recorded words from John the Baptist in Matthew's gospel are "Repent, for the kingdom of heaven is near" (Matt. 3:2). It's a short sermon — just eight words in my Bible — but these few words sure got a powerful response. Verses 5 and 6 record that "[p]eople went out to him [John] from Jerusalem and all Judea and the whole region of the Jordan. Confessing their sins, they were baptized by him in the Jordan River." Short messages like this can solicit a big response only if the hearer understands the context of the message, and reading John's words and seeing the urgency with which he preached, I was baffled at his results. Why did John's audience respond in droves to this short message? What did they hear in these eight words that I was missing? What were they anticipating? I knew that to understand what they were hearing in John's message, I'd have to look beyond the New Testament. To really understand the kingdom, I had to go back to the Old Testament Scriptures, to the prophetic book of Daniel.

Looking Back at Daniel

During the time of Daniel, the Jews had been conquered by the Babylonians and dragged off to Babylon. The Babylonian captivity in 605 BC "marks the beginning of the times of the Gentiles (Luke 21:24), the prophetic period when Jerusalem is under Gentile control."[89] It was believed that the "times of the Gentiles" would come to an end when the Messiah returned. Daniel records that one night Babylon's king, Nebuchadnezzar, had a perplexing dream about "an enormous, dazzling statue, awesome in appearance" (Dan. 2:31). Perplexed about the dream, he called in his soothsaying "magicians, enchanters, sorcerers and astrologers" (2:2), but they were unable to tell him of his dream and its meaning. Those who failed to interpret were rounded up to be put to death. But Daniel, who was in the king's service, told Nebuchadnezzar that "there is a God in heaven who reveals mysteries" (2:28). He stepped forward, not only interpreting the dream but also recalling the very details of it. Daniel told Nebuchadnezzar that the four metals of the statue (gold, silver, bronze, and iron) symbolized four kingdoms. Babylon was the first kingdom. Three other kingdoms were to follow the Babylonians in influence and domination. Daniel ended his message to Nebuchadnezzar by telling him of one more kingdom — the kingdom of God. "In the time of those kings, the God of heaven will set up a kingdom that will never be destroyed, nor will it be left to another people. It will crush all those kingdoms and bring them to an end, but it will itself endure forever" (2:44).

Later Daniel had a dream of four beasts, again representing four kingdoms that dominate the earth. His dream ended with "one like a son of man, coming with the clouds of heaven … [who] was given authority, glory and sovereign power; all peoples, nations and men of every language worshiped him. His dominion is an everlasting dominion that will not pass away, and his kingdom is one that will never be destroyed" (7:13–14). His dream ended with the hope that "the saints of the Most High will receive the kingdom and will possess it forever — yes, for ever and ever" (7:18). "Then the sovereignty, power and greatness of the kingdoms under the whole heaven will be handed over to the saints, the people of the Most High. His kingdom will be an everlasting kingdom, and all rulers will worship and obey him" (7:27). With Daniel's prophecy, the stage was set for this coming king and his kingdom.

> The stage was set for this coming king and his kingdom.

The Kingdom and the Birth of Jesus

At the time Jesus was born, Israel had been chafing and languishing under foreign control for over six hundred years. The Babylonians had been conquered by the Persians, who were in turn conquered by Alexander the Great and the Greeks. Greece eventually yielded to the mighty hand of Rome, an empire of 50 million inhabitants.[90] The Romans were the kingdom du jour. Every Jew who understood history and understood the Scriptures knew that the next kingdom on the horizon, according to Daniel's prophecy, was the promised kingdom of God. The air was thick with anticipation. The births of John the Baptist and Jesus had been foreshadowed by prophecies and speculation that pointed to a coming messianic king. John would lead the way as the one to precede Jesus, who would "rescue [them] from the hand of [their] enemies" (Luke 1:74).

The angel Gabriel visited Mary and told her that she would bear the coming king: "You will ... give birth to a son.... He will be great and will be called the Son of the Most High. The Lord God will give him the throne of his father David, and he will reign over the house of Jacob forever; his kingdom will never end" (Luke 1:31–33). After the birth of Jesus, magi from the East came to King Herod in search of the "king of the Jews" who had been recently born (Matt. 2:1–12). Herod, though currently the king of the Jewish people, knew exactly what they were talking about. He knew they were referring to the prophetic king promised by Daniel, so he consulted the chief priests and scribes and sent the magi on their way to Bethlehem to see the newborn king. Their gifts and homage were proof that they believed they had found him. When the baby Jesus was dedicated in the temple, days after his birth, the eighty-four-year-old prophetess Anna excitedly "spoke about the child to all who were looking forward to the redemption of Jerusalem" (Luke 2:36–38).

THE CENTRALITY OF THE KINGDOM MESSAGE

Matthew records for us John the Baptist's first public words — "Repent, for the kingdom of heaven is near" (Matt. 3:2) — and now, hopefully, we have a better understanding of what John was saying to the people. In anticipation of the long-awaited kingdom, prophesied long ago, the crowds from Jerusalem and Judea came out to the desert and responded to the call to turn from their sin, confess, and be baptized in the Jordan (Matt. 3:4–11). If the king was coming soon, these people wanted to be ready for him!

Soon afterward, we read, Jesus was baptized by John and, returning from the desert, found himself in his hometown of Nazareth (Luke 4:14–30). As we saw in our last chapter, when the scroll of Isaiah was handed to Jesus, he read from Isaiah 61: "The Spirit of the Lord is on me, because he has anointed me to preach good news to the poor" (Luke 4:18). This passage fleshed out and confirmed the "great commission" of Jesus. Isaiah 61:1–6 depicts the gospel being preached through proclamation ("proclaim") and demonstration ("bind up the broken-hearted," "comfort all who mourn," "provide for those who grieve," etc). It speaks of the kingdom as a place of beauty, not ashes; gladness, not mourning; praise, and not despair (v. 3). The transformed people of the kingdom — referred to as "oaks of righteousness" — are those who "rebuild," "renew," and "restore" the city.

Jesus' Message and Ministry

As Jesus began his public ministry, the words of his sermon were identical to the message proclaimed by his older cousin, John — "Repent, for the kingdom of heaven is near" (Matt. 4:17). Jesus, like John, announced the nearness of the coming kingdom, and the next three years of his life would define and shape a vision for that kingdom, leading to his bloody death and triumphant resurrection. Wherever he went, Jesus spoke about the kingdom: "I must preach the good news of the kingdom of God to the other towns also, because that is why I was sent" (Luke 4:43); "Jesus went through all the towns and villages, teaching in their synagogues, preaching the good news of the kingdom and healing every disease and sickness" (Matt. 9:35; see also Luke 8:1; 9:11).

> "Unless Matthew, Mark, and Luke are totally wrong, all who want to preach and live like Jesus must place the 'kingdom of God' at the center of their thought and action" (Arias Mortimer).

The kingdom was central to the message and the ministry of Jesus. The first petition that Jesus taught his disciples to pray was a cry for God's kingdom to be a reality on earth: "[Y]our kingdom come, your will be done on earth as it is in heaven" (Matt. 6:10). Jesus taught his disciples that they should seek first (in priority and importance) his kingdom (Matt. 6:33). Even after his death and resurrection, the kingdom of God was central to his teaching and message: "He appeared to them over a period of forty days and spoke about the kingdom of God" (Acts 1:3). Theology professor Arias Mortimer notes, "Unless Matthew, Mark, and Luke are totally wrong, all who want to preach and live like Jesus must place the 'kingdom of God' at the center of their thought and action. This phrase (or Matthew's equivalent, the 'kingdom of heaven') appears 122 times in the first three Gospels — most of the time (92) on the lips of Jesus himself."[91]

THE MINISTRY OF THE DISCIPLES

Jesus' message of the kingdom was not confined to his own preaching. When he sent out his disciples, he instructed them, "As you go, preach this message: 'The kingdom of heaven is near'" (Matt. 10:7; see also Luke 10:9) — the very same message that he and John had been preaching. The central teaching of Phillip is summarized in Acts 8:12 as "the good news of the kingdom of God and the name of Jesus Christ." Similarly, we find evidence that the apostle Paul also preached the kingdom of God. When Paul came to Ephesus for three months, he spoke out boldly, "arguing persuasively about the kingdom of God" (Acts 19:8). For two years, Paul set up shop in the school of Tyrannus, where he taught about the king and the kingdom (19:9). In Paul's farewell address to these same Ephesians, he said, "Now I know that none of you among whom I have gone about preaching the kingdom will ever see me again" (20:25). When Paul arrived in Rome, he arranged, even under arrest, to meet with Jewish leaders, and "[f]rom morning till evening he explained and declared to them the kingdom of God" (28:23). Finally, the closing curtain on the book of Acts finds Paul under house arrest, welcoming all who came to see him: "And without hindrance he preached the kingdom of God and taught about the Lord Jesus Christ" (Acts 28:31). In Paul's writing, he refers to the kingdom no fewer than sixteen times.

A KINGDOM MUST HAVE A KING

While the kingdom was the central message preached, it was just as clear to those listening that Jesus was the king of that kingdom. A careful student of the Gospels will note that the bookend passages of Jesus' earthly life indicate his kingship. He was king in the manger (Matt. 2:1–2), and he was king before Pilate — "You are right in saying I am a king. In fact, for this reason I was born, and for this I came into the world" (John 18:37; see also John 19:12; Luke 23:2). Jesus was even called a king while hanging on the cross, when a thief asked to be remembered as Jesus entered his kingdom that Friday afternoon (Luke 23:42). And the central message of Paul's teaching not only was about the kingdom but also focused on the king of that kingdom: "These men who have caused trouble all over the world have now come here.... They are all ... saying that there is another king, one called Jesus" (Acts 17:6–7).

WHAT IS THE KINGDOM OF GOD?

As I studied the Scriptures, it occurred to me that the kingdom of God is found anywhere God has operative dominion. Although "[t]he earth is the LORD's, and everything in it, the world, and all who live in it" (Ps. 24:1), the kingdom of God is present in those places, spiritual or material, where God is honored as sovereign and his values are operative. The kingdom of God has a king, and his name is Jesus (Matt. 2:1 – 12; John 18:37). So preaching the message of the kingdom, among other things, demands that we tell people through our words and communicate with our actions who this king is and what he values. We tell an alternative story of what life should be, can be, and one day will be. As we mentioned in the previous chapter, there are several places in Scripture that give us a physical description of what community life looks like when God's reign is fully operative.

If the kingdom of God is a place where God's perfect will is operative, then any place where there is sorrow, weeping, infant mortality, hunger, premature death, or other signs of original sin's effects on the world is an affront to that kingdom. This helps us to understand why the miracles of Jesus were so significant to people. When Jesus taught the crowds and found five thousand Jews who were hungry, it was an affront to God's kingdom, so he fed them. When four thousand Gentiles in the region of the Decapolis were hungry, he also fed them (Mark 8:1 – 8), because the kingdom of God is not limited by geographic or ethnic boundaries. When Jesus met people who were sick or paralyzed, he saw their condition as an affront to the kingdom and healed them. And when a twelve-year-old girl died, Jesus raised her from the dead (Luke 8:40 – 56). Why? Because children don't die in the kingdom, and the king had come to her home. Even when Jesus' friend Lazarus died, Jesus chose to raise him from the dead (John 11:38 – 44), because his premature death was an affront to the kingdom of God. Because the broken, natural world will one day be restored, Jesus calmed the raging seas. Through his miracles, Jesus gave us a picture of what the kingdom of God is and will be like. Admittedly, Jesus didn't heal everyone, he didn't feed everyone, and he didn't raise every dead person. But Jesus created a compelling and alternative vision called the kingdom of God. When he later sent his disciples out to minister, they preached the message of the coming kingdom and did the very same things that Jesus had done to show the people, in living color, what the kingdom of God looked like (Luke 7:21; 9:2; 10:8 – 9; etc.).

> We tell an alternative story of what life should be, can be, and one day will be.

SHOWING THE LOVE IN ASIA

My (Eric's) son Andy and his wife, Natalie, (and their two young children) have been working in East Asia for the past six years. When Andy shares the gospel with students on college campuses, he starts by saying, "God loves you and has a wonderful plan for your life. Part of his plan is to use you to change the world. When Jesus was on earth, he fed the hungry, healed the sick, loved the children, and as followers of Jesus, we do the same. What would our campus be like if all of our students followed Jesus and lived as he lived?"

After some thought, students inevitably respond, "We would love each other and help each other." Then Andy asks, "And what if every person in our city became a Christ follower; what would our city be like?" "Well," they answer, "there would be no homeless, or hungry, or street children, and our city would be an awesome place, and everybody in our country would want to move to our city." Wow! Even those who don't know Christ know that the kingdom is a better story than the one we have. Life in the kingdom is universally attractive. The gospel is much bigger than just a personal relationship with God — the gospel of the kingdom can literally change the world!

> "There would be no homeless, or hungry, or street children, and our city would be an awesome place, and everybody in our country would want to move to our city."

Parables about the Kingdom of God

When Jesus preached about the kingdom of God, he frequently used parables to reveal different facets of the kingdom. Each parable in itself is unable to adequately describe all the workings of the kingdom, but taken together, they provide a thick, three-dimensional picture of how the kingdom operates. Though it would be extremely beneficial, we don't have space to develop the teaching of each parable — that's something you can do on your own. What's important, though, is recognizing just how many different stories Jesus has given us to help us understand the kingdom, each one with a unique twist on the kingdom. Jesus taught us that the kingdom of God, or heaven, is like

- "a man who sowed good seed in his field" (Matt. 13:24);
- "a mustard seed, which a man took and planted in his field" (Matt. 13:31);
- "yeast that a woman took and mixed into a large amount of flour until it worked all through the dough" (Matt. 13:33);

- "treasure hidden in a field. When a man found it, he hid it again, and then in his joy went and sold all he had and bought that field" (Matt. 13:44);
- "a merchant looking for fine pearls" (Matt. 13:45);
- "a king who wanted to settle accounts with his servants" (Matt. 18:23);
- "a landowner who went out early in the morning to hire men to work in his vineyard" (Matt. 20:1);
- "a king who prepared a wedding banquet for his son" (Matt. 22:2);
- "ten virgins who took their lamps and went out to meet the bridegroom" (Matt. 25:1);
- "a man going on a journey, who called his servants and entrusted his property to them" (Matt. 25:14);
- "a man [who] scatters seed on the ground. Night and day, whether he sleeps or gets up, the seed sprouts and grows, though he does not know how. All by itself the soil produces grain" (Mark 4:26–28).

Light shining through each kingdom parable reveals a unique and attractive facet of kingdom life. These kingdom parables help us develop and envision an alternative and more compelling story of what life can be like in our communities. The parables of Jesus, like all good stories, give the listener an ending they want … but not an ending they would expect.

Teachings and Values of the Kingdom

The kingdom of God is a place where worldly values are turned upside down and things are not as we expect them to be. One of the clearest places to catch a glimpse of these unexpected values is in the Sermon on the Mount (Matthew 5–7; Luke 6:17–49). Since he is the king of the kingdom, we will assume that whatever Jesus values is a kingdom value and whatever Jesus taught is kingdom teaching. Again, we lack the time and space to give you a complete treatise on the teachings and values of the kingdom, but we offer the following summary of select kingdom values, drawn from the teachings of Jesus.

- Children are valued and held in high esteem (Matt. 18:1–4; Mark 10:14).
- The poor are blessed and given a place of honor (Luke 6:20).
- Servanthood is valued over power (Matt. 20:20–28).
- We love our enemies, do good to those who hate us, bless those who curse us, and pray for those who mistreat us (Luke 6:27–28).

- It's a life where we treat others as we wish ourselves to be treated (Luke 6:31).
- It's a life of peacemaking (Matt. 5:9).
- It's a life filled with faith and free from worry (Matt. 6:25 – 34).
- It's a life of giving (Matt. 6:1 – 4).
- It's a life of prayer (Matt. 6:5 – 14; 7:7 – 12).
- It's a life of love (Matt. 5:43 – 48).
- It's a life of forgiveness (Matt. 6:14; 18:21 – 35).
- It's a life where marriage is honored (Matt. 5:27 – 32; 19:3 – 9).
- It's a life of reconciliation (Matt. 5:23 – 26; Luke 15:11 – 31).
- It's a life of good deeds (Matt. 5:16).
- It's a life of honesty (Matt. 5:33 – 37).
- It's a life of good neighboring (Luke 10:25 – 37).

These values are a sample of what is most attractive when people live together the way God intended them to live. Often, when people are honored and prizes are given for humanitarian efforts, those who are being honored represent in some way a kingdom value, whether or not they identify that value as such.

What Is Kingdom Work?

Kingdom work involves two aspects. It involves introducing people to the King (Jesus), and it involves bringing his perspective, his values, and his generative structures into the world in which we live. It's about being active participants in answering the prayer, "[Y]our kingdom come, your will be done on earth as it is in heaven" (Matt. 6:10). Many of the parables describe this work of the kingdom as sowing and reaping, which are commonly understood as the ministries of evangelism and discipleship. One side of kingdom work involves evangelism — introducing people to the King — while the second side of the work is about helping them grow in that relationship as they learn and embody kingdom values. Most would probably agree with what we've said thus far, but now we'd like to venture out upon a supporting limb as we consider a broader notion of kingdom work. In this broader sense, we would like to suggest that anytime we are involved in making this world more reflective of God's coming kingdom (Rev. 11:15) and are redeeming something that was lost or broken because of the fall, we are involved, to some degree, in kingdom work. In this sense, cleaning a park or painting a mural that covers graffiti can be considered kingdom work. Why? Because the kingdom is also a place of beauty. Isaiah 61:4 speaks of transformed people who "will rebuild the ancient ruins and restore the places long devastated; they will renew the ruined cities that have been devastated for generations." Those involved in rebuilding, restoring, and renewing the city are, in this broader sense, doing kingdom work.

Whenever we are involved in correcting and making right social ills, seeking to address injustice, and fighting against the wrongs of this fallen world because they are an affront to the character of God, we are involved in kingdom work. Anytime we are involved in healing the sick, preventing an illness, or building a hospital, this too is kingdom work. Anytime we are caring for children as Jesus did, this is kingdom work. The peacemakers of the world and those who work toward forgiveness and reconciliation, in this broader sense, are involved in kingdom work.

> Kingdom work is intro-ducing people to the King, and it is helping to bring his perspective, values, and generative structures into the world we live in.

This broader understanding of kingdom work implies that more people are doing the work of God's kingdom than just those involved in the "direct ministries" of evangelism and discipleship. By affirming that acts of kindness and mercy are kingdom work, we can present a compelling vision to those who are caring for the sick, teaching our children, and cleaning our parks that they too are involved in building the kingdom of God — regardless of their personal faith. They may protest that they don't attend our church, are of another faith persuasion, or don't have any faith at all, but God can still use them to further his kingdom purposes.

Another Look at the Good Samaritan

You may remember the story of the man who is waylaid by robbers while traveling from Jerusalem to Jericho. As he lies there beaten, naked, and half-dead, we see that God gives the first opportunity to respond with compassion and mercy to the people of faith, a priest and a Levite. But when they choose to go their own way and not engage with the need that lies in front of them (probably for very spiritual reasons), Jesus discloses that it is the Samaritan — the person despised by the religious people of that day — who becomes the hero of the story. In the same way, God would love to use the church today to heal the hurts of a bruised and battered world, but when the church fails to respond or is more focused on counting nickels and noses, God will raise up just about anyone to carry out what he wants done — that's how much he cares for our broken world.

In the Old Testament, we see that God used Pharoah, Artaxerxes, Cyrus, and Nebuchadnezzar as tools to accomplish his work. The kingdom of God is larger than the church—it is built by people of *goodwill* working together with people of *good faith* to accomplish God's agenda.

We believe that Jesus still invites unbelievers to be part of his miraculous work. When Jesus told the servants at the wedding feast in Cana to "fill the jars with water" (John 2:7) and take the newly transformed wine to the banquet master, he was giving them the opportunity to be involved in the work of God. Jesus is always looking to invite people to be part of his work. Sometimes the opportunity is given to four friends of a paralytic; sometimes the opportunity is given to a boy with a small lunch. Sometimes opportunities are given to Samaritans and individuals outside the church, like Bill Gates and Warren Buffet, Bono and Jon Bon Jovi, who give their time, fortunes, and influence to make life better for millions of people.

How Do We Enter the Kingdom?

Now, before you set this book down because you disagree with what we are suggesting here, we feel that it is important to affirm that kingdom work does not in any way, shape, or form *merit* our entrance into the kingdom. Doing the work of the kingdom does *not* make one a member of the kingdom. In John 3, in his discourse with Nicodemus, Jesus explains exactly how a person enters the kingdom of God: "I tell you the truth, no one can see the kingdom of God unless he is born again.... I tell you the truth, no one can enter the kingdom of God unless he is born of water and the Spirit " (vv. 3, 5). Jesus is quite clear about one thing: we must be spiritually reborn. We enter the kingdom through a personal faith encounter with Jesus, not by merit of any good works we may do.

> Doing the work of the kingdom does *not* make one a member of the kingdom.

The Kingdom without a King, and a King without a Kingdom

As we consider what it means to do kingdom work, we need to remember that the kingdom always, and by definition, includes a king. Historically, the church (God's outpost of the kingdom and his workforce for expanding the kingdom) has drifted to one side of the pendulum or the other—trying to bring the King to people without helping to bring the kingdom, or bringing the kingdom to people while failing to tell them about the King. Both approaches fall short. The kingdom, by definition, must have a king, and people need to meet him. Conversely, if we are telling people about the King (Jesus), then it is entirely appropriate that we help them answer the question, "What is he king over?" The answer? "Well, that would be his kingdom." To be kingdom Christians, we must be committed to helping build the kingdom as well as introducing people to the King. The kingdom of God will not be realized in its fullness until the day described in Revelation 11:15, when the final transformation occurs and "[t]he kingdom of the world has become the kingdom of our Lord and of his Christ, and he will reign for ever and ever." Until that day, we must be committed to helping people enter the kingdom *and* live under the rule of the King.

FORTY YEARS OF REPURPOSING

Have we settled for too little in thinking about what God has for us? Unless we have a kingdom perspective, we are likely to reduce the ministry we do outside the walls of our church to mere programs with an emphasis on tactics and strategies. Our evangelism and outreach to our community will not flow out of the core of who we are as a church. Kingdom work is not a program. It's not something we can fit into a forty-day campaign—it's more of a forty-year plan! Kingdom Christians can truly rejoice anytime they see God's kingdom manifested, regardless of whether it results in their particular church growing. Sometimes people who come to faith in Christ end up joining another congregation. Sometimes, working in an after-school program or mentoring a child, we may not see the fruit of our efforts for ten or fifteen years! We'd like to promise you that engaging your community and focusing your time and energy outside the walls of your church to expand the kingdom will lead to significant church growth, but the truth is that sometimes it does ... and sometimes it doesn't. Some churches will glowingly report that they really started growing when they began engaging their communities, but some churches may do the same thing and see little immediate growth. It's not just about growth and numbers, though. God calls us to be the church and to live out the kingdom—whether it builds our individual church or not. It's about God, not about us. It's about the welfare of the city, not about the well-being of our church.

MOVING FROM CHURCH TO KINGDOM

The church is *different* than the kingdom. Jesus builds his church (Matt. 16:18), and the church helps to build the kingdom, the embodiment of what life looks like when people are living under the reign of God. The church serves as a living proof of the kingdom, a community where the world can see what marriage, family life, business practices, work habits, generosity, mercy, race relations — all of life — look like when lived under the rule and authority of Jesus Christ. But the church is not a closed community. We are commanded to go out into the world, serving as witnesses to the King and his kingdom. Spreading the kingdom of God is more than simply winning men and women to Christ. It involves working toward *shalom* and the redemption of structures, individuals, families, and relationships as well as surprising others with unexpected deeds of grace, mercy, and justice (Mic. 6:8). The church is called to create an attractive and compelling alternative, showing what life is like when lived under the reign of God.

> The church is called to create an attractive and compelling alternative, showing what life is like when lived under the reign of God.

ENGAGING OTHERS IN THE KINGDOM

A few years ago, I (Eric) read Joseph Campbell's *The Hero with a Thousand Faces*, the seminal work on comparative mythology. After studying the myths of ancient Greece, Rome, China, India, Persia, Australia, and the Americas (including the stories of the Bible, the *Bhagavad Gita*, the Koran, and other religious texts), Campbell concludes that all mythology follows a similar story line — the "monomyth." In every great story, an average person is called to do something great. Campbell identifies this as "the call to adventure." Normally, the call to adventure is followed by a refusal of the call (think of people like Moses, Jonah, Luke Skywalker, or Frodo Baggins). The person is then given supernatural aid (a ring that gives magic powers, or a cape that makes them invisible), and the adventure begins. After crossing thresholds and battling foes, the potential hero eventually acquires what he or she was sent to find, but the new setting is now so good, he or she refuses to return. Campbell notes that the hero's cycle is never complete until he returns to his homeland and blesses humanity with what he has attained (like Prometheus returning from the sun and blessing humanity with the gift of fire).

Reading Joseph Campbell did not lead me to mythologize the Scriptures (or my faith, for that matter), but it did help me to see yet another apologetic for the universal message of the Scriptures. God has placed within every human being a desire for a certain story line: the kingdom story. Isn't the story line—the narrative of the gospel—a call to adventure, to give ourselves away to a noble and worthy cause—to follow Jesus in his redemptive and transformational work? Like Campbell's reticent hero, though, we want to keep what we have received and make our faith private and personal rather than public and transformational. We refuse to return to those in need and bless them with what we've been given. That's the real adventure of faith. Have we co-opted God's story by making faith in Christ the *end* of a journey rather than the *beginning* of an adventure? In doing so, have we reduced the gospel to simply a way of escaping from danger, rather than embracing the compelling call to follow Christ into our broken world—a call to adventure?

This seems like a good place for a personal confession. I (Sam) was a pastor of three churches over a period of thirty-five years. Two facts were true at the end of each of those pastorates: the church was larger ... and the surrounding community was worse off when I left than it had been when I arrived. I don't know that there was a direct cause-and-effect relationship between my presence and either of those facts. I do know this: my focus as a pastor was all about growing the church, not about transforming the community. If it were possible to have a "do-over," I would love to go back and change the focus of my ministry, from the church to the kingdom. The first step? Assuming pastoral responsibility for the *community* as well as the church, proclaiming the gospel as a call to adventure rather than simply an escape from danger.

FOR REFLECTION AND DISCUSSION

1. What resonates most with you from this chapter? What did you disagree with, if anything, and why?
2. What are some of the consequences of churches focusing on growing the church rather than manifesting the kingdom?
3. Is it possible to be the church *and* build the kingdom? How?
4. Tim Keller says, "Every 'world-view' has to answer the question: 'what is wrong with life and how can it be fixed?'" What do you think is wrong with life? How can it be fixed? How does the answer to that question relate to doing kingdom work?
5. What agendas or programs do we have that most often substitute for a kingdom agenda?

CHAPTER FOUR

TRANSFORMING POWER

> We are subjects of the city and involved in its condemnation, and yet we are the possible artisans of her adoption by God.
>
> — Jacques Ellul, *The Meaning of the City*

Wherever we go around our country and around the world, we are asked by leaders, "Where is this working?" "Are there any examples you can give me?" "Can cities really be transformed?" Our answer is that not only can cities be transformed; history shows that entire societies have been transformed. That's what this chapter is about.

Historian Thomas Cahill's *Desire of the Everlasting Hills: The World Before and After Jesus* is one of his books about the "hinges of history" — the people and events that greatly shaped the values, culture, and thinking of the Western world. In this book, Cahill seeks to answer the two questions, "Did Jesus make a difference?" and "Is our world any better today than it was before Jesus walked this earth?"[92] Cahill notes that there seem to be two streams of Christianity that flow through history — the transformational and life-giving gospel of the cross (which is the model we want to advocate) and the dark "subterranean river" of Christianity that is a fount of suppression and exclusion (the inauthentic Christianity that many reject). Cahill concludes that for the past two

> For the past two thousand years there have been those, in every age, who have read the Gospels with fresh eyes and become agents of grace and transformation for their communities.

thousand years there have been those, in every age, who have read the Gospels with fresh eyes and become agents of grace and transformation for their communities.[93] We believe that transformation of a city is predicated on our learning to read the Scriptures with new eyes and rediscovering the ancient message once again, learning what it means to be an agent of grace in our generation.

The Early Christians

At least one lesson that we can learn from the story of the early church is that you don't need seminaries, church growth seminars, elaborate youth programs, and large buildings to grow and see lives changed by the gospel. Sociologist Rodney Stark notes that Christianity grew at a rate of 40 percent *per decade* for the first three hundred years of its existence.[94] There were many sociological, political, and spiritual factors that contributed to the spread of the gospel. The first century was indeed a "fullness of time" (Gal. 4:4) moment for Jesus to enter the world. There were definite benefits that a common language, the safety of travel, and the availability of Roman roads provided to the early church. But beyond these external factors, the early Christians lived in such a way that the world noticed something different about them, for they had a distinctive lifestyle that could not be ignored. As followers of Christ, they would seek to follow in his steps—living as he lived, loving as he loved, caring as he cared—and if the ultimate price was to be paid, they would pay that price and be welcomed into the company of Jesus himself.

Early Christians were captivated by the gospel and were profoundly influenced by the teachings and the values of Jesus Christ. It was easy to see that these early believers had been changed, since they were now consumed with the values of the kingdom of God. They became more than salt and light in their communities. In some cases, they became the "soul" of their communities. In the *Epistle of Mathetes to Diognetus*, dated around AD 150, Mathetes writes about the distinctive lifestyles of these believers.

> For the Christians are distinguished from other men neither by country, nor language, nor the customs which they observe. For they neither inhabit cities of their own, nor employ a peculiar form of speech, nor lead a life which is marked out by any singularity.... But, inhabiting Greek as well as barbarian cities ... and following the customs of the natives in respect to clothing, food, and the rest of their ordinary conduct, they display to us their wonderful and confessedly striking method of life. They dwell in their own countries, but simply as sojourners. As citizens, they share in all things with others, and yet endure all things as if foreigners. Every foreign land is to them as their native country, and every land of their birth as a land of

strangers. They marry, as do all [others]; they beget children; but they do not destroy their offspring. They have a common table, but not a common bed. They are in the flesh, but they do not live after the flesh. They pass their days on earth, but they are citizens of heaven. They obey the prescribed laws, and at the same time surpass the laws by their lives. They love all men, and are persecuted by all.... They are poor, yet make many rich; they are reviled, and bless; they are insulted, and repay the insult with honor; they do good, yet are punished as evil-doers.... In a word, what the soul is in a body, the Christians are in the world.[95]

Captivated by the gospel, these early Christians freely moved against the flow of the predominant culture. In a world that devalued children, the early Christians followed the example of Jesus, who welcomed little children. Rodney Stark writes about the low value attached to the lives of children and infants in Greek and Roman cultures: "Seneca regarded the drowning of children at birth as both reasonable and commonplace.... It was common to expose an unwanted infant out-of-doors where it could, in principle, be taken up by someone who wished to rear it, but where it typically fell victim to the elements or to animals and birds. Not only was the exposure of infants a very common practice, it was justified by law and advocated by philosophers. Both Plato and Aristotle recommended infanticide as legitimate state policy."

In a city where children were abandoned and left to die, the followers of Christ would comb the city for abandoned babies and raise them and love them as their own. They deplored both abortion and infanticide and swam against the cultural tide by raising their own children as well as rescuing those children abandoned by others.

Tertullian tells us how Christians looked out for the needs of others.

Each of us puts in a small amount one day a month, or whenever he pleases; but only if he pleases and if he is able; for there is no compulsion in the matter, everyone contributing of his own free will. These monies are, as it were, the deposits of piety. They are expended upon no banquets of drinking-bouts or useless eating-houses, but on feeding and burying poor people, on behalf of boys and girls who have neither parents nor money, in support of old folk unable now to go about, as well as for people who are shipwrecked, or who may be in the mines or exiled in islands or in prison—so long as their distress is for the sake of God's fellowship, and they themselves entitled to maintenance by their confession.[96]

The teachings of these early leaders in the church emphasized the importance of love and service to others. Tertullian, writing around 215, said, "It is our care of the helpless, our practice of loving kindness that brands us in the eyes of many of our opponents. 'Only look' they say, 'look how they love one another!' "[97] Practicing mercy and loving-kindness, while evident in the church community, also extended beyond the walls of the church. Recording how Cyprian, the bishop of Carthage, instructed his flock around the year 250, his biographer, Ponianus, wrote, "The people being assembled together, he first of all urges on them the benefits of mercy.... Then he proceeds to add that there is nothing remarkable in cherishing merely our own people with the due attentions of love, but that one might become perfect who should do something more than heathen men or publicans, one who, overcoming evil with good, and practicing a merciful kindness like that of God, should love his enemies as well.... Thus the good was done to all men, not merely to the household of faith."[98]

> Practicing mercy and loving-kindness, while evident in the church community, also extended beyond the walls of the church.

Early Christ followers, in addition to caring for their own, were focused outside themselves and beyond their own comforts. They loved and did good to all. They embodied the teachings of Jesus by living out the Sermon on the Mount.

Stark notes that in the first three centuries (in AD 165 and AD 251), there were at least two great plagues that were instrumental in the nascent church's incredible growth rate.[99] The plagues were severe, wiping out one-fourth to one-third of the population of the Roman Empire, with an estimated five thousand people a day dying in Rome.[100] When the plagues came, those who were able to leave fled the city, but the Christians did not. They stayed and ministered to the sick and dying—to fellow Christians and non-Christians alike. Dionysius, Bishop of Alexandria, writing of how believers responded to the plague of AD 251, observes,

> Most of our brother Christians showed unbounded love and loyalty, never sparing themselves and thinking only of one another. Heedless of danger, they took charge of the sick, attending to their every need and ministering to them in Christ, and with them departed this life serenely happy; for they were infected by others with the disease, drawing on themselves the sickness of their neighbors and cheerfully accepting their pains. Many, in nursing and curing others, transferred their death to themselves and died in their stead.... The best of brothers lost their lives in this manner, a number of presbyters, deacons, and laymen winning high commendation so that death in this form, the result of great piety and strong faith, seems in every way the equal of martyrdom.[101]

Writing of the response of those who were not followers of Christ, Dionysius continues, "The heathen behaved in the very opposite way. At the first onset of the disease, they pushed the sufferers away and fled from their dearest, throwing them into the roads before they were dead and treated unburied corpses as dirt."[102] Stark observes that just by providing some basic care of food and water to those too weak to care for themselves, the Christians would greatly reduce the mortality rate of the victims. He estimates that 80 percent of Christians survived the plagues, compared with only 25 percent to 50 percent of the general population. As the plagues subsided, the believers who had survived constituted a substantially higher portion of the population. Even beyond this differential in mortality, as non-Christians were nursed to health by believers, many of them became Christians themselves, responding to the mercy they had been shown. And when those who had fled the city returned to find their loved ones alive and well, their admiration for the Christians increased, and many of these people also became ardent followers of Christ. It is a universal reality of human nature that people tend to never forget how they were treated during the worst of times.

The kind of love that is willing to sacrifice in this way cannot be manufactured or faked — it has a ring of authenticity to it. In the year 362, the emperor Julian wrote to the high (pagan) priest of Galatia "that the recent Christian growth was caused by their 'moral character, even if pretended,' and by their benevolence toward strangers and care for the graves of the dead."[103] Government officials began to notice that the church had developed an effective strategy for growth — loving people in need.

In a letter to another priest, the emperor Julian wrote, "The impious Galileans (Christians) support not only their poor, but ours as well, every one can see that our people lack aid from us."[104] These observations led Julian to launch a campaign to institute pagan charities, "but for all that he urged pagan priests to match … Christian practices, there was little or no response because there were no doctrinal bases or traditional practices for them to build upon."[105] Stark concludes that it was the gospel's overwhelming growth and influence that caused Emperor Constantine in AD 313 to *acknowledge* the triumph of Christianity rather than to cause Christianity's triumph through his Edict of Milan. It was the selfless conduct of believers that attracted people to their God. Church historian Eusebius wrote,

> Then did they show themselves to the heathen in the clearest light. For the Christians were the only people who amid such terrible ills showed their feeling and humanity by their actions. Day by day some would busy themselves with attending to the dead and burying them (for there were numbers

to whom no one else paid any heed); others gathered in one spot all who were afflicted by hunger throughout the whole city and gave bread to them all. When this became known, people glorified the Christians' God and, convinced by the very facts, confessed the Christians alone were truly pious and religious.[106]

Theologian and Christian thinker Augustine of Hippo (AD 354–430) argued against a self-serving church, as he "insisted that the church was not a refuge from the world but existed for the sake of a world that was hurting."[107]

> Augustine of Hippo "insisted that the church was not a refuge from the world but existed for the sake of a world that was hurting."

Through its clear thinking and practice, the early church set a pattern for the future of the church as it engaged the world. This DNA is what Thomas Cahill calls "the substance of the original gospel," and it was essential for the survival and replication of the gospel. Cahill writes, "Through the history of the West since the time of Jesus, there has remained just enough of the substance of the original Gospel, a residuum, for it to be passed, as it were, from hand to hand and used, like stock, to strengthen, flavor, and invigorate new movements that have succeeded again and again—if only for a time—in producing *alteri Christi*, men and women in danger of crucifixion. It has also produced repeatedly and in the oddest circumstances, the loving-kindness of the first Christians."[108]

EARLY MEDIEVAL TIMES

After the fall of Rome in the fifth century and the collapse of the Roman Empire, western Europe entered what is sometimes referred to as the early medieval or Dark Ages, which lasted from approximately AD 476 to 1000.[109] Literature and the arts went dormant in the West, but Christianity continued to spread along the trade routes, and many of the barbarian conquerors adopted the Christian faith. Time does not allow for a thorough treatment of the church's role in distributing mercy during this epoch, but we do want to note that the church's light, though dim, was not extinguished. One historian writes, "In the absence of law and order, citizens tended to look to the bishops for civic leadership. In some cities, the bishop served as mayor and magistrate. The bishops of Spain and France set up vast networks for social welfare, so that the poor did not freefall now that Rome's safety net had disappeared."[110] Regarding the monks and the monastic movement, historian David Bosch notes that "humanly speaking, it was because of monasticism that so much authentic Christianity evolved in the course of Europe's 'dark ages' and beyond."[111] He goes on to say the monks "worked incredibly hard; they plowed, hedged, drained morasses, cleared away forests, did carpentry, thatched, and built roads and bridges ... they lifted the hearts of the poor and neglected peasants."[112]

In the British Isles, God was at work in a unique way. Celtic Ireland had been considered too barbaric for the Romans to conquer and civilize. But at the turn of the fifth century, a man named Patrick, who had been captured and had worked as a slave on the island for over six years before escaping, returned to Ireland with a dozen other Christ followers. After twenty-eight years of sustained ministry, Patrick (later to be known as Saint Patrick) had "planted around 700 churches and ordained perhaps 1000 priests.... [W]ithin his lifetime, 30–40 (or more) of Ireland's 150 tribes became substantially Christian."[113] Patrick did more, though, than simply plant churches. He was also committed to creating a better life for the Irish people.

Patrick's gospel had community implications as well. Thomas Cahill notes that Patrick was the first to publicly crusade against slavery. "Within his lifetime, or soon after, 'the Irish slave trade came to a halt, and other forms of violence, such as murder and intertribal warfare decreased,' and the communities Patrick founded modeled the Christian way of faithfulness, generosity, and peace to the Irish."[114] In the years that followed, "Patrick's movement blanketed the island: 'In Ireland alone there are more than 6,000 place names containing the element Cill—the old Gaelic word for church.'"[115] The gospel that Patrick preached penetrated each community, profoundly shaping the culture.

THE MIDDLE AGES

During what is now called the High Middle Ages (AD 1054, marking the split between the Latin Church and the Greek Church, to the 1400s), the social influence of the church was also felt throughout Europe. Though we often think of this time period as the time of the Crusades, this period was not without external, transformational ministries of mercy. Some of our earliest social institutions date back to the High Middle Ages. It was Pope Innocent III, in the thirteenth century, who established the modern city hospital "to care for the acutely ill who may have no one to take care of them properly, as well as for those who have been injured or who have been picked up on the street and whose friends are not in a position to care for them."[116] After establishing his then state-of-the-art hospital,

Pope Innocent III invited bishops to Rome to observe his modern hospital ... and then sent them away to replicate it.

Not surprisingly, this led to an explosion of hospital building throughout Europe. The numbers of doctors and surgeons, as well as their expertise, increased greatly. Germany soon had a hospital for every town of five thousand residents. In England, in addition to the medical services provided by the monasteries, there were 750 hospitals to meet the needs of about two million people. As a result of this, leprosy was eradicated from England, without the aid of drugs.[117]

Catholic scholar Thomas Massaro sheds light on the innovative and practical role of the church during the Middle Ages: "Modern labor unions and group insurance policies are an outgrowth of various activities of guilds and sodalities, agencies through which members of the medieval church practiced mutual support, often under direct religious auspices."[118] Despite the shortcomings of the crusading medieval church, it was not without charity. Beryl Hugen writes, "In one respect at least, the medieval church protected the poor. Only the church was large enough and universal enough to speak for those outside the [feudal] system.... It is significant that the three services most typical of the church at that time were the hospital, the hospice, and the sanctuary."[119]

In addition to the work of the institutional church, God was raising up individuals like Francis of Assisi (1182–1226), who rediscovered the gospel and eventually established his own monastic order. Historian Matthew Arnold writes of Saint Francis in his *Essays in Criticism* (1865), "He [Francis] transformed monachism by uprooting the stationary monk, delivering him from the bondage of property, and sending him, as a mendicant friar, to be a stranger and sojourner, not in the wilderness, but in the most crowded haunts of men, to console them and to do them good. This popular instinct of his is at the bottom of his famous marriage with poverty. Poverty and suffering are the condition of the people, the multitude, the immense majority of mankind; and it was towards this people that his soul yearned. 'He listens,' it was said of him, 'to those to whom God himself will not listen.'"[120]

Francis's Christianity was a faith that had clear, external social implications and greatly impacted those in the lower strata of society.

The Reformation

Though Martin Luther, the spark that ignited the Reformation, repudiated good works as a means of salvation, he was quite clear that he never meant for salvation to be void of good works altogether. "We are not saved by works," he said, "but if there be no works, there must be something amiss with faith."[121] A couple of years ago, we had the opportunity to visit Luther's home in Wittenberg, Germany. We saw the library containing hundreds of Luther's manuscripts. We saw the table where Luther held his nightly "table talks" with whoever dined with his family that evening. And we saw the "common chest" that through Luther's influence found its way into every church. This chest was used to collect funds for the poor, funds that the deacons distributed where most needed.

The reformer John Calvin also recognized the need to serve the poor and minister to the needs of the community: "When 60,000 refugees flooded into Geneva from France beginning in 1550, Calvin funded a private, church-based ministry that became a model throughout Europe. The ministry cared for a broad range of needs, serv-

> "But if there be no works, there must be something amiss with faith."

ing the sick, orphans, elderly, incapacitated, travelers, the aged, disabled, and terminally ill. Aid to the needy was tied to a work ethic. Deacons were trained to find long-range solutions to poverty—job-retraining, temporary housing, tools to set up a trade ..."[122]

Eventually the reformation of the church resulted in a growing fragmentation among the Protestants. An emphasis on the purity of doctrine, in some cases, led to a loss of emphasis on mission. For some Calvinists, the belief in predestination "paralyze[d] the will to mission."[123] For Lutherans of the seventeenth century, "the Great Commission became a theme for discussion, not missionary action."[124]

But there remained some bright spots in Germany. August Hermann Francke (1663–1727) had the dual vocation of professor (at the University of Halle) and pastor. Impressed by God that he had a responsibility toward the outcast children of his community, he began his "ragged school," and by "1698 there were one hundred orphans under his charge to be clothed and fed, besides five hundred children who were taught as day scholars."[125] He worked tirelessly for thirty-six years, simultaneously feeding and catechizing orphans and the poor. During the course of several decades, he transformed the town into a showcase of social and cultural reforms. The large cluster of buildings housing the institutions he began, including an orphanage, hospital, library, and missionary center, is still preserved today as a monument to his labors.[126]

Following in the steps of Franck were individuals like Count Zinzendorf and spiritual movements among the Moravians and the Anabaptists, whose efforts "included both the preaching of the Lamb and initiatives of social and cultural healing. They cared for the sick, established schools and provided for the aged, widows and orphans."[127] These movements gave hands and feet to the body of the church.

CARING CATHOLICS

Interestingly, during these fractured times of the Reformation, the Catholic Church experienced a renewal of mission. The Society of Jesus, better known to us as the Jesuits, was founded by Ignatius of Loyola in 1534, when he was forty-nine years old. The Jesuits cut a huge swath for the gospel across the globe. Having no prior experience with schools, the Jesuits focused on education and founded thirty colleges in their first ten years of existence and eventually founded more than seven hundred secondary schools and universities on five continents.[128] By the 1800s, author Chris Lowney notes, one out of every five Europeans was educated in a Jesuit school.[129] These men crossed mountains, forded rivers, and filled in many of the white spaces on the maps. They were confidants to European kings, Indian moguls, and Chinese emperors. Their mission: "By traveling through the various regions of the world ... to preach, hear confessions, and use all other means ... to help souls."[130] In 1540 there were only ten Jesuits, but by 1556, the year of Ignatius's death, there were a thousand, and by 1580 there were over five thousand. Vladimir Lenin once said, while sighing, that with only a dozen cadres as talented and dedicated as the Jesuits, his Communist movement would change the world![131]

As the gospel penetrated China in the 1500s, it was the merciful actions of the Jesuits that awakened the Chinese to the good news of the gospel. The Chinese were intrigued with the idea of serving one's fellowman, a concept that had no parallel in Confucianism. In 1582, the Chinese were impressed with the "themes of [Jesuit leader] Ricci, the first of which concerns the practice of public charity; the management of hospitals and orphanages, the pious foundations and charitable societies caring for the poor, for destitute widows and prisoners, and the practice of almsgiving."[132] Ricci's effect on China was so profound that "at his death the emperor made him an honorary citizen of China."[133]

These Catholic missionaries practiced the "[s]even bodily and seven spiritual works of compassion"[134] found in the New Testament. As early as 1630, the Christian Humanitarian Society in Hangzhou, China, was founded. "[I]t was the Christian contribution to a larger movement of setting up 'societies for the performance of good deeds,' that was very popular in late Ming times."[135] It was practices such as these that engendered a great admiration for the morality of the believers and led thousands to become Christ followers.

THE INFLUENCE OF WESLEY

It is impossible to discuss the history of the church engaging the needs of society without addressing John Wesley. Wesley was a man with a mission and a vision—"to redeem the nation" and "to spread scriptural holiness throughout the land."[136] In a country where in "1736 every sixth house in London was licensed as a grogshop,"[137] England was a country of drunkenness, despair, and moral decay. Children as young as three and a half worked in the mines, the mills, and brickyards, and "[l]ess than one in twenty-five had any kind of schooling."[138] The rural poor migrated to the cities in droves, looking for work, as the primitive wheels of the Industrial Revolution began to turn. This created urban slums never seen before. "The reins of economic power were completely in the hands of the wealthy few. Beneath the sophisticated veneer of the governing classes, the English populace was gripped in a vise of poverty, disease, and moral decay."[139] But where was the church? The Church of England at that time catered to the upper strata of society. Churches were subsidized by the government, and of the eleven thousand pastors who were on the payroll, six thousand of them never even set foot in their parishes, residing in England or on the continent while farming out their ministry to underlings.[140]

Wesley's goal was formidable, but his mission was clear. Wesley knew that preaching to the masses alone was insufficient. His contemporary, George Whitefield, would often preach to crowds exceeding twenty thousand. (Ben Franklin once calculated that Whitefield could be heard by thirty thousand people, an amazing feat for that time!)[141] But because Whitefield had no mechanism for preserving the fruit of his preaching, near the end of his life he called his own converts "a rope of sand."[142] Wesley tried to learn from Whitefield, and building on Whitefield's "field preaching," he added his class meetings—a small group system—and it was these class meetings that began to shape character and change behavior, effecting the redemption of the nation.

Wesley's approach to ministry was influenced by the biography of Catholic nobleman Gaston Jean Baptiste de Renty (1611–1649). "Throughout his life, Wesley continued to refer to de Renty as the epitome of Christian holiness coupled with concern for the poor and effective methodology."[143] De Renty's small groups formed the model for Wesley's own class meetings—small groups of people that met regularly for encouragement and accountability. More important, though, de Renty helped shape Wesley's spiritual growth model. "The focus of the Anglican groups was personal growth through careful attention to themselves; de Renty concentrated on personal growth by ministering to the needs of others. The Anglicans hoped that Christian service would be the eventual outcome of their quest for personal holiness; de Renty viewed Christian service as the context in which personal holiness developed.... [F]or Wesley, de Renty's model of growth-through-service enabled him to steer his groups around the dangers of morbid introspection and mysticism."[144]

Wesley practiced what he preached — "There is no holiness apart from social holiness."[145] Among other things, he campaigned against the slave trade, agitated for prison and labor reform (including child labor), set up loan funds for the poor, opened a dispensary to distribute medicines to the poor, worked to solve unemployment, and personally gave away considerable sums of money to people in need.[146] Wesley's life was contagious. "The church was producing a different kind of lay person, people who were spending three hours daily for the work of the kingdom and giving much of their income toward its building."[147]

> The story of John Wesley may well be the best-kept secret of the past two and a half centuries of church history.

In many ways, the story of John Wesley may well be the best-kept secret of the past two and a half centuries of church history. On February 24, 1791, at age eighty-eight, six days before his death, Wesley wrote the last letter he would ever write, to a man named William Wilberforce, who was converted under Wesley's ministry.[148] In this letter, Wesley urged Wilberforce to continue his fight to end the slave trade. Relentlessly, for the next sixteen years, Wilberforce pressed on to end slavery. Eventually the British Parliament outlawed England's participation in the slave trade in 1807, finally ending slavery in 1833, a few days before Wilberforce's death. Eight hundred thousand slaves were set free. Wesley's revolutionary concepts and his vision for what the church could be shaped not only the denominations that developed from his churches but also an approach to externally focused ministry that continues to influence churches all over the world today.

The Industrial Age

In America there were also signs of spiritual awakening. The revivals of 1726 to 1825 had not just spiritual but social implications as well. David Bosch writes, "It was those touched by the Awakenings who were moved to compassion by the plight of people exposed to the degrading conditions in slums and prisons, in coal-mining districts, on the American frontier, in West Indian plantations and elsewhere."[149] Thomas Cahill captures what *awakening* means when he writes, "When in the late seventeenth century George Fox and his fellow Quakers began to read the gospels, Acts, and the letters of Paul, it seemed to them as if no one had ever read them before, for they rediscovered there the blueprint for Christianity as the radical 'society of friends' it had once been and the theological courage to oppose slavery, prisons, capital punishment, war, and even unholy union of church and state."[150]

D. A. Carson adds, "These Christians [converts of Wesley, Whitefield, and their contemporaries] were instrumental not only in getting slavery banned throughout the British Empire but also in passing laws outlawing child labor in the coal mines and in reforming the prison system. They began countless institutions to help the indigent and they founded trade unions to tame the rapacity that sprang from the first flush of the Industrial Revolution."[151]

Jim Wallis gives some insight into how and why the now-familiar altar call was originally invented. "The Billy Graham of his day, [Charles] Finney [1792–1875] called people to faith in Jesus Christ and then to enlist in the anti-slavery campaign. Finney actually pioneered the 'altar call' so he could sign up his converts for the anti-slavery campaign."[152]

In 1797, Catholic parishioners met and organized an orphanage for children whose parents had died following an outbreak of yellow fever. By the mid-1830s, Bishop John Dubois in New York ordered that all church collections on Christmas Day should go for the care of orphans. Within a few years, all collections on Easter Sunday were being used for that same purpose. "These collections were the forerunners of the Campaign for Human Development, which annually distributes some $50 million to community-based social services that address poverty and empowerment."[153]

THE BLACK CHURCH

In *The Black Church in the African American Experience*, authors C. Eric Lincoln and Lawrence H. Mamiya insist that the black church has been the one stable social unit for African Americans. The church has been the "enduring institution" of the black community—the one place where blacks have had unfettered opportunities for leadership development. Quoting a representative pastor, they write, "The church has many critics but no rivals in what it has meant in the life of the people—in saving and developing them. Without the Black Church, black leadership and black organization would hardly have developed. Especially as a positive influence in the black experience, black consciousness would have been devoid of real hope and black life would have been completely dehumanized. The Black Church is the biggest happening in the black experience in the United States of America."[154]

The authors propose that it is the black church that nurtured the slaves and was the cradle and ideological seedbed for those who fought for the salvation and liberation of black Americans. Harriett Tubman, Sojourner Truth, Booker T. Washington, Frederick Douglass, Martin Luther King Jr., and nearly all black legislators throughout history have come from the black church.

In his book *The Beloved Community: How Faith Shapes Social Justice, from the Civil Rights Movement to Today*, Charles Marsh puts forth the argument that in America, civil rights leaders from Martin Luther King Jr. to John Perkins have led in response to the leading of God in their lives. Citing Catholic monk and writer Thomas Merton, Marsh affirms that "the civil rights movement [is] the greatest example of Christian faith in action in the social history of the United States."[155] He goes on to say that "[Martin Luther King Jr.'s] concept of love was … the passion to make human life and all social existence a parable of God's love for the world. It was agape: the outrageous venture of loving the other without conditions—a risk and a costly sacrifice."[156] As Christ followers, aren't we glad to be associated with such an accolade?

THE GREAT REVERSAL

Despite all of the positive signs we have outlined thus far, there was also a counterweight to the externally focused ministry of the church. Toward the end of the nineteenth century, the eschatological teaching of premillennialism became the popular theology of the day. One tenet of premillennialism is the teaching that the world will grow progressively worse before Christ intervenes to judge the world through his personal and physical return. Though premillennial beliefs do not necessitate this belief, some churches interpreted this to mean that any effort Christians made trying to make the world a better place, helping the poor and healing the sick, served to delay the return of Jesus Christ. This belief exempted these believers from engaging in the ills and hurts of the nation. The Christian's main concern was not the repair of a wrecked world but the rescue of ruined souls—getting individuals off the sinking vessel of this world and into the lifeboat of salvation."[157] Slowly but surely, the historic Christian mandates of love

> The historic Christian mandates of love and mercy that had been coupled with gospel proclamation were abandoned in favor of an exclusively verbal message addressing individual salvation.

and mercy that had been coupled with gospel proclamation were abandoned in favor of an exclusively verbal message addressing individual salvation. The widespread effect that this teaching had upon churches was devastating. David Bosch writes, "[B]y the 1920s the 'great reversal' . . . had been completed; the evangelicals' interest in social concerns . . . had been obliterated."[158]

Reversing the Reversal

Beryl Hugen writes, "The justice and love of God set forth and exemplified in the Judeo-Christian tradition has given drive and direction to much of western culture's charities."[159] It is clear the church has had a defining role in caring for those on the margin in every generation. As we think about our own churches and the world we live in today, what would the world look like if the church and those who follow Christ did not step forth to live out the good news of the gospel in their communities? As we look back on the past and are inspired by the historic work of the Christian church, one question emerges: what are we doing to write the next chapter for our generation?

For Reflection and Discussion

1. What stories from history were you most impressed with? Why?
2. In your city, are there any areas of need where Christ followers today could make an impact as dramatic as these examples?
3. How have the theological doctrines of your tradition positively or negatively affected your own church's impact on the city?
4. What do you think your city would be like if there were no churches or Christ followers in it? Would there be a difference in the quality of life?
5. If time travel were possible and early Christians were transported to our world today, what social issues do you think they would likely be involved with?
6. If your church were to close its doors tomorrow, would anyone in the community notice? And if they did notice, would they care?

CHAPTER FIVE

THE WHOLE CHURCH

For the strength of the pack is the wolf and the strength of the wolf
is the pack.

—Rudyard Kipling, *The Jungle Book*

In a classic *Peanuts* cartoon by Charles Schultz, Lucy demands that Linus
change TV channels, threatening him with her fist if he doesn't comply.
"What makes you think you can walk right in here and take over?" asks Linus.

"These five fingers," says Lucy. "Individually they're nothing, but when I
curl them together like this into a single unit, they form a weapon that is terrible
to behold."

"Which channel do you want?" asks Linus. Turning away, he looks at his
fingers and says, "Why can't you guys get organized like that?"

Our good friend Higgins, from Auckland, New Zealand, has the same idea
when he refers to his "five-point management plan" (a closed fist) for encouraging cooperation with his teenage boys and staff. Thankfully, he doesn't have to
use it very often!

The church certainly does not impact the city through force or threats, but
it often fails to have much of an impact when individual churches aren't willing
or able to work together. We believe that transformation of our cities will occur
when the church in the city is intent on becoming exactly what God wants it to
be—a visible, united presence that seeks the city's good.

ONE CHURCH ... MANY CONGREGATIONS

Wherever we go and speak to city leaders who are interested in the transformation of their city, we begin our time by sharing a phrase adopted from the

Lausanne movement.[160] We say that transformation can only occur when "the whole church takes the whole gospel to the whole city." But that definition, while it sounds nice, requires us to address three questions. What is the *whole* church? What is the *whole* gospel? And what do we mean by the *whole* city? This chapter and the following two will address what these phrases mean and why they are helpful to bringing transformation to our cities and communities.

> "The hope of the world is the church, but not necessarily the local congregation" (Jim Herrington).

To speak of the whole church is a shorthand way of speaking about the unity of the church in a given city. This concept, that the church is really only *one* church in a city made up of many different congregations that meet at various locations and times, has been explored in detail by people like Joe Aldrich, Jack Dennison, George Otis Jr., Ray Bakke, and others. We believe it is important for us to note that when the apostle Paul wrote his letters to Christians in a city, he wrote them to the church of *the city*—for example, "the church of God *in Corinth*" (1 Cor. 1:2, emphasis ours), "the church *of the Thessalonians*" (1 Thess. 1:1, emphasis ours). Though there were likely multiple house churches and various groups of believers meeting at different times and locations in these cities, every city has one church. This is a helpful concept to consider, not just as we think about the power of unity but also as we look at how spiritual gifts are distributed within the church. Have you ever considered that while all of the necessary gifts for ministry and maturity are contained within the church, they may not all reside in a particular local congregation? If this is true, we really do need to work with other congregations if we want to accomplish the work that God has given his church to do in a city. As Jim Herrington of Mission Houston says, "The hope of the world is the church, but not necessarily the local congregation."[161]

Why Was Jesus So Concerned with Unity?

On the night of his betrayal, Jesus allowed his disciples to overhear his verbal prayer to the Father in the garden as he prayed for them and for their spiritual offspring—"those who will believe in me through their message" (John 17:20). He prayed that his followers "all ... may be one" (v. 21) and that they will make progress toward "complete unity" (v. 23). Jesus knew, better than anyone, how different and unique his disciples were — in disposition, temperament, background, and values. Without a deep commitment to loving one another and working together, they wouldn't have a chance of impacting the world as his witnesses.

When Jesus initially chose his team of disciples, it was after an extended time of prayer, and he intentionally selected those men whom he felt were best suited for the task, but they certainly were not alike! Matthew, employed by Rome as a tax collector, was now serving on the same ministry team with Simon the (patriotic) Zealot (read: *religious fanatic*). Or consider the volatile and power hungry "sons of thunder," James and John. Jesus chose Andrew, who seemed ready to believe everything, but he also chose Thomas, who struggled to believe what he could not see or experience. Among his disciples, it was no secret that Jesus also had his inner circle (Peter, James, and John), the men who accompanied him most frequently. But only one disciple was given the trusted position of taking care of Jesus' mother. The situation was ripe for conflict and disorder. It's no wonder he beseeched his Father for supernatural unity and love.

THE EARLY CHURCH

As the young church grew, its early leaders fought to maintain the unity that Jesus had prayed for … and it wasn't easy. They appointed the first deacons to look after those who were being slighted in the distribution of food (Acts 6). Although they eventually came around (Acts 11:18), there were some stuffy separatists who balked when Peter suggested converting the pagan Gentiles and including them in the church. James had to speak out, in his letter, against the sin of favoritism that divides the body (James 2:1 – 13), and Paul was frequently writing to remind the churches of the need for unity (Rom. 12:4 – 21; 1 Corinthians 12; Eph. 4:1 – 16). Imagine Paul's frustration when he discovered that the Corinthian church had divided into factions supporting different Christian leaders, in much the same way that we might divide over our favorite sports teams or our preferred political parties. In Corinth, there were those who proclaimed, " 'I follow Paul' ['Give me a P!']; another, 'I follow Apollos'; another, 'I follow Cephas'; still another, 'I follow Christ' " (1 Cor. 1:12). (As a side note, it's always nice to speak last in situations like these so you can come up with the most spiritual-sounding answer.)

Councils were convened to address doctrinal questions (Acts 15), and when the Gnostic Christians tried to separate themselves by claiming a special knowledge of Christ, they were soundly rebuked. By the end of the first century, a fragile peace existed between the different groups of Christians. And a modicum of unity was preserved through the foundation of structures and systems that would lead to the institutionalization of the church in the beginning of the fourth century. Even then, the Eastern and Western branches of the church eventually parted ways in 1054, in what is now known as "the Great Schism." Preserving unity has never been easy, and the church has had its own share of problems in this regard.

How did we get so divided?

Looking centuries later to the time of the Reformation, we begin to see further fragmentation of the fragile unity of the church as institutional structures split and divided. David Bosch, in his classic book *Transforming Mission*, makes a key observation about the role the Reformation played in the division of churches: "The Reformational descriptions of the church thus ended up *accentuating differences rather than similarities* [emphasis ours]. Christians were taught to look divisively at other Christians. Eventually Lutherans divided from Lutherans, Reformed separated from Reformed, each group justifying its action by appealing to the marks of the true church."[162]

While there were many positive aspects to the Reformation, the seeds of division that were sown at that time have now left us with (according to Bosch) over thirty-four thousand different denominations. Individuals and groups found unique ways to differentiate themselves from one another — each believing they were the closest expression of what the New Testament church ought to be. Isn't it just a wonderful thing to know that you are in the right denomination, the only true and biblical church? (If you didn't smile just now, you may have missed our point.)

So where are we now?

In many ways, we find ourselves in a situation similar to that of the Scotsman who was marooned for a year in the Hebrides Islands. When rescued by his family, the marooned man said, "Let me show you what I built with me own two hands. Here is my house, and here are the two churches I built." "But why on earth did you build two churches?" they queried. "Well, *this* is the church I go to ... and *that* is the church I don't go to!" Historically, we've often defined ourselves both by what we are *and* what we are not — the things we stand against. Christians seem to have a gift for finding the smallest things to split over. Recently I (Eric) was in Pennsylvania doing an Externally Focused Church seminar for a Mennonite church. In preparation for my visit, I read up on the Mennonites. They are a very missional people, but they have often divided and formed new denominations around the smallest of distinctions ... like how many folds a woman's bonnet should have. The most interesting group I found is called "Black Bumper Mennonites." This group believes in using automobiles, but they feel it is too ostentatious to have shiny chrome accoutrements on the cars, so they paint the bumpers black! (Our apologies to any Black Bumper folks who might be reading this page.)

Despite a long history of fragmentation and division in the body of Christ, the past few years have seen some positive indications that the body of Christ is now coming together through movements of reconciliation and unity. In the years following World War II, thousands of young people from hundreds of denominations began gathering, despite their different backgrounds, in para-church settings where personal faith was emphasized over denominational distinctives. Youth for Christ, Campus Crusade for Christ, the Navigators, Camp Christ Sports, Young Life, and groups like Intervarsity Christian Fellowship forged a path and introduced a necessary discussion about the *essentials* of the faith. Thought leaders like C. S. Lewis, John Stott, and Paul E. Little wrote books about being a *Christian* as opposed to being a Baptist or a Methodist. As Christians entered into marriage, finding a potential spouse with personal faith in Christ became more important than marrying inside the denomination. Many pastors and church leaders, especially those of younger generations, now tend to gather in groups based on common desires for fellowship and learning or on common practices and ministry styles, rather than common belief or a common denomination.

> Unity does not require that we have uniformity of doctrine, uniformity of programming, or unity in the way we pray or worship.

WHAT *UNITY* DOES NOT MEAN

Unity does not require that we have uniformity of doctrine, uniformity of programming, or unity in the way we pray or worship. Consider the primary illustration the apostle Paul used to encourage unity in the church: a body. Unless you see your job as that of Dr. Frankenstein — gathering diverse body parts from various corpses around the city, somehow hoping to make them work as one — "[t]he body [already] is a unit, though it is made up of many parts; and though all its parts are many, they form one body" (1 Cor. 12:12). Paul does not stipulate that every body part needs to do the same thing in order to demonstrate its commitment to the rest of the body. In fact, he suggests the very opposite!

The various parts of the body may not have the same functions, but they are able to work in concert to achieve a common purpose. The toe doesn't have to ask permission from the eyes to function as a toe. The toes and the eyes just have to do what they do and learn to work together, if there ever comes a day when the body needs to kick a football past a defender and into a net to score a goal. Teamwork requires us to use our different skills and work as one.

Three Expressions of Unity

Admittedly, *unity* is a difficult word to define. Scripture speaks of at least three expressions of unity, each necessary for city transformation—the unity of the family, the unity of fellowship, and the unity of purpose or function. We believe that taken together, these three expressions of unity lead to the complete unity that Jesus prayed for in John 17:23.

Unity of Family

> Make every effort to keep the unity of the Spirit through the bond of peace. There is one body and one Spirit—just as you were called to one hope when you were called—one Lord, one faith, one baptism; one God and Father of all, who is over all and through all and in all.
>
> —Ephesians 4:3–6

Family unity is the unity we have because of our common spiritual birth. All Christians have a common Father, and they have been adopted into the same family. We are brothers and sisters. Family unity is true about us as members of the body of Christ, whether we acknowledge it or not—even whether we like each other or not. Theologians describe this as "positional unity," so called because God *positions* us in this relationship with one other. This is not a unity we can really seek after; instead it is something God gives us that we must work to preserve and protect ("make every effort to keep").

Unity of Fellowship

> May the God who gives endurance and encouragement give you a spirit of unity among yourselves as you follow Christ Jesus, so that with one heart and mouth you may glorify the God and Father of our Lord Jesus Christ. Accept one another, then, just as Christ accepted you, in order to bring praise to God.
>
> —Romans 15:5–7

The second biblical expression of unity is found when we pursue God together ("follow Jesus Christ"), praying and worshiping together ("with one heart and mouth ... glorify") and actively reconciling with one another ("accept one another ... just as Christ accepted you"). Among church leaders, this expression of unity occurs when pastors begin meeting together for prayer and worship. International Renewal Ministries (IRM) and Frontline Ministries have done an excellent job of facilitating hundreds of multiday "prayer summits" in cities around the globe, where pastors seek the face of God through worship and prayer.

These meetings are often transformational times filled with personal and corporate brokenness flowing out of repentant hearts, as pastors unite together around their love for Jesus Christ rather than dividing over doctrinal differences. It is also a time when many pastors discover that other pastors in their city have the same dreams, the same burdens, and a similar heart for the people of the community (not to mention the same kinds of problem people).

This expression of unity should not be taken to suggest that doctrines are unimportant or that we should try to come to a common belief on every Christian doctrine. But it does suggest that we may need to reconsider our reluctance and our fears when it comes to partnering with others in ministry. When we had our four-day prayer retreats, many pastors expressed that for the first time they felt real unity with other pastors in their community, *and they wanted to see their congregation tied into a bigger church of their city.* This type of unity, based on fellowship, is often sustained throughout the year as pastors continue to meet weekly or monthly to pray together, as well as seek each other out during times of difficulty or discouragement.

A few years ago, we were with a group of pastors in Banska Bystrika in Slovakia at the invitation of a good friend. We had been part of a city event sponsored by DAWN (Discipling a Whole Nation) in Budapest. In Budapest, we had been enjoying one of the most delightful cities in eastern Europe. Now we were driving north to meet up with our friend, Doug. After arriving in Banska Bystrika, we took a walking tour of the town center and went to dinner with our friend, his wife, and his children. The next day, during the course of our seminar, we noticed how committed these pastors were to one another, so we asked how they had grown to be so unified. One pastor answered, "We have eaten a lot of salt together." This expression meant that they had shared many, many meals together. These were pastors who loved hanging out together. They were friends.

Once leaders get a taste of the unity that comes from friendship with other pastors, the city movement can go in one of two directions. Because this unity engenders pastoral friendships and collegial relationships, pastors can get stuck at this stage, focusing their attention only on nurturing their relationships. While this may serve a personal need, it serves no greater purpose for the church or the community. We've also seen pastors and leaders who unify around friendship but then come to the conclusion that it's not about *my* church; it's really about *the* church. They discover that being a missional church is not about them; it's about the community they are called to serve. They start to think, "Now that we like each other, we really ought to do something together."

> "We have eaten a lot of salt together."

This was an important step we had to take with the pastors of our own community. For three consecutive years, approximately twenty to thirty key pastors from the city spent four uninterrupted days at a Catholic retreat center in the Rocky Mountains. Each of us had simple, private, TV-deprived rooms, and we enjoyed rich times of corporate and individual prayer. The times of gathered worship were uplifting. Forgiveness was sought and extended between pastors who had spoken against each other. Meaningful relationships were begun, and they were nurtured long after we had come down from the mountain and returned to the city. But as wonderful as these personal relationships were, something else developed during our time — the desire to have a shared impact in our city. And so the fourth year of our meeting together was devoted to praying for our city, which led us to the third and final expression of unity.

Unity of Purpose

> If you have any encouragement from being united with Christ [unity of family], if any comfort from his love, if any fellowship with the Spirit [unity of fellowship], if any tenderness and compassion, then make my joy complete by being like-minded, having the same love, being one in spirit and purpose [unity of purpose or function].
>
> — Philippians 2:1 – 2

Uniting around purpose means that the church in the city shares a common function or *raison d'être*. That common purpose is given to us by Jesus in his prayer in John 17:20 – 23: "My prayer is not for them alone. I pray also for those who will believe in me through their message, that all of them may be one, Father, just as you are in me and I am in you. May they also be in us so *that the world may believe that you have sent me.* I have given them the glory that you gave me, that they may be one as we are one: I in them and you in me. May they be brought to complete unity *to let the world know that you sent me and have loved them even as you have loved me*" (emphasis ours).

Who is Jesus praying for in this passage? He is praying for you and me and the millions of other Christians throughout history, as well as the generations to come, who would believe in him through the message of his disciples. And what is he asking the Father for? He is praying that we would be one, *just as he and the Father are one.* Upon first glance, it seems as though the purpose of this prayer is greater unity, but a closer look reveals that Jesus has a different goal. Jesus actually mentions two results that grow out of our unity. The first is that our unity would communicate to the world that God sent Jesus. The second is that it would communicate to the world that God loves the world just as much as he loves Jesus. The end of our unity is not simply good relationships between fellow Christians. Instead it is the proclamation and demonstration of the gospel to the world.

> The end of our unity is not simply good relationships between fellow Christians. Instead it is the proclamation and demonstration of the gospel to the world.

It is through verbal *proclamation* that people discover that Jesus was sent by God. No one comes to that conclusion through reason or intuition alone. It must be revealed to them through a written or spoken proclamation. Along with that, however, we see that it is through *demonstration* that people experience the truth that God loves them as much as he loves his own Son. Most people have never experienced the love of God in a tangible way. Just as the incarnation of Christ brought heaven to earth, it is the responsibility and privilege of the church, the body of Jesus Christ, to bring heaven a bit closer to the people in our world through defining acts of love and service.

How Do We Unify?

Unity, then, is a means and not an end. This helps us to understand why most ecumenical movements fail. If unity is our primary goal, we will never arrive at our destination. Phill Butler, in a paper titled "Fifteen Key Principles for Success in Kingdom Collaboration," writes, "Successful networks/partnerships develop in order to accomplish a specific vision or task. Cooperation for cooperation's sake is a sure recipe for failure. Warm 'fellowship' is not enough. This means lasting cooperation focuses primarily on 'what' (objectives) rather than 'how' (structure). Form always follows function — not the other way around."[163]

God's intention, as evidenced in the John 17 prayer of Jesus, is that we would be unified through a shared mission — helping people understand, through

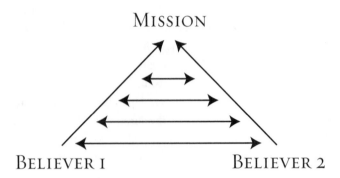

Figure 5

words and deeds, that Jesus is sent from God and that God loves every person on earth as much as he loves his own Son. Figure 5 helps us to visualize unity around mission or purpose.

As believers or churches pursue a common mission, they grow in unity. By pursuing their own separate purposes, however, they walk the path of disunity. Individual congregations may have different roles in this mission, but they are all motivated by the same common purpose. They are the body of Christ in their city.[164] A. W. Tozer saw and understood this relationship between unity and a shared focus: "Has it ever occurred to you that one hundred pianos all tuned to the same fork are automatically tuned to each other? They are of one accord by being tuned, not to each other, but to another standard to which each one must individually bow. So one hundred worshipers [meeting] together, each one looking away to Christ, are in heart nearer to each other than they could possibly be, were they to become 'unity' conscious and turn their eyes away from God to strive for closer fellowship."[165]

This same principle is true of congregations, whether you have two or two hundred, all focused on Christ's mission in their city.

In fact, we are not aware of a single, sustained city transformation movement that is not centered on mission. If churches aren't working together on something, trying to accomplish a dream together that they cannot accomplish as a single congregation, then there is no purposeful unity between them. There are at least a couple of reasons why this is true. First, it is a fact that the longer people live in relationship with each other, the more they are likely to discover how different they really are. It's the truth in the axiom "Familiarity breeds contempt." It is very difficult to sustain the unity of fellowship over an extended period of time. Unless congregations share something in common with each other that is significant enough to motivate them to "accept one another" (Rom. 15:7), their embrace of unity will be short-lived. A shared mission that proclaims *and* demonstrates the love of God to the city provides that motivation.

A second reason why we should seek unity in mission is that most leaders are naturally biased toward action. Few will not attend more than a couple of prayer meetings if they sense that these gatherings lack a clear purpose. CitiReach International founder Jack Dennison writes in his book *City Reaching*, "We see repetitive efforts to demonstrate our unity through citywide worship events, prayer vigils ... and other similar events. These activities ... are wonderful symbols of our unity but they rarely produce real substance. They make us feel good and sometimes result in great newspaper coverage, but the cities remain unchanged."[166]

> If churches aren't working together on something, trying to accomplish a dream together that they cannot accomplish as a single congregation, then there is no purposeful unity between them.

We can diagram a path to the complete unity that Jesus prayed for, as in figure 6.

Sometimes unity comes about by this neat process of progression. At other times, unity of fellowship is experienced *as* believers unite around a common purpose. A recent Leadership Network survey about church partnerships asked the question, "Which [activity] originally triggered your church's involvement [with other churches]?" As many churches listed "doing a community service

UNITY OF FAMILY (EPH. 4:3–6)	UNITY OF FELLOWSHIP (ROM. 15:5–7)	UNITY OF PURPOSE (JOHN 17:23)
"Make every effort to keep the unity of the Spirit through the bond of peace. ... one body ... one Spirit . .. one hope ... one Lord, one faith, one baptism; one God and Father of all, who is over all."	"May ... God ... give you a spirit of unity among yourselves as you follow Christ Jesus, so that with one heart and mouth you may glorify ... God. ... Accept one another, then."	"May they be brought to complete unity to let the world know that you sent me and have loved them even as you have loved me."

Figure 6

UNITY OF FAMILY
(EPH. 4:3–6)

UNITY OF PURPOSE
(JOHN 17:23)

UNITY OF FELLOWSHIP
(ROM. 15:5–7)

Figure 7

project together" as indicated "meeting together for prayer."[167] Pastor Rick War-ren of Saddleback Church summarizes the motivation for unity in this way: "We need to mobilize a billion Catholics and Orthodox [believers]. I'm not really that interested in interfaith dialogue. I am interested in interfaith projects. Let's do something together. You are probably not going to change my doctrinal distinc-tives. We have different beliefs but the fact is, we do serve the same Lord. Let's work on the things we can agree on."[168]

Striving together with a common purpose brings us into fellowship with one another. In this case, the progression of unity can be better diagrammed as in figure 7.

Does this mean that our new goal is to get every church in the city unified in both fellowship and purpose? No! That is not likely to happen, nor does it really need to happen for us to effectively transform the city. City transformation won't *include* all churches (some just prefer to play by themselves or don't play well with others), but it should not *exclude* any churches.

Everywhere we turn, we see more and more pastors and Christian leaders thinking in these broad categories and looking for partnerships outside their own churches and denominations. *Leadership* journal reported the results of a May 2008 survey of seven hundred evangelical pastors who responded to the question, "As a leader, do you see church evangelism efforts primarily to grow 'my' church or 'the' church?" Ten years ago, the results of the survey showed that 39 percent of pastors answered "my church." But in 2008, 93 per-cent of pastors answered "the church." In 1998, only 51 percent of pastors agreed that "partnerships are essential in accomplishing the gospel mission." But by 2008 that number had grown to 75 percent.[169] There is a growing desire among church leaders to pursue this kind of purposeful unity with other congregations.

> City transformation won't *include* all churches, but it should not *exclude* any churches.

PROJECTS ARE NOT PURPOSE

Uniting the church in a city around a common purpose is *not* simply doing common cooperative projects together. Jack Dennison reminds us that we align ourselves "in unity to pursue the same goals for our community while each participant determines the part it should play."[170] Functional unity does not exclude doing cooperative projects together, but each church can still act with a degree of sanctified independence. Churches do not need to wait for permission from other churches to serve their community, and there may be times when they choose not to join a cooperative project, but they can still be working toward the agreed-upon vision of a healthy, transformed community. This understanding is helpful, particularly if we want to preserve the unity of the body over time, as churches grow and leaders change.

City transformation serves as a macro strategy around which individual congregations and ministries can execute their tactical initiatives in line with their unique capacity and calling. It's the body of Christ working together. With this in mind, we'd like to reread Jesus' prayer in John 17:23 one last time: "May they be brought to complete unity *to let the world know that you sent me* and *have loved them even as you have loved me*" (emphasis ours). As we have shown, unity was intended not to be an end in itself but to be a critical step in letting the world know that Jesus is God's Son and just how much he loves people! Without unity of purpose, it's difficult to move outside of our own ministries to impact the greater community around us, and the prayer of Jesus remains just that—an unfulfilled prayer.

ORGANIZING FOR USEFULNESS

Understanding the basis of our unity helps inform the way a city transformation movement is organized. The principle here is simple: less is more. Many citywide movements have split and fallen apart because they have tried to overorganize activities or have created a litmus test (attendance at a weekly leadership prayer meeting, commitment to quarterly all-church worship events, participation in a joint evangelistic event, adherence to detailed doctrinal statements) that determines who is "in" and who is "out"—who is committed or not committed to city transformation. While there can be some honest need for accountability, ironically, it can sometimes be the very desire to unite that turns into the most divisive force among churches in the city. City leader Copi Valdiviez of Toledo, Ohio, says it this way: "All church leaders are part of city transformation. Some leaders of those churches come to the meetings, while others don't even know they are part of a movement." We want to reiterate a key point: transformation movements won't *include* every church, but they shouldn't *exclude* any church. The unity of fellowship in the church is fragile at best, so by all means keep your organization simple. The less there is to "join," the less chance that your leaders will "leave" because of disappointment or unmet expectations. Keep your organizational expectations low and your purposes broad. Author Anne Lamott poignantly summarizes our advice when she writes, "Expectations are resentments under construction."[171] Be steadfast and clear about the purpose of a citywide movement and allow pastors and churches to move in and out as their time and opportunity allow them to be involved.

Even with more organized city movements, membership and affiliation is quite simple. In 2006, Willow Creek Multisite Pastor Jim Tomberlin began meeting with pastors and network leaders in the greater Chicagoland area. This was the beginning of Catalyst—a robust city transformation movement whose vision is "to see the body of Christ mobilized in order to experience a sustained Christ-awakening that transforms the people, churches, and communities of Chicagoland." Now under the visionary leadership of Bill Yaccino and operating under the name Christ Together, this vibrant movement of more than seventy-five churches is shaping the face of the church in Lake County, Illinois, through its own initiatives as well as what the churches of Lake County do through existing community partnerships. They come alongside schools, feed the hungry, serve the poor and visit those in prison, begin Alpha courses, and provide marriage enrichment opportunities for the community.

Churches become a participating church of Christ Together simply by participating in any Christ Together initiatives, and all churches are welcome. But there is another level of engagement. Churches can become "partner churches" by contributing 0.5 percent of their annual budget to Christ Together, with a maximum annual contribution of $12,000. Currently, more than thirty churches have stepped up to the partner level. This level of buy-in provides camaraderie among leaders as well as the finances critical to impact a community with good news and good deeds.

Unity and Affinity

It is also important that we don't confuse "unity" with "affinity." Affinity is what forms between people who believe and enjoy the same things. City transformation movement meetings (prayer meetings, organizational meetings, vision meetings, joint worship) are really an expression of an affinity, and there are certain leaders who enjoy such activities. Those who don't enjoy them usually stay away and find something else that they enjoy doing. Leaders often mistakenly assume that because they personally see these gatherings as vital and essential, all Christian leaders should also see them as vital and essential if we are to have true unity. Others may feel as if they have failed or begin to think that Christian leaders in the community are fragmented and uncooperative. The unity that Jesus prayed for is much deeper than mere affinity for certain activities. The unity Jesus prayed for was a love and a commitment to identify and serve with other believers, even those with whom we have no affinity whatsoever. We must continue to bless and speak well of our brothers and sisters, even though they may never come to our meetings or share our specific passions.

GETTING STARTED

So ... how do you get started? In January 2009, a good friend of ours, Pastor Dave Runyon of Foothills Community Church in Arvada, Colorado, initiated a city transformation movement in the northwest quadrant of Denver. Using Jim Tomberlin's[172] simple, eight-step template for starting a transformation movement, we'd like to unpack the simple steps that Dave took to begin a citywide movement.

1. *Define geographical regions. This should happen organically, from the grass roots.* Dave identified the quadrant of the Denver metro area — west of I-25 and north of I-70 — where his city (Arvada) is located and where he has significant relationships with pastors. The entire metro area was too big a bite to take, but the northwest quadrant seemed reasonable.

2. *Identify the "anchor church" pastors in those regions.* Dave identified the pastors of five influential churches in the quadrant — pastors with impact and influence who would act as magnets to the other churches.

3. *Gather the anchor church pastors together to consider the question, "What could we accomplish together that we could not do alone?"* Dave met with each pastor individually on one or more occasions to begin discussing what they could accomplish together that they could not accomplish alone. All of the key pastors indicated they were "in."

4. *Develop personal pastoral relationships by praying, planning, and playing together.* The individual appointments with these key leaders led to a meeting of about twenty pastors to pray about and plan "what it would look like for the churches in our area to come together to serve our community."

5. *Partner to address a community need.* Never do anything in the community alone. Always do things with other local congregations. To discover

the needs of the community, the group of pastors invited Arvada mayor Bob Frie to address them regarding his dream for the city, along with the issues that were hindering that dream from becoming a reality. Bob came with a grocery list of pervasive issues that he wanted to address, among which were at-risk kids, elderly shut-ins, dilapidated housing, and hunger. And after addressing these issues, he said to the gathered pastors, "After thinking about all of these things, it occurred to me that what our city really needs are good neighbors. . . . The majority of the issues our community is facing would be eliminated or drastically reduced if we could just become a community of people who are great neighbors." To this statement one pastor responded, "Here we are, asking the mayor what areas of the city are most in need, and he basically tells us that it would be great if we could just get our people to obey the second half of the Great Commandment."

6. *Plan a community catalytic event to stimulate and inspire collaboration.* The twenty churches decided to "come together and with one voice challenge the people in their congregations to 'Rediscover the Art of Neighboring.'" Each church took the three weeks following Easter to preach through a common series of messages called "Building Blocks— Rediscovering the Art of Neighboring." The outcomes included each congregant creating a block map identifying each neighbor by name. The second outcome was to host a block party. The potential impact was 48,000 households in the northwest quarter of Denver. Dave says, "In our quest to be good neighbors we ask ourselves, 'If our family was to move out of the neighborhood, would our neighbors notice . . . would our neighbors care?' We want to be a city full of neighbors that the community would miss."

7. *Celebrate regularly with your local congregation what God is doing in the community through the body of Christ.* Celebrating milestones of accomplishment through the use of stories is a great way to spread the message.

8. *Cooperate with the Holy Spirit as you pray, plan, and do together.* Dave and the other city pastors continue to follow God's guidance as they move forward in making the kingdom tangible for those who live in their community. Dave has also identified and met with other pastoral leaders in the other quadrants of the city.

Above all, remember that God is already at work in your city. As you pray and initiate, God will continue to open the doors that only he can open.

CATALYTIC EVENTS

We believe in the importance of catalytic events. There are countless stories of cities like Atlanta, Boulder, Little Rock, Greensboro, Costa Mesa, Dallas, and San Diego that annually host events like ShareFest, CareFest, Serve Day, Faith in Action, Inside Out, Agents of Grace, Go and Be, Beyond Our Walls, Step Out, or similar concerted weekend efforts. These collaborative efforts engage thousands of volunteers from dozens of churches who give tens of thousands of hours in service to make a difference in their cities. Among the variety of projects churches are engaged in, many are work projects in which churches partner with schools to do painting, landscaping, deep cleaning, repair work, and other maintenance and improvements that shrinking school budgets simply cannot afford. Such projects don't require any previous screening or background checks and can include the contributions of people of all ages—from babies in backpacks to senior adults. There is something very valuable and enduring about parents and children working side by side for a day. Service puts shoe leather on our spiritual words. These events often lead to ongoing engagement for a large percentage of congregants. The financial value to the city is often somewhere in the hundreds of thousands of dollars. And the value of these events in the lives of the people served is priceless. We'd like to share just a few examples of how congregations are working together to transform their cities using these weekend or weeklong initiatives.

> Service puts shoe leather on our spiritual words.

Manchester, England

The Luis Palau Evangelistic Association has a strategy that brings churches together for a six-month Season of Service that precedes a two-day open-air evangelistic festival.[173] We first became familiar with Palau's ministry in Manchester, England (soccer fans will know where Manchester is), in August 2003. Some five thousand young people from western Europe camped out in Heaton Park, one of the largest parks in Europe, in a "tent city." There were two phases to this week's activities—On the Streets and In the Park. Each morning, the youth were bused to Hot Zones, some of the worst neighborhoods of Manchester, where they "blessed the city through social action." Working together with people from the neighborhood, they transformed a trash-littered vacant lot into a freshly sodded soccer field, beautified parks, removed graffiti, planted flowers, and pulled weeds to show God's love in practical ways. During the week, the young people built relationships with people in the community as they served them and worked alongside them, and then invited them to the weekend festival in the park or to nightly evangelistic events in one of three circus tents around the city. Between four hundred and seven hundred neighborhood youths attended the nightly meetings, where they heard and responded to the words of the gospel.

During a lull in the action, we met with project leaders and Policeman Bob, who served as the liaison between the police and the leaders of the Make a Difference projects. Bob described his experience: "At six foot one and 220 pounds, my job is to break doors down, but for ten straight days we've not had one crime. These are the most fantastic people I've ever met. The impact of two thousand people working in the last city project permanently reduced crime by fifty percent. They removed over six hundred tons of trash in four days. I've never seen anything so impactful as these kids cleaning and restoring neighborhoods. These people are superb. If I do become a Christian, it will be because of people like you."

The weekend festival, In the Park, drew over fifty thousand people of various ethnicities and ages. The good deeds created goodwill, and the goodwill drew thousands to hear Luis Palau share the good news about Jesus, resulting in hundreds of people being introduced to Jesus for the first time.

Florida

If the problems of cities were simple, they would have been solved long ago. The persistent problems of most cities are so large and complex that they require the concerted efforts of every domain in the city (to be discussed more in chap. 7). Unfortunately, if churches aren't working with one another, it is unlikely that they will work well with other organizations and groups in the city. This is where churches need to ask the kingdom question. City leader Doug Small from Tampa Bay, Florida, says, "The most dangerous question is asking other pastors, 'Is there something God would want us to do, that we can do better together, that would advance the kingdom?'" Jack McGill from Orlando shared with us what happened when he began asking that question:

> "The most dangerous question is asking other pastors, 'Is there something God would want us to do, that we can do better together, that would advance the kingdom?'" (Doug Small).

The big issue we faced in Orlando is that there were lots of churches doing great things in serving our city. But, just like droplets of rain, the impact was good, but the issues seemed so overwhelming. We began to ask ourselves this: "What would happen if a few times a year we put all those raindrops into one bucket and poured them out over the city?" What would the impact be? There was a group of ten to twelve church leaders who began to meet every other month to pray, plan, and strategize. We felt the Lord gave us a mission and vision that we could all get excited about — "Connecting the church to do together what cannot be done alone." That same group of churches met over the course of about a year to form a simple but very specific strategic plan. We would "mobilize people to serve" and we would "engage leaders in the systemic issues of the city."

Chennai, India

Transformational impact can sometimes go beyond a weekend or onetime event. Mark Visvasam, Campus Crusade's associate national director of India, is part of Chennai Transformation Network (CTN, *www.ctn.org.in*). Chennai is a city of eight million people with over twenty-five hundred churches, many of which are part of CTN. These CTN leaders have identified forty-five thousand people who live on the streets of Chennai, called "pavement dwellers." In many cases, these are the third generation of pavement dwellers. Together the churches in Chennai are adopting city blocks where these street people live, providing them with food and medical assistance. Mistakes are sometimes made, but they are learning as they go. When they discovered that people's illnesses don't always correspond to a weekly visit by doctors, they figured out a way to provide medical insurance cards for street people so they would have access to the local hospitals. These leaders have also identified each of the city's seventeen thousand streets, with plans to make sure there are churches in proximity to each of these streets. In the planning and learning to work together, it was the Catholic bishop who took the initiative and hosted the first meeting. Soon various parachurch organizations joined the cause, and the project is now having a noticeable impact on the physical and spiritual lives of the pavement dwellers.[174]

Penang, Malaysia

When we were in Penang, Malaysia, in 2008, we met with a group of pastors whose churches had adopted a housing development known as the Rifle Range — a housing project filled with thousands of displaced people, many immigrants from India. This initiative, begun by three people in their late sixties and seventies, brought medical help, food, furniture, and spiritual hope to over five hundred residents. Good deeds create such goodwill that the good news often falls on fertile soil. Over a thousand Rifle Range residents have since put their trust in Jesus. A Tamil Indian, the maintenance man from a local Christian seminary, has led dozens of fellow Tamils to faith and is now serving as their pastor.

Colorado Springs, Colorado

Jaan Heinmets, director of Here's Life Inner City in Colorado Springs, knows firsthand the difference that partnering with other churches can make. Nine years ago, Jaan went to the human-services offices in Colorado Springs asking what they, as a group of churches, could do to serve the city. One particular group of people who were falling through the cracks were the single mothers. Jaan and others suggested that the human-services office ask entering moms if they would like a faith community to work with them. If any of the single moms indicated that they would prefer to work with a faith-based program, they would be sent down the hall to another room. Out of this visit, an initiative called Faith Partners was born. Faith Partners' goal is to train mentors from local churches to serve by empowering single moms for an entire year. Their responsibility for that year is to assist single moms as they move from a culture of poverty to a state of self-sufficiency. The mentors are trained in providing life skills, job training, and childcare and can even help with transportation needs. They teach these single moms how to solve their own problems and are *never* allowed to give them money—"not even one dime." This creative partnership between the city and the churches has a 90 percent success rate for moving single moms out of poverty into self-sufficiency.[175]

What Could You Do Together?

Without question, every community has huge problems that the church united could lead in alleviating. One of the most critical needs in education is for children in third grade to learn to read at a third-grade level. This is probably the most determinative aspect that affects a child's future. Third-grade reading levels are directly tied to high school graduation, teen pregnancy, drug use, and incarceration. We've heard that over 80 percent of men in federal prisons in the United States are functionally illiterate. I (Eric) shared this correlation during a sermon I was giving, and afterward an administrator came up to me and said, "You are exactly right. We tell parents, 'Up to third grade we learn to read, and after third grade we read to learn." Imagine how it feels to get farther and farther behind every year because you lack that one critical skill! What if the churches in your city came together and made a commitment to every third-grade class in every elementary school in your city that every student would be able to read at a third-grade level?

Like tutoring, mentoring can make a transformational difference in the lives of others. In our Boulder community, over two hundred volunteers work with high-risk children from third through twelvth grade through the "I Have a Dream" Foundation. Now in its tenth year of operation, this organization reports that "[e]ighty-two percent of our first three Dreamer classes graduated from high school. Of these graduates, 86 percent went on to some level of post-secondary schooling."[176] What is most impressive is this graduation rate compared with the peer graduation rate among similarly situated students, which is a painful 35 percent. The economic impact to future families and the contribution to greater society through greater tax contributions and lessened burden on the tax system are nothing less than astonishing. Nationwide, "[i]f the students who dropped out of the class of 2008 had graduated, the nation's economy would have benefitted from an additional $319 billion in income over their lifetimes."[177] Could the churches in your city unite to take on youth mentoring?

How about issues like children in poverty? Plenty of evidence links poverty to increased likelihood of maltreatment, academic failure, delinquency, and violence. In fact, poverty is the largest predictor of child abuse and neglect. Children living in families with annual incomes below fifteen thousand dollars are twenty-two times as likely to be abused or neglected than are children in families with annual incomes of thirty thousand dollars or more. Ron Sider and Heidi Unruh note, in their book *Hope for Children in Poverty*, that each year that we allow thirteen million children to live in poverty will cost our

> God always gives capacity and strength to help others.

society over $130 billion in future economic output, as poor children grow up to be less-productive and less-effective workers than those who don't grow up in poverty.[178] God always gives capacity and strength to help others. What could the church in your city do?

What other needs could the unified church lean into? How about single moms or shut-in elderly or parents with special-needs children? Look at the following chart as a way to identify needs, gaps, and opportunities in your city.[179] What could the church do together that any church could not do by itself?

	Orphans James 1:27	Widows James 1:27	Immigrants Lev. 19:33–34	Prisoners Heb. 13:3	Sick/Disabled Matt. 25:36	Poor Gal. 2:10	Aged 1 Tim. 5:9
Physical • food/nutrition • shelter/housing • clothing							
Spiritual • salvation • discipleship							
Social • loneliness • addictions • mentoring							
Emotional • grief • stress							
Educational/ Training • literacy • tutoring • language • career guidance							

The idea for this chart was inspired by Dr. Raymond Banke.

PRAYING OR DOING?

Are city movements about praying and waiting, or planning and going? Our answer is … yes. In the past, city movements have coalesced around a choice between two approaches. The first approach might be called the "revival" approach: gathering for prayer and then waiting for a divine visitation. The idea behind this approach is that when God moves, he can do more in a moment than mere humans can hope to achieve in a lifetime. The other approach is seen as the "missional" responsibility of the church, advancing the kingdom in the city. To these folks the mandate is clear: they just need to trust and obey. They pray, but they also plan and take action. These are the leaders who, after attending one city gathering where they hear, "We're just going to keep meeting and praying till we hear from God," respond by saying, "Give me a call when he tells you what he wants to do — I'll join you when you know." Rather than seeing these approaches as competitive, we see them as parallel tracks running in the same direction. Some people gravitate toward prayer, while others gravitate toward action, and much of this is determined by gifting and temperament. Rather than competing with or disparaging one another, we believe that God uses both approaches and will continue to do so. Prayer alone is insufficient if it never leads to action. But acting without prayer often leads to futility. We certainly need the strengths of both approaches, and we need to affirm and appreciate those with different but complementary passions.

THE ROLE OF MEGACHURCH PASTORS

City transformation movements certainly don't require the active participation of megachurch pastors, but it sure helps to have them in the mix. There are a number of reasons why the lead pastors of megachurches might choose to stay on the sidelines. First, these churches tend to be fairly self-sufficient, and they are large enough to create their own weather patterns and set their own direction for ministry. Cooperating with other pastors has, historically speaking, not been critical to their success or growth. Second, some of the pastors are strong leaders and don't play well with others if they are not actually leading the movement. They feel most effective when they are casting vision and leading the charge, and less effective in a support position. In some cases, this is simply a matter of giftedness and making sure that the right people are using their gifts in the right way. Third, these leaders frequently have more than enough to do, a full-time job that takes all of their time … and then some. Like senior pastors from churches of every size, they feel that their first responsibility is the mission and welfare of their immediate congregation. They generally aren't looking for more gatherings to attend, especially if that could lead to the neglect of their congregations. Fourth, leaders are wired to lead, not sit in meetings. Jim Tomberlin reminds us that "leaders don't get 'invited into a process,' they launch movements!... Prayer and fellowship are not motivators for leaders. They see prayer as a means to an end and fellowship as a by-product of taking a hill together."[180]

> City transformation movements certainly don't require the active participation of megachurch pastors, but it sure helps to have them in the mix.

Despite these challenges, there is a definite advantage to engaging megachurch pastors — especially when the movement is in the formative stage. First, the size of the vision is often proportionate to the combined visionary capacity of those who cast it. Large-church pastors tend to have a higher visionary capacity than pastors of smaller initiatives. Second, because city transformation movements will involve the engagement of domain leaders from government, business, media, and education, these domain leaders will likely want to meet with the most influential leaders of the faith community. When Reggie McNeal and I (Eric) formed our Missional Renaissance Leadership Communities (communities of cross-domain leaders from ten to twelve cities from around North America that meet four times over two years), we required the senior pastor of each of the sponsoring churches to attend these gatherings, because we were also asking the sponsoring churches to invite other cross-domain leaders from their cities to participate. The result was that we had the participation of mayors, executive directors of major nonprofits, and two president/CEOs of billion-dollar companies. Like attracts like. Leaders attract leaders. Influence usually does not flow uphill, so the senior pastors had to lead the way.

So if megachurch pastors are so important to the success of a city transformation movement, how do we get them to engage? The answer is simple! Comedian Steve Martin has a great sketch where he proposes to speak on the topic "How to Become a Millionaire." His answer? "First, get a million dollars!" That's helpful. We recognize that this is something of a catch-22, but the truth is that the single most effective way to get megachurch pastors to the table is to have megachurch pastors *at* the table. With that in mind, we follow the sage advice of Jim Tomberlin, who recommends that you start by praying that God would raise up a couple of local megachurch senior pastors who have a vision for their community, beyond the walls of their church, and who are willing to give of their time. If you can find one or two who have that passion, and tap into that, you may be able to propel your city movement forward at an exponential rate.[181]

What if you don't have the involvement of megachurch pastors? Is it still worth moving forward? Our short answer is to say, "Yes ... go with who you have." We firmly believe that even unstrategic action is preferable to strategic inaction. *Some* movement is better than *no* movement, and God is always in the business of surprising us by raising up Gideons, Davids, and little lads carrying a few fish. It might be possible to start by asking for the sponsorship of megachurch senior pastors without burdening them down with administrative or operational roles.

Megachurch pastor Randy Pope of Perimeter Church in the Atlanta area planted Perimeter with the dream that it would be the church that would transform the city of Atlanta. In the decades since the church launched, that dream has not dimmed for him. But to be most effective, Randy has decided to free up two (and a half) staff members to give leadership to the citywide Unite! movement in Atlanta. Randy's endorsement of the movement, and his presence at key events, is a wonderful support to this powerful city transformation movement.

It's also important to note that as city transformation movements grow and spread, we may see even more involvement by megachurch leaders as they recognize the profound impact they as megachurch pastors can have for the kingdom. In 2007, senior pastor Joel Hunter from Northland, A Church Distributed pulled together the pastors from eight of the largest and most influential denominational churches in Orlando to lead a common church-based effort for disaster relief. This effort has since emerged into a growing city transformation movement. In early 2008, Gary Kinneman, pastor emeritus of City of Grace Church in Mesa, Arizona, convened the lead pastors of twenty of the largest churches in the Greater Phoenix area (churches with an average weekend attendance of over five thousand) for three days in Sedona to cast vision and talk about city transformation. Scott Chapman, multisite and megachurch pastor of The Chapel, in Lake County, Illinois, personally called on more than fifty senior pastors, inviting them into relationship and greater kingdom impact through Christ Together (formerly Catalyst). We expect to see even more trends like these as senior leaders begin thinking in fresh ways about the kingdom.

We said earlier that a city transformation movement will not include every church but it can't *exclude* any church. In other words, Christian leaders will tend to coalesce around the things they have passion for and have the capacity to do, and the sum total of these various passions and abilities is what leads to city transformation. Megachurch pastors can be supportive of a city transformation movement, lending their influence to the movement, without actively participating in its operation. Likewise, leaders of a city transformation movement can support the efforts and initiatives of megachurch pastors, even though the pastors' names are not listed on the letterhead. It's all good!

Why Transformation Movements Falter

We want to end this chapter with a few prudent and helpful insights from Jim Herrington and Steve Capper of Mission Houston into why transformation movements falter and fail. Mission Houston (*www.missionhouston.org*) was begun by Jim over ten years ago and is one of the largest and most mature expressions of city transformation that we know. Mission Houston focuses on cross-domain collaboration and has received many civic awards for the work they do to serve the Greater Houston area. Jim and Steve agreed to offer us some clear and practical reasons why movements sometimes end up moving in the wrong direction.

1. Leaders do not have a clear idea of where they are going and a workable map to get there.
2. Leadership teams move from a catalytic role to one of sponsoring and owning ministries.
3. Current leaders fail to engage senior leaders from the diversity of the body of Christ, especially prominent leaders from the African American and Hispanic communities.
4. Leaders are not able to move beyond prayer and relationships.
5. Leaders are committed to the transformational *process* but are not engaging in community-based ministry.
6. Senior leaders are not leading the way.
7. A low level of commitment by leaders leads to an administrative movement rather than a catalytic leadership role in the community.
8. The strategic initiative is sometimes hijacked by another competing agenda.
9. The initiative is underfunded, typically beginning with the leadership team.
10. Leaders do not give enough emphasis to fostering spiritual vitality and relationships within the pastoral community.
11. Leaders do not really understand the holistic and comprehensive nature of transformation, so they settle for something less.

12. Leaders think too regionally and don't develop local relationships and initiatives.
13. Leaders fail to mobilize believers and leaders from the marketplace.

As you can see from this list, we have tried to address many of these concerns in this chapter by highlighting successful examples and distilling key, practical principles for launching and leading a successful city transformation movement. As you gain experience working with a movement, you may end up developing a list of your own downfalls. True wisdom is the ability to learn from the successes *and* the failures of others, and we hope that this list will provide an outline of key issues that should be considered should you choose to move forward.

For Reflection and Discussion

1. What expressions of unity are you currently seeing in your city?
2. How does the concept of the three expressions of unity deepen or develop your understanding of unity?
3. What problems in your city could churches work together to address and really make a difference?
4. Who are possible "conveners," or anchor churches, in your community?
5. What community service events could possibly be turned into a citywide, catalytic event around which churches could unite?
6. Where is your city movement "stuck"? What are some additional reasons why a city movement may falter or fail?

Chapter Six

THE WHOLE GOSPEL

You know the message God sent to the people of Israel, *telling the good news* of peace through Jesus Christ ... how God anointed Jesus ... with the Holy Spirit and power, and how he *went around doing good* ... because God was with him.

—Acts 10:36–38 (emphasis ours)

In Luke 10:1, Jesus appoints and commissions seventy-two of his followers and sends them "two by two ahead of him to every town and place where he was about to go." Their job was to serve as the lead team, preparing the way for Jesus to enter these cities. As followers of Jesus, we need to be doing the very same thing in our own communities. So how can we best prepare the way for Jesus to enter a city? Are there things we can do that will welcome Jesus into our cities, preparing the way for him to transform them by his presence?

The life and ministry of Jesus were absolutely transformational. Through his ministry of mercy (his response to those in distress), through his ministry of empowerment (his healing ministry), and through evangelism (speaking the message of the kingdom), he improved the lives of people, not just on that day but for all of eternity. Through a holistic ministry of teaching, preaching, and healing, he led the recipients of his grace to conclude that "God has come to help his people" (Luke 7:16). God was manifested in the words, works, and loving presence of Jesus.

As we have seen, though, the church has a tendency to detour from this type of holistic ministry. For some believers, the key to transformation is "saving the lost," and transformation is the trickle-down effect that comes after preaching and proclamation. Others suggest that we start by "serving the least of these" and emphasize deeds of mercy toward those in need. Jesus didn't operate from an either-or approach to ministry. The incarnational message of Jesus was made manifest through word *and* deed. He would both show *and* tell, and his words clarified his deeds while his deeds verified the truth of his words. When Jesus was once asked for his credentials by the disciples of John the Baptist, he responded, "Go back and report to John what you have *seen* and *heard*: The blind receive sight, the lame walk, those who have leprosy are cured, the deaf hear, the dead are raised, *and* the good news is preached to the poor" (Luke 7:22, emphasis ours).

Good News and Good Deeds Working Together

N. T. Wright describes a faith void of deeds as an opiate that serves to promote complacency rather than a remedy to redeem a broken world: "But my impression is that religion is an 'opium' when the religion in question includes the Platonic downgrading of bodies and of the created order in general, regarding them as the 'vain shadows' of earth, which we happily leave behind at death. Why try to improve the present prison if release is at hand? Why oil the wheels of a machine that will soon plunge over a cliff? That is precisely the effect created to this day by some devout Christians who genuinely believe that salvation has nothing to do with the way the present world is ordered."[182]

But here is the good news: we don't have to be trapped in the tyranny of either-or thinking. The church has historically taken the approach of both-and rather than either-or. After all, Jesus is *both* fully God *and* fully man. At her best, the church can be about justification *and* justice. Richard Lovelace helps us at this juncture. He writes, "The classical evangelical position has been that of holistic witness to

> He would both show *and* tell, and his words clarified his deeds while his deeds verified the truth of his words.

the gospel including evangelistic preaching directed toward the redemption of individuals conjoined to works of love and prophetic social action. The church should neither withdraw from involvement in the structures for society nor try to dominate them in the Constantinian fashion, but should operate as a transforming agent both in changing hearts and changing structures."[183]

Wow! That's good. We often use a quadrant to help explain the way in which good deeds and good news can both be embraced. A truncated version of this

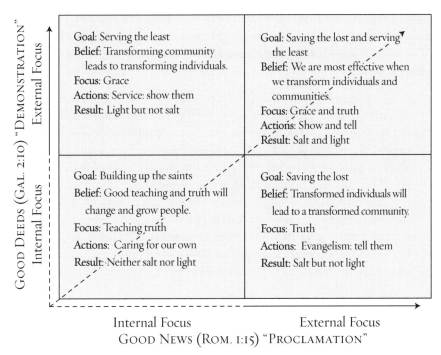

Figure 8

diagram was originally published in the book *The Externally Focused Church*,[184] but we have here further developed this idea of holistic witness (see fig. 8).

Consider the diagram carefully. If you look at it long enough, like those pictures you have to stare at for a while in order to see the 3-D image, it will start to make sense. A few months ago, I (Eric) received an email from a pastor who attended a seminar I gave at Dallas Theological Seminary. He was excited because he had just figured out that his church didn't need to be an either-or church but could be what he described as a fourth-quadrant church—saving the lost *and* serving the least. The goal that we are seeking is that upper-right quadrant, where we see the church doing both of those things. We don't have to choose between changing our communities and changing lives; we can focus, like Jesus did, on both truth *and* grace (John 1:14, 17) without ever having to compromise either one.[185]

GOOD DEEDS, GOODWILL, AND GOOD NEWS

Good deeds almost always produce goodwill with others. When people are observers or recipients of unmerited acts of kindness, they sit up and take notice.

Albert Einstein's spiritual journey oscillated between deism, Judaism, and agnosticism, but there is evidence that at various times in his life he was openly seeking God. In the December 23, 1940, issue of *Time* magazine, Einstein is quoted as saying,

> Being a lover of freedom, when the revolution came in Germany, I looked to the universities to defend it, knowing that they had always boasted of their devotion to the cause of truth; but no, the universities were immediately silenced. Then I looked to the great editors of the newspapers, whose flaming editorials in days gone by had proclaimed their love of freedom; but they, like the universities, were silenced in a few short weeks. . . .
>
> Only the Church stood squarely across the path of Hitler's campaign for suppressing truth. I never had any special interest in the Church before, but now I feel a great affection and admiration for it because the Church alone has had the courage and persistence to stand for intellectual and moral freedom. I am forced to confess that what I once despised I now praise unreservedly.[186]

When the church defends the innocent, stands up to the evil in this world, and serves the community with good deeds, these actions often result in goodwill toward the church. Even people like Albert Einstein take note. But remember this — goodwill is not the same thing as good news. Winning the goodwill of the community should not imply that something of eternal, salvific significance has occurred! The goodwill generated by our actions provides an opportunity to share the good news about Jesus. Without this, we are simply a social service agency with Bibles in our pockets. We must never forget that the church has the opportunity to do what no one else in the community can — point people to Jesus for forgiveness of sin.

> Winning the goodwill of the community should not imply that something of eternal, salvific significance has occurred!

With this in mind, how can churches best utilize the goodwill generated by their acts of community service, using it as a springboard for sharing the good news? We must first recognize that when people are recipients and observers of unexpected grace or mercy, two questions immediately arise in their minds — even if asked with a note of suspicion: (1) "Who are you?" and (2) "Why are you doing this?" Selfless service provides the opportunity for others to see, taste, smell, and feel the kingdom of God. The real "evangelistic questions" of our generation are not the ones being asked *by* us ("If you were to die tonight, do you have the absolute assurance that you would go to heaven?") but also include the two questions people ask us when we graciously serve them in the love of Christ. Our friend Reggie McNeal, in his book *The Present Future*, writes, "Pastor Cho [pastor of the world's largest church] in South Korea instructs the people of his church what to say when they are asked about the intentional acts of kindness they perform (this is part of their small group evangelism strategy). When asked by those who are blessed by them why they do their kind acts, they are told to say: 'I am a disciple of Jesus. I am serving him by serving you because that's what he came to do.' That response is brilliant. It signals to people that God is for them, not against them, but also provides content to what it means to be a follower of Jesus."[187]

As we train people in methods of evangelism, we also need to train them to be sensitive for that "God moment" when we sense that God is at work in our conversation and people grow surprisingly open to deeper conversations about him. These God moments can usually be identified as people ask us questions and express curiosity about what we are saying and doing. We find examples of this type of curiosity in the biblical stories of Nicodemus, the rich ruler, and the woman at the well. In chapter 5, we gave several examples of thousands of people from scores of churches serving the community together. Now, think of the evangelistic and kingdom conversations that would follow if each person who served told five people during the following week, "I had a *great* weekend!" and then just shut up. If God is at work, people will respond with curiosity and questions that can easily lead to tens of thousands of gospel conversations.

Let us give you another example of this. We would probably all agree that a car wash for one dollar is a great deal. But what if a church were to give car washes for even less than a dollar? What if they were even *less* than ... free? After I (Eric) finished speaking about this topic of curiosity and questions at a seminar, a pastor came up to me and said, "You're right! We do Dollar Car Washes in our community. One hundred percent of the people we serve ask us, 'Who are you?' And after washing and wiping down their cars with a clean chamois and giving the driver a dollar bill for letting us serve them, people are surprised and ask, 'Why are you doing this?' These questions give us two great opportunities to tell him or her about the grace and goodness of God. It's been wonderful."

People who receive underserved grace simply have to know the "who" and "why" of the situation. As Christ followers begin to recognize these God moments, they will soon discover opportunities to have thousands of unlikely conversations about the King and his kingdom. Tim Keller writes, "[T]he ministry of mercy is a dynamic witness to those with whom you share the gospel, because it builds a 'plausibility structure' for our message. Most Christians in evangelism seek only to make the gospel credible, to make it cogent and persuasive intellectually. But people believe in a message mostly for non-rational reasons. A belief appears convincing to the degree that it is supported by a consistent, loving group or community. The mercy ministry of Christians provides tremendous social and psychological support for the validity of the gospel.... It convinces a community that this church provides people with action for their problems, not only talk. It shows the community that this church is compassionate."[188]

> People who receive under-served grace simply have to know the "who" and "why" of the situation.

Good deeds and good news, when matched in partnership, raise questions that demand answers, answers we are eager to share with those who are spiritually curious.

SAINT FRANCIS OF ASSISI

Saint Francis of Assisi was a godly man who devoted himself to proclaiming the gospel and serving the poor. His gospel went forth in both word and deed. Unfortunately, many Christ followers have misrepresented his actual ministry, hiding behind a phrase that is dubiously attributed to him (most scholars agree that it was not said by Francis): "Preach the gospel at all times, and *if necessary* use words." While this statement might be appropriate as a greeting card slogan, it is hardly a missional strategy. There is no preaching of the gospel without words, and make no mistake, Francis certainly used words to preach.

In Romans 10:14, the apostle Paul asks his readers to consider a rhetorical question: "How can they believe in the one of whom they have not heard?" In other words, how can people come to faith in Jesus if there is no one to tell them about him? Paul answers his own question a few verses later, emphasizing the necessity of the *spoken* word: "Faith comes from hearing the message, and the message is heard through the word of Christ" (10:17). If we don't provide a verbal witness that explains our actions of love and mercy, then people, left to themselves, will just guess at our motives. The "who" and the "why" will remain unanswered.

Our goal is to answer the questions and clarify misunderstandings. On the day of Pentecost, as people began speaking in languages they had never learned, the bystanders wrongly concluded that these men were drunk (Acts 2:13). They saw what was happening and wanted an answer. The idea that the men had drunk "too much wine" seemed reasonable enough. But their guess was wrong.

Peter's first words were a God-honoring corrective: "These men are not drunk, as you suppose" (2:15). He then went on to preach the gospel and teach the crowd about Jesus, resulting in the salvation of three thousand people.

In Acts 3, we see another situation where actions needed answers. After Peter and John healed the paralytic on their way to the temple, a crowd gathered around them, "filled with wonder and amazement at what had happened to [the man]" (3:10). Peter then spoke to offer a corrective to their misunderstandings: "Why do you stare at us as if by our own power or godliness we had made this man walk?" (3:12). Again, Peter turned the conversation to Jesus, and at least a couple more thousand people were added to the kingdom. These examples from the Scriptures remind us that people, when left to their own, will often come to the *wrong* conclusion regarding the motive for our good deeds. Deeds can verify the truth of our words, but it is our words that clarify the reason for our deeds.

Let's consider one final example, from Acts 14. Paul and Barnabas were in the Roman city of Lystra, and they healed a crippled man who was lame from birth. When the people of Lystra saw the crippled man jump up and walk, the people began shouting, "The gods have come down to us in human form!" (14:11). They collected wood and rounded up several bulls to offer sacrifices to Barnabas and Paul — assuming one of them was the Greek god Zeus and the other Hermes (not a bad compliment, if you think about it). Paul's words, like Peter's, were a helpful and necessary corrective: "We … are only men, human like you" (14:15). Paul then went on to tell the assembled group about Jesus. Left to themselves, without this explanation, the people would have understood these acts of kindness and mercy in the light of their own worldview. They would have missed the amazing and radical message of the gospel.

By now you have probably realized that we aren't talking about a new type of friendship evangelism. Serving people in your city and your community is not a substitute for other evangelistic efforts you are currently engaged in. Again, we want to emphasize a key point: *we serve because Jesus serves.* Still, we have found that there is often no richer and more fertile ground for evangelistic conversation than a heart that has been softened through service. We are not saying that

> We must never lose sight of the fact that we are kingdom workers, not just community volunteers.

every time you serve, you must include a gospel presentation as part of your service or as a qualifier for whether you will serve someone, but we must never lose sight of the fact that we are kingdom workers, not just community volunteers.

Rethinking the Thickness of the Gospel

Viv Grigg, a friend of ours from New Zealand, was an engineer by education and was trained by the Navigators. Since I (Eric) was also involved in the Navigator ministry while in the Army Reserves, I deeply respect the level of commitment and training shown by those involved in this ministry. As a young man, Viv sensed the call of God on his life to go and minister to the poorest of the poor in Manila in the Philippines. In preparation for his life among the poor, Viv read and memorized 254 verses about God's care for people living on the margins of society. After a bit of time in language school, learning the language Tagalog, Viv moved into the squatter community of Tatalon and rented a room above a shack. As he met the people, they asked, "What's a white-face like you doing here?" Viv would simply answer, "Jesus said the poor are blessed and I came here to find out why."[189] As Viv began telling people about Jesus, the people of Tatalon responded to his message—often presented as "the Bridge" diagram (fig. 9). I have also used this method to share my faith on multiple occasions.

As people began coming to faith, Viv realized that the good news he was sharing merely addressed the *spiritual* consequences of sin and did not directly address the economic or social consequences of sin. Since poverty was so rampant in this barrio, Viv found himself thinking, "Women need Jesus Christ to help them stay

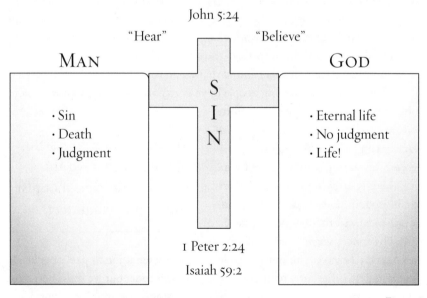

John 5:24

"Hear"   "Believe"

MAN   GOD

S
· Sin   I   · Eternal life
· Death   · No judgment
· Judgment   N   · Life!

1 Peter 2:24

Isaiah 59:2

Figure 9

out of prostitution—and an alternative income.... Drinking men need Jesus Christ—and a job.... Exploited workers need Jesus Christ—and assistance in the right ways to relate to their oppressive employers."[190] That was when he realized that the gospel he was sharing was *true*, but it was incomplete. It primarily addressed the *spiritual* consequences of sin. It was a thin gospel. "Jesus might be the answer, but as Christians, we had not been asking the right questions. Western notions of the gospel and discipleship were irrelevant in the Two-Thirds World except to the upper and middle class, whose problems were primarily psychological and emotional needs."[191]

> Jesus came to redeem *all* that is broken and invites us to join him in this wonderful work.

Viv understood that the fall affected not only our relationship with God but also our relationship with other people and our relationship to all of creation. The fall had profound spiritual consequences, as well as social, economic, and environmental consequences. Indeed, all of creation groans under the "bondage to decay," waiting for its final redemption (Rom. 8:21–22). Every aspect of God's original design is marred, broken, and flawed. But here is the news that is the basis of the good news: everything that was lost in the fall was redeemed at the cross and one day will be totally restored. Colossians 1:19–20 tells us that "God was pleased to have all his fullness dwell in [Jesus], and through him to reconcile to himself *all* things, whether things on earth or things in heaven" (emphasis ours). The redemption of the cross goes far beyond simply bringing us to heaven. In light of this, the gospel we share should address not only the spiritual consequences of our sin and rebellion but also the social and economic consequences. The good news Viv shared became *thicker*. His bridge diagram now looks something like figure 10.[192]

When I (Eric) first saw this diagram, it was like a light went on as it helped me understand that for the gospel to be transformative, it has to touch every area of life. This helped explain why Jesus could start with any area of life, because the gospel was going to touch every area of life. So with Nicodemus he could begin with his spiritual life; with the woman at the well, her social life; with the rich young ruler, his economic life. This *thick* gospel brings transformation to the totality of life. Christianity is not a form of Gnosticism, which values the soul but ignores the body and the material world. Jesus came to redeem *all* that is broken and invites us to join him in this wonderful work.

Recently I (Eric) was in Europe meeting with leaders of a worldwide parachurch ministry who had gathered together from different nations. All of them

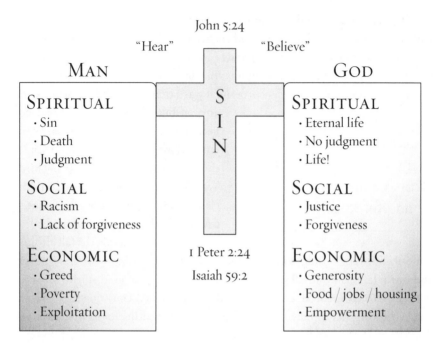

Figure 10

were experiencing this same shift from a proclamation-focused ministry to a more holistic approach. Some shared that there was concern among some of the leadership that this holistic gospel would lead to an abandonment of the guiding principle of Matthew 28:18–20: "Go and make disciples." As the discussion deepened, someone read the passage to us all and pointed out that Jesus further encourages us, as we make disciples, to teach them to "obey everything I have commanded you." Perhaps the problem was really an issue of mission—that our goals for mission were not thick enough and we were neglecting the full responsibility of making disciples who obeyed *everything* Jesus had taught his disciples to do and believe. We concluded that ministering holistically was not an abandonment of our mission and calling in Matthew 28:18–20. It was actually a deeper fulfillment of that mission!

> We concluded that ministering holistically was not an abandonment of our mission and calling in Matthew 28:18 – 20. It was actually a deeper fulfillment of that mission!

Understanding the larger picture of God's story suggests at least two things to us. First, it encourages us to think and live *missionally*. Reggie McNeal defines the missional church as "the people of God partnering with God in his redemptive mission in the world."[193] We love that definition, since it emphasizes our partnership with God, in which we serve as his agents to bring healing and fix what is broken in the world. Second, understanding the thickness of God's story helps us understand why so many nonbelieving "image bearers" want to help heal our broken world. Intuitively, human beings know that our relationships with one another are out of whack. They know that dirty water and polluted air are not right. They may be passionate environmentalists or working to end sex trafficking, but they know that something is broken, and they want to be part of the solution. They want to bring change to the world. Rather than writing these people off, perhaps we should see them as those who look in a mirror and dimly sense what God is doing as he restores our world. We may have unique opportunities to help them connect their story to God's bigger story of the kingdom and show them how their passion fits in with God's bigger plan for our world. We may even have an opportunity to introduce them to the King so they can come to know him personally.

> We may have unique opportunities to help them connect their story to God's bigger story of the kingdom and show them how their passion fits in with God's bigger plan for our world.

THE ENGLE SCALE … AND THE GRAY SCALE

Several years ago, the brilliant missiologist, sociologist, and marketing expert James Engle developed a diagram that helped believers think more effectively about evangelism. Rather than treating non-Christians as a single, monolithic category of people, Engle suggested that unbelievers actually have different amounts of awareness and differing sensitivities to what God is doing in their lives. He believed that understanding that level of awareness could help the church determine the best tactical approach to take in helping them come to faith. An approximate representation of the Engle Scale, read from bottom to top, looks something like figure 11.

This diagram has proved to be quite helpful for many evangelists, but it is not without its own shortcomings. As a scale, it mainly represents our *cognitive* response to the gospel. But if this scale were accurate, then why is it that the Jews who lived at the time of Jesus and saw his miracles and heard his teachings

ENGLE SCALE

+2	Initiation into the church
+1	Evaluation of decision
− 1	Repentance and faith
− 2	Challenge and decision to act
− 3	Awareness of personal need
− 4	Positive attitude toward the gospel
− 5	Grasp implications of the gospel
− 6	Awareness of basics of the gospel
− 7	Interest in Christianity
− 8	Initial awareness in Christianity
− 9	No awareness of Christianity
− 10	No awareness of a supreme being

Figure 11

rejected him? They should have been most receptive to him, but they were not. Perhaps something is missing, a way of making the Engle Scale more accurate?

Recognizing this shortcoming of the scale, another missiologist, Frank Gray, added a horizontal vector representing "attitude toward the gospel," combining it with Engle's vertical vector of "knowledge of the gospel." Gray's Matrix can be represented as in figure 12.[194]

MOVING PEOPLE TOWARD JESUS

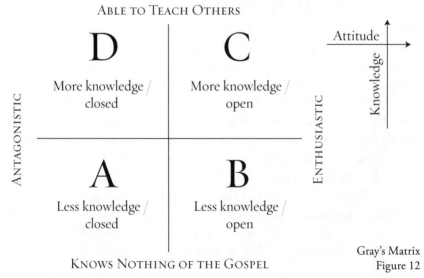

ABLE TO TEACH OTHERS

D	C	Attitude
More knowledge / closed	More knowledge / open	Knowledge
A	B	
Less knowledge / closed	Less knowledge / open	

ANTAGONISTIC   ENTHUSIASTIC

KNOWS NOTHING OF THE GOSPEL

Gray's Matrix
Figure 12

Gray's Matrix suggests how good news and good deeds can work together. Good news helps people move up the vertical vector—from "knows nothing of the gospel" to "able to teach others"—but history attests that it is often good deeds that move people along the horizontal vector—from being antagonistic to the gospel to enthusiastically embracing it. We can summarize by saying that good deeds create an *openness to the gospel,* while good news creates *knowledge of the gospel.*

This was the attraction of Jesus. People came to him to hear his words and his teaching—but also to be healed of their diseases (Luke 6:18). If we want to be engaged in moving nonbelievers "up and to the right," then perhaps we need to begin sharing the good news *verified* by our good deeds and engaging in good deeds that are *clarified* by the good news that opens hearts and minds to the truth about God. The good news is what helps people *know* that Jesus is sent from God (this is not necessarily intuitive), but it is often through love and sacrificial service that people *experience* the truth that God loves them as he loves his own Son (John 17:23). Sometimes the hardest soil can be softened and made receptive to the seed of the gospel message through deeds of mercy and grace.

Recently I (Sam) was invited to a Middle Eastern country to share the principles of city transformation with a group of Christian leaders who live and serve in predominately Muslim countries. As I was sharing this "good deeds, goodwill, good news" continuum, one of the participants shared a personal example from her own life. She and her husband are expatriates who serve in a predominately Muslim North African country. He is a medical doctor, but since he cannot officially practice medicine for profit in the country, the two of them own and run a coffee shop in a nice neighborhood in the city. Each week, however, they venture into the poorest parts of the city and provide free medical care to the sick and dying. A resident of the community where they run their coffee shop, upon learning that they were Christians, began a campaign to try to destroy their business. He would stand in front of the coffee shop, loudly proclaiming that the doctor and his wife were Christians, and attempt to keep people from going in. He had some success in turning people away. Not sure how to best confront this angry man, the doctor invited his adversary to spend the day with him.

Throughout the day, they visited some of the poorest parts of the city, and the protestor watched as this Christian doctor cared for and comforted the sick in the name of Christ. Moved by what he saw and experienced, this man completely changed his attitude toward the couple and their shop and is now an "evangelist" for the coffee shop, encouraging people to frequent it. Why? Because "these people go into parts of the city our own people won't go to, and care for people we don't even care for." Good deeds are a universal language of love.

Discovering Common Ground

In October 2003, we were in Riga, Latvia, meeting with a small group of pastors. These devoted servants had joined us for breakfast on the west side of the
Daugava River, overlooking this beautiful medieval city. On the back of a place-
mat we sketched out a diagram for them as we explained the concept of being
a "serving church" (this is now a permanent part of our presentation on city
transformation). This sketch of three intersecting circles provides a visual way
of focusing our understanding of city transformation. To transform a city, there
are always three entities at play—the needs and dreams of the city, the mandates
and desires of God, and the calling and capacity of the church. Take some time
to examine figure 13. We would encourage you to refer to it as we unpack the
content of these circles and their intersections.[195]

Needs and Dreams of the City

First, let's look at the circle labeled "Needs and Dreams of the City." What
exactly does this refer to? We have found that every city has needs, which are
often quite obvious—pressing problems that need to be addressed. In addition,
communities also have dreams, aspirations, and hopes for what they would like

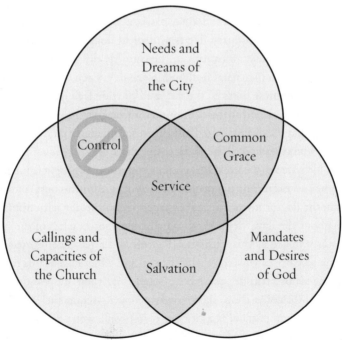

Figure 13

to become and what they would like to be known for. So how do we discover the needs and dreams of the city? The simplest way we have found is to *ask* those who are in a position to know, the people who are actively serving the city—servants in government, education, and human services.

As we mentioned earlier, over a two-year period we hosted monthly luncheons and met with the leaders who serve our city. We asked each of these leaders to tell us what they did, to share their vision for what a healthy community looked like, and to let us know of three impossible things they needed to get done (things that no person could do for them right now). These last items became their prayer requests as we prayed for them. As they presented their vision for a healthy community, all of them described the kind of city we wanted to live in and raise our families in. These common dreams formed common ground between governmental and church leaders and served as a catalyst for transformation. Interestingly enough, the dreams of the city officials did not include seeing the city "saved." Dreams and needs tended to focus on physical and material problems rather than spiritual ones.

Mandates and Desires of God

The second circle in the diagram represents God's vision for a healthy city. In the Bible there are hundreds of passages about cities. As we learned earlier, when God envisioned building a city from scratch in Isaiah 65:17–25, he created a blueprint of the physical, social, and economic aspects of a healthy city. What God wants spiritually for a city is probably best reflected by the words of Jesus when he spoke to the city of Jerusalem in Luke 13:34: "O Jerusalem, Jerusalem, ... how often I have longed to gather your children together, as a hen gathers her chicks under her wings...." God wants a spiritual reconciliation with the city through Jesus.

Calling and Capacity of the Church

The last circle in the diagram represents the calling and capacity of the church. Each church may have a different capacity, based on its size and gifting, but all churches share a common calling. Throughout the Old Testament, we learn that God has given to his people the responsibility and privilege of defending the powerless and speaking up for those without a voice in our communities— the poor, widows, orphans, single moms, prisoners, immigrants, elderly, sick, and disabled. Every church has the capacity to change their neighborhood by ministering to those on the margins of the community. Remember God's word regarding King Josiah: "He defended the cause of the poor and needy.... Is that not what it means to know me?" (Jer. 22:16).

Intersection 1: Common Grace

The diagram gets interesting when we start to look at the areas where the circles overlap. While the circles represent the hopes and dreams of the different entities of the city—the secular community, the church, and God—the intersections represent where there may be common ground to work and serve together. Consider the first intersection, the intersection between the secular interests of the city and the desires of God. *Common grace* is the term we use to describe the space where the needs and dreams of the city intersect with the mandates and desires of God, apart from the church. Common grace is a term John Calvin used to describe the things which God wants to do for a city that he doesn't need the church to accomplish. So, for example, Calvin referred to the city wall as an expression of God's common grace, in that it protected both believers and nonbelievers. Common grace is a way of talking about God's beneficence toward all people, a concept reflected in the words of Jesus in Luke 6:35 ("[God] is kind to the ungrateful and wicked") and Matthew 5:45 ("He causes his sun to rise on the evil and the good, and sends rain on the righteous and the unrighteous"). God desires that all people would live in safety and with justice. The common grace of God includes blessings like schools, streetlights, traffic lights, sewers, roads, bridges, and police and fire protection.

> God desires that all people would live in safety and with justice.

Whenever people are excluded from God's common grace in a city, the church has historically served as an advocate for those persons or groups, putting its members in harm's way for the cause of justice. The church has defended the civil rights of people, working to guarantee access to fair housing, abolish slavery, and establish orphanages to care for children in need. Martin Luther King defined the role of the church in this regard: "The church is neither servant of the city nor master of the city but the conscience of the city."[196]

Intersection 2: Control

"Control" is the intersection between the city and the church, apart from the will of God. The history of this intersection has generally been negative and problematic. This intersection represents both attempts by the state to control the church and attempts by the church to control the state. In either case, control by one entity over the other has failed to lead to a sustained impact for the gospel and has not furthered the growth and expansion of the kingdom. We've represented this intersection with a universal prohibition sign over the word *control* to say, "Don't go there."

Intersection 3: Salvation

"Salvation" is the third intersection, where we see what God wants for the city and what the church has the calling and capacity to do for the city—bringing the message and the work of salvation to the community. The Scripture passage that best describes this intersection is 1 Timothy 2:4, where we see that God "wants all men to be saved and to come to a knowledge of the truth." But our diagram (and our experience) tells us that no one in the city is necessarily asking to be saved. None of the city officials we invited to our monthly luncheons described a healthy Boulder by expressing a desire to see the city saved—at least not in a spiritual sense. If that is true, how can we bring salvation to the city if no one really seems to want it? That dilemma brings us to our fourth and final intersection.

Intersection 4: Service

"Service" is the only intersection where we see the needs and dreams of the city, the mandates and desires of God, and the calling and capacity of the church meet together. We often refer to this intersection as the sweet spot. Cities resist being "reached," but they love being served, loved, and blessed. Cities may care little about our efforts to evangelize them, but they will listen when we speak to their own needs and dreams. Meeting those needs and participating in those dreams in the context of meaningful relationships generates goodwill which, in turn, provides a platform for sharing the good news. Increasingly, Christian leaders are finding themselves invited into opportunities of ministry where they were never welcome before, and that service has become a bridge to bring the good news of salvation. It is God's kindness that leads to repentance (Rom. 2:4), and barriers to the gospel often melt away when people experience God's kindness through acts of service and blessing.

THE PASTORS IN RIGA

Back to our breakfast in beautiful Riga. After we shared a few illustrations of people coming to Christ at this sweet spot of service, one of the older pastors sighed in resignation. "Oh, we're a very poor church," he said. "What could we ever do to serve the city?" Immediately a young pastor, Peter, jumped in. "I know what we could do right now. Last month there were seven children killed during the first two weeks of school. It was a tragedy because the city provides no crossing guards. If we had two lat [four U.S. dollars], we could supply safety vests for our church people and cover every crosswalk in the city!" He got it! The safety and well-being of children is something the city cares about, God cares about, and the church cares about. Providing crossing guards would be their sweet spot. When we told this story to our friend Phil Olson of Network 9:35, he built on that vision: "Could you imagine the impact of an adult believer, knowing each of these kids by name, asking them their concerns of the day and letting them know they'd be prayed for ... and then greeting them after school, anxious to find how their days went? Do you think that would make a difference over the course of a year?" Our point is not to say that the next new thing is for churches to have a crosswalk ministry. We're saying that every church has something that they *uniquely* can do that will minister in the sweet spot of the needs and dreams of the city, the mandates and desires of God, and their own calling and capacity as a church and further the kingdom in their city.

> Every church has something that they *uniquely* can do that will minister in the sweet spot of the needs and dreams of the city, the mandates and desires of God, and their own calling and capacity as a church and further the kingdom in their city.

We want to pause once again and remind you of something we said earlier, that while salvation is our *ultimate* motive in what we do, it should not be our *ulterior* motive. People quickly sniff out ulterior motives and "bait and switch" events. Again, we serve not to convert but because we ourselves have been converted. As we serve with genuine concern and authenticity, we often discover (by God's grace) that there is no richer evangelistic environment than a church serving the community.

CHINA

In our travels to the East, we often have the opportunity to meet with church and business leaders. While in East Asia one time, we met with some factory owners who have a unique sense of calling. We asked them the question, "What do you do?" and they answered, "I'm the pastor of a church of five hundred ... but they don't know it yet!" What do they mean? Well, these are business leaders who hire and house migrant workers when they come to the city looking for jobs. But they aren't just looking to make money. These business leaders also hire doctors and dentists and manicurists (what good is a winning smile with dirty fingernails?) to look after their employees and provide for their needs. They also employ several house church evangelists who bring a message of good news to complement the good deeds that are done. One man candidly shared, "They are seeing between 40 and 60 percent of these workers come to faith. Service is powerful because the gospel shouts when it comes through love."

> "The gospel shouts when it comes through love."

TURNING GOODWILL INTO GOOD NEWS

Recently I (Eric) was talking to Randy Chestnut, a church planter from a large city in Ohio. He went to the mayor of his city and asked him what he and a group of volunteers could do to serve the city. At first the mayor was hesitant, but he thought about it a bit and asked the group if they could paint houses. The mayor explained that the city had been given financial grants of four hundred dollars per house to paint the homes of elderly and disabled people. This amount barely covered the cost of the paint and was nowhere near enough to hire and pay professional painters. Randy shared that over the past four or five months, he and his teams had painted twenty-nine houses and had led twenty-five people to Christ through this work. Curious, I asked Randy how they went about the work of evangelism. He said,

> We are very intentional about evangelism. We expect that when we go in as servants that we are never more like Jesus, and so we expect Jesus to show up. Sometimes the person whose house we are painting comes to Christ. We also have people "prayer walking" the neighborhood, and sometimes people they talk to come to faith. The last person who came to Christ was a next-door neighbor who walked over to ask the question, "Why would a dozen people give up their vacation days to help paint the house of a person they've never met?" We've started a Bible study in this man's home and are hoping to turn it into a house church.

Over the course of this two-year initiative, the team mobilized nearly nine thousand volunteers in the city, partnered in starting fifteen new churches, and saw over twenty-five hundred people make first-time professions of faith and start following Christ. Writer and pastor Steve Sjogren sums up the power that good deeds can have in situations like this: "The easiest entrance point into someone's life is a simple deed done in kindness."[197]

Kingdom Conversations in the Public Square

As the world becomes more globalized, tribalized, and sectarian, there is always a danger that government leaders, political pundits, and philosophic thought leaders will push for a world where society and civil conversation are truly secular, where religion is relegated to private life and kept from public view. We believe the exact opposite needs to happen. In pluralistic societies like America, the best way for society to progress is to keep religious dialogue in the public sphere, allowing each religious tradition, through its teachings and behaviors, an opportunity to present society with a vision for a common good—a more compelling story that describes what the future could be for the nation. In this regard, we appreciate David Hollenbach's insight regarding the Second Vatican Councils' position on the purpose of religious freedom. He writes, "For the council stated, 'It comes within the meaning of religious freedom that religious bodies should not be prohibited from freely undertaking to show the special value of their doctrine in what concerns the organization of society and the inspiration of the whole of human activity.' The free exercise of religion is a social freedom and the right to freedom of religion includes the right to seek to influence the policies and laws by which a free people will be governed and the public culture they share."[198]

In other words, everyone should have the opportunity, in the free marketplace of ideas, to put forth their vision for the future—including the church. Let's be at the forefront of not only sharing that vision with our words but also *demonstrating* that vision as the church embodies the gospel of God's grace.

For Reflection and Discussion

1. What are some expressions of common grace in your city?
2. What are the needs and dreams of your city leaders? How would you find out?
3. What are some of the unique callings of your church? What is your church's capacity to serve the city?
4. What is at the intersection of the needs and dreams of the city, the mandates and desires of God, and the calling and capacity of the church in your life and city? Where could your congregation, or a group of congregations, make the biggest difference?
5. Where have you seen or experienced good deeds creating goodwill which led to the passionate proclamation of good news?

CHAPTER SEVEN

THE WHOLE CITY

Organizations must competently perform the one social function
for the sake of which they exist—the school to teach, the hospital
to cure the sick, and the business to produce goods, services, or the
capital to provide for the risks of the future. They can do so only
if they single-mindedly concentrate on their specialized mission.
But there is also society's need for these organizations to take social
responsibility—to work on the problems and challenges of the community. Together these organizations are the community.

—Peter F. Drucker

Cities, especially large ones, often seem like these impenetrable, amorphous
entities that resist any and all efforts at transformation. Churches often
recognize opportunities but don't know where to begin, or get lost in the overwhelming needs they see. There are many ways to subdivide a city and break
it down into manageable pieces. We can divide it by zip codes, neighborhoods,
ethnic groups, or a combination of ethnography and geography. Regardless of
the way we use to understand and address the problems and needs of the whole
city, we must first find a way of breaking it down to a finer level of detail.

To transform a city, we find it helpful to think and plan based on the idea
that there are *sectors* of society. Economists and social scientists recognize at least
three major sectors in every society. The exact size of each sector and what is
or is not included may vary from society to society, but each city, regardless of
geography or ethnography, can be divided into these three sectors—the private
sector, the public sector, and the social sector.

1. *The private sector.* The first sector we must consider is the *private* sector,
   composed of privately owned businesses, companies, corporations, small

businesses, and banks which are not controlled by the state. These institutions are profit motivated.

2. *The public sector.* The second sector is commonly referred to as the *public*
   sector. The public sector is that part of economic and administrative life
   that deals with the delivery of goods and services by and for the government at the local, state, or national level. The public sector is owned by
   the state and exists to provide services that reflect the public interest. In
   some developed countries, these would include police and fire service,
   clean water and sanitation, and possibly waste management and garbage
   removal.

3. *The social sector.* The third sector of every society is sometimes called
   just that—the *third* sector, or the *social* sector. It represents the wide
   range of community, voluntary, religious, and not-for-profit activities
   in society. The activities and programs of Christian churches would be
   included in this sector of society.

Although there are three separate sectors, there is often cooperation and contribution between them. A robust private sector (business) fuels both the public
and social sectors of a city. The private sector pays taxes to supply the funding for
the public sector. Often both the private sector and the public sector contribute to
the social sector by providing goods or services that the social sector does not want
to or is unable to provide. Sometimes the opposite is also true, and social sector
enterprises will have private sector (profit-making) components to their work. We

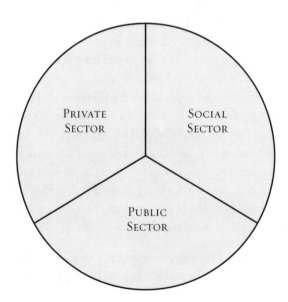

Figure 14

would suggest that the best way to get an overview of a city is to recognize each of the three sectors diagramed in figure 14 and then begin to note the ways they overlap in what they provide and the ways they are distinct from one another.

Community transformation, if it is to be genuine, lasting, and holistic, will need to take into account all three sectors of society. In his book *The City: A Global History*, Joel Kotkin suggests that all three sectors of society must prosper and fulfill their respective purposes for a city to thrive: "What makes cities great, and what leads to their gradual demise? . . . [T]hree critical factors have determined the overall health of cities—the sacredness of place, the ability to provide security and project power, and last the animating role of commerce. Where these factors are present, urban culture flourishes. When these elements weaken, cities dissipate and eventually recede out of history."[199]

Pastor Rick Warren comes to the same conclusion as Kotkin, emphasizing the necessity of addressing all sectors of society and not just one or two of them. In an interview with *Christianity Today*, Warren says, "When I was at the Davos World Economic Forum for the first time, I kept hearing people talk about public and private partnership. What they meant was that government and business need to get together to work on poverty, disease and illiteracy. I'm thinking, 'Wait a minute. You are close but no cigar. You are missing the third leg of the stool—the church. You are missing the component that has the most distribution, the most volunteers, that already has boots on the ground, and that already has the motivation to do it for free.'"[200]

Warren recognizes that the key to successful community transformation requires all three sectors—public, private, and social (the church)—working together for the good of the city.

DOMAINS

The three sectors of society can also be subdivided into what are commonly referred to as the "domains" of society. These domains are the major social and economic structures that make up the building blocks of every society. They represent the spheres of life that influence how we live, work, learn, play, and worship. The thought leaders and activists of each domain determine the future influence of that domain. Each domain can play a redemptive role in God's intention for a city or a nation. Although there is no common agreement on the number of domains, and there are certainly other ways of slicing and dicing the city (neighborhoods, ethnicity, etc.), most would agree that the transformation of individual domains provides an excellent starting point for planning a holistic strategy to transform the city.

In 1975, Campus Crusade for Christ founder Bill Bright and Youth With A Mission (YWAM) founder Loren Cunningham came together and identified what they called "Seven Mountains of Influence" — pillars or domains of society that need to be transformed if the world is to be transformed. The seven mountains they identified were:

- Education: entities that engage in teaching and training
- Arts/Entertainment: entities that consciously produce or arrange sounds, colors, forms, movements, or other elements in a manner that affects the sense of beauty; entities that afford pleasure, diversion, or amusement
- Government: entities (local, regional, or federal) that serve the greater common good of society by restraining evil and promoting the good
- Religion: religious or nonprofit service organizations, such as churches, synagogues, mosques, United Way, Boys & Girls Clubs, and so on
- Family: the fundamental social group in society, typically consisting of one or two parents and their children
- Media: entities that transmit information to the masses via radio, television, print, or the internet
- Business: enterprises that engage in the sale of goods or services

While we recognize that these seven domains may not appear to cover every aspect of society, we have found they serve effectively as "big buckets" to hold more distinct subgroups like law, healthcare, agriculture, military, and so on.

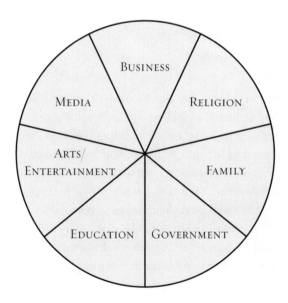

Figure 15

The seven key domains in every society, according to the breakdown developed by Bright and Cunningham, look something like figure 15.

Here's why we think domains are critical to transformation: For many years, church leaders assumed that their job was to pull the most committed believers out of their various domains and get them involved in the *religious* domain, doing "church work." So church leaders would try to woo and recruit people from the domains of education and business and out of the home to serve in full- or part-time, programmed ministry. But what if that was the wrong way to bring lasting change? What if instead we understood that God had placed these believers into each domain for a specific purpose—so they could be agents of change and community transformation! Understood in this sense, then, the church is not a *separate* domain but is called to be the transformational salt, light, and leaven in each and every domain in the city. Reflecting on this idea, Landa Cope of YWAM has even suggested that God has designed each domain to reflect a particular attribute of his character. The domain of government is intended to reflect the justice of God, the domain of the family is meant to express the nurture and love of God, the domain of business exemplifies the provision of God, and the domain of education expresses the knowledge of God.[201] Every domain represents to the world a different aspect of who God is.

> What if God had placed these believers into each domain for a specific purpose—so they could be agents of change and community transformation!

WHO SERVES WHOM?

Tim Svoboda of YWAM has helped us to understand this idea by contrasting the way things are right now with the way things ought to be from a missional perspetive. We first met Tim in Nagpur, India, back in November of 2001. We met with Tim and a number of leaders from around India to talk city transformation and the role of the church. Tim had been serving in Chennai, India, for several years and was aware of the challenges of his city—as well as the opportunities. Over a glass of chai tea, he sketched out a couple of diagrams for us. He had observed that most churches have a "church-centric" view of life, a model of ministry that pulls people away from their particular domain to help with the ministry of the church. Musicians could help with the worship service, educators could help teach Sunday school, and businesspeople could write some big checks to help support the church's ministries. In this faulty model, the church becomes the gravitational center, and all ministry is defined by what happens within its four walls. Not all churches would say it this bluntly, but in many churches this is the reality of how ministry is done. Talent is pulled from the domains of society into the church, and the church draws the resources of the community to itself (see fig. 16).

Tim suggested that we need to change this diagram if we really want to see a change in our communities. No longer should the church be the center of our thinking. Instead it is the Christians in the city, working and operating in their respective domains, who should be at the center of our thinking, with the church as one of the outer circles. A revised diagram (fig. 17) has arrows pointing outward to each of the domains, indicating that the influence is directed *from* individual Christians in the community into each of the domains of society, including the church. The fields of service, in this model, are truly unlimited. In the first diagram (fig. 16), the fields of service are quite limited. People can serve a ministry of the church—as an usher, deacon, elder, board member, Sunday school teacher, volunteer, or staff member—but there is little room for those who do not have a gift that fits the needs of the church. The second diagram (fig. 17) shows us that all kinds of gifts and talents can be employed to serve the

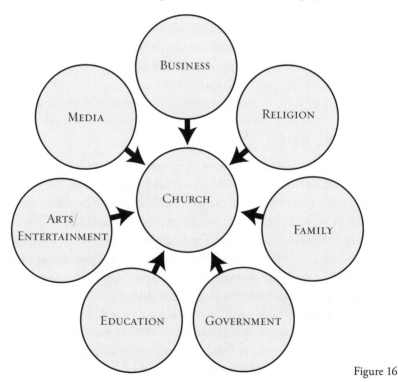

Figure 16

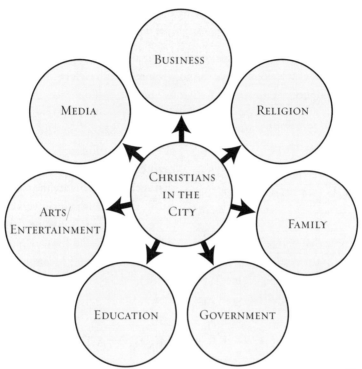

Figure 17

Lord and build his kingdom, even gifts that do not fit the particular ministries of the church and its programs.

How does an artist, an educator, a media person, a businessperson, or a government servant serve the Lord best? Tim reminds us that "there are two questions that every Christian who is working in the secular field must answer. The first is, 'How can I be an effective witness in the sphere of society to my other non-Christian friends?' And a second question is this: 'How can I impact society with the values of the kingdom through the sphere that I am serving in?'"[202] Tim's insight is mirrored by the thoughts of Bob Roberts, pastor of NorthWood Church in Keller, Texas:

> The lowest common denominator of the church for engaging society is not the religious leader but the everyday disciple because each disciple is in a different domain. We've made the preacher the hero of the church. The hero must be the disciple. The job of the pastor must be to equip, mobilize, and help the disciple engage his or her world.... As their lives are transformed, disciples transform the domains of society where they work and live. We're talking more than a Bible study at work, but rather how people use their

vocations for transformation by living out the gospel in a natural way with those around them. This allows the gospel to be viral.[203]

Believers living out the gospel in their domains can have a potentially more powerful evangelistic effect, since the gospel spreads through the natural societal channels as opposed to being a "religious" program. The research of Rodney Stark also confirms the importance of working in domains: "By now dozens of close-up studies of conversion have been conducted. All of them confirm that social networks are the basic mechanism through which conversion takes place. To convert someone, you must first become that person's close and trusted friend."[204] Friendships are most often made within the domains of communities — educators with educators, businesspeople with businesspeople, media people with media people. Social connections are often the pathways that God uses to lead us to eternal life.

> Social connections are often the pathways that God uses to lead us to eternal life.

The Power of Transformation

Christians living out the gospel in their respective domains can also be catalysts of broader domain and societal transformation. Here are just a few examples representing the opportunities in each domain.

From the Domain of Business

Business and job creation is a powerful component of societal transformation. All other domains flourish or languish in proportion to the robustness of the business domain. Wouldn't it be great if every community had business leaders who provided well-paying jobs, treated their employees well, and motivated their workers to deliver excellent goods and services by giving opportunities for growth that reflected the character and values of God? Wouldn't it be wonderful if these employers trained and employed the underemployed of their communities? Wouldn't it be great if they saw themselves as "pastors" of their businesses, with the goal that each employee would somehow reach his or her God-given potential? Does such a business exist? Could it exist?

Consider, for example, Truett Cathy, the founder and CEO of Chick-fil-A, a chain of over twelve hundred restaurants that employs over forty-five thousand young people and produces nearly two billion dollars in annual revenue. Chick-fil-A's purpose statement is posted in their corporate office and in every Chick-fil-A franchise. It reads, "To glorify God by being a faithful steward of all that is entrusted to us. To have a positive influence on all who come in contact with Chick-fil-A." As an extension of Cathy's Christian convictions, all restaurant locations are closed on Sundays so that employees can attend church or spend time with their friends and family. To help local families in distressing situations, the Cathy family runs a "soup kitchen" where they feed up to six hundred people a day in their hometown. Because they believe in empowering people through education, they offer one thousand dollars in tuition payments for each of their employees. In 1989 Cathy received the Horatio Alger Award, and in 1990 he was named Atlanta's "Most Respected CEO" by *Business Atlanta* magazine.

Another kingdom-centered businessman, Bill Job, went to China in 1987 to learn Mandarin. While he was there studying, he learned of a new policy that allowed foreigners to own business enterprises. He jumped at the opportunity and started an innovative stained glass business called Meixia.[205] But this was no low-end factory struggling to survive. Their clients included the likes of Coca-Cola, Disney, and Tiffany Lamps. The vision of Bill's company was "transforming people and communities through profitable business." His core conviction is that "eternal things are more important than temporal things" — and his vision and values are more than just empty words. A large percentage of the more than six hundred workers are former beggars or people with physical handicaps. Before they ever start working at the factory, new employees are taken to the local hospital and given a complete physical; any operation or medical care the employee needs is taken care of before they begin their first day of work. Employees are also given temporary housing until they earn their first paycheck. These employees first experience the grace of the gospel, and then hear the message of the gospel through fellow employees who have also experienced the same incarnate love and grace. Meixia is very active in the local community as well, sponsoring foster care initiatives, helping orphanages, and paying for expensive surgeries. For Bill, his job is his ministry. Bill Job reminds us that there is no welfare program we can offer that is as effective at changing lives or as empowering to an individual as a full-time job with benefits — especially when those benefits are given with the grace and love of the gospel.

The July 3, 2008, edition of *Business Week* featured the story of Richard Chang, a Taiwanese American chief executive of Semiconductor Manufacturing International in Shanghai. Chang's company does $1.5 billion in sales each year, and on Christmas Day 2005, Chang opened Thanksgiving Church for his employees in Shanghai, in partnership with several other churches around China. Thanksgiving Church in Shanghai now attracts eight hundred people each week. Chang exemplifies the qualities of a kingdom-minded business owner. It's not just about making a profit or furthering his own advancement. Chang has funded schools and training programs for company workers, he donated $140,000 to the 2008 Sichuan earthquake victims in central China, and he provides every one of his employees with stock and stock options.[206]

Business leaders with kingdom vision truly have an opportunity to influence more than their own employees, though. They can help to literally change the world! In 1983, a civil contractor named Graham Power started a company in Capetown, South Africa, which eventually grew to become what is today known as the Power Group of Companies. The Power Group has received numerous construction, environmental, and community awards for the way they conduct business and help to improve life in local communities. In 2003, for example, one of their projects was constructing homes for 1,374 low-income families. Employing a management team of only ten team leaders, the company employed 311 local contractors and 1,200 local workers and artisans to build the homes, empowering some 1,500 people with job opportunities in the process.[207] Their values and policies are outlined on their company website, and they reflect the values of God's kingdom.[208] Each company in the Power Group donates 10 percent of its profits to the Power Group Charitable Fund, which distributes the money to four charitable organizations.[209]

> Business leaders with kingdom vision can influence more than their companies. They can help to change the world!

When a company decides to adopt and model kingdom values, God often multiplies and expands the vision and reach of the movement. In 2001, Graham Power called the people of Cape Town together to pray for their community. This movement of prayer eventually spread to other cities and countries in Africa. Five years later, in June 2006, over *500 million* Christians (that was not a typo) gathered at event centers in 199 countries of the world for the Global Day of Prayer![210] In June of 2007, they decided to add ninety days of community service as a follow-up to the daylong prayer event. Can half a billion people make a difference in our communities?

From the Domain of Arts and Entertainment

Filmmakers, screenwriters, artists, poets, and writers shape the thinking and values of a generation. Shakespeare recognized the transformational power of entertainment when he wrote, "The play's the thing, wherein I'll catch the conscience of the king" (*Hamlet*, act 2, scene 2). How would arts and entertainment be different if more missional believers were encouraged to pursue excellence and express kingdom values in the public square through the domain of arts and entertainment? Recently I (Eric) was with a group of Christian artists in China who had spent two weeks with a minority tribal group in a remote mountain village, whose faith and style of worship reflect the work of two English missionaries, Sam Pollard and James Fraser, over a hundred years ago. These diligent servants of God created a written language for this people and with the help of others translated a complete copy of the New Testament. Thousands of Lisu people came to faith as a result of their faith-filled efforts. Back in their studios, the artists painted what they saw and experienced. Their plan is to take their exhibit, entitled A Spiritual Love for China, back to England in order to thank the British people for bringing them the gospel, with an eye toward re-evangelizing England.

The recognized "father of English pottery" is Josiah Wedgwood (1730 – 1795).[211] Wedgwood's practical and innovative work graced the tables of English and Russian royalty, and his glazing techniques revolutionized his industry. His work is on display in some of the greatest museums of the world, and his company continues to thrive after nearly three hundred years. But in addition to being a successful craftsman and businessman, Wedgwood used his craft to speak out against the slave trade. In 1787, Wedgwood joined the Society for the Abolition of the Slave Trade. He also "designed the Society's seal which showed a black slave in chains, kneeling, his hands lifted up to heaven. The motto read: 'Am I Not a Man and a Brother?' "[212] Wedgwood reproduced the design in a cameo and donated hundreds of these to the society for distribution. The upper-class ladies of England had them fashioned into broaches, hairpins, and necklaces, and this "fashion statement" was instrumental in piercing the conscience and shaping a critical mass of opinion that helped lead to the abolition of the slave trade in England.

While a work of art can certainly have influence, is it possible for a soap opera to change a nation? During the 2007 elections in Kenya, tribal protests over extreme poverty and corruption left almost fifteen hundred people dead and three hundred thousand displaced. Political leaders often manipulate the tribalism of different factions, using this to their advantage by pitting one tribe against another. To combat the hatred raised by tribalism, a group of ambitious actors and producers have come up with a popular television show called *The Team*, which is now watched by over two million Kenyans. *The Team* is a program about a soccer team made up of players from different tribes who "work together to overcome historic rivalries and form a common bond." Their hope is that by showing the commonalities between those of different backgrounds, they can inspire harmony in the real world among Kenya's forty-two diverse tribes.[213]

Transformation is also possible within the domain of music. In 2005, Irish rock star Bono, of the band U2, was named, along with Bill and Melinda Gates, as *Time's* Person of the Year. Bono started One.org—a viral web-based network bent on ending global poverty. Bono uses his popularity and influence with the leaders of some of the world's richest nations to work at gaining forgiveness of forty billion dollars in debt owed by the poorest countries in Africa. The hope is that by having these debts eliminated, these countries can instead spend the money on health and schools rather than interest payments. Bono also lobbies the U.S. government, urging them to give even more money toward eradicating poverty, ending hunger, and fighting HIV/AIDS around the world. How can a musician change the world? Bono says, "I'm a musician. I write songs. I just hope that when the day is done, I'll have torn a little corner off of the darkness."[214]

Musical lyrics can be a powerful transformational force. Steve Garber, director of the Washington Institute for Faith, Vocation and Culture, challenges young Christian rock stars, whom he mentors, with the following question: "How can you find ways to write words, rooted in the truest truths in the universe, in a language that the world can understand?"[215]

In 1975, Jose Antonio Abreu launched a musical initiative in Venezuela with a strong social mission: to help "the fight of a poor and abandoned child against everything that opposes his full realization as a human being."[216] The program, called El Sistema, trains students from poor families, teaching them how to play music in the classical style. Although 90 percent of the students are from Venezuela's lowest economic class, in the past thirty years El Sistema has made "classical musicians out of half-a-million young Venezuelans and ... has transformed the lives of many underprivileged and at-risk youths in the process."[217] The musicians trained by this program are so good that the famed opera singer Placido Domingo cried when he saw the Venezuelan Youth Orchestra perform, confessing that "the concert evoked the strongest emotions he had ever felt."[218] The youth in this program have inspired twenty-three countries in the Americas to launch similar music education programs. Many have noted a young person's need to belong, often met by turning to gangs, can be better satisfied as students perform in an orchestra. For a dose of inspiration (and to see with your own eyes what one musician with vision can do), go to YouTube or Google and type in "Venezuelan Youth Orchestra." Then sit back and enjoy. Just one thought as you listen: if we truly believed that the poor need a way of expressing the beauty of God as much as they need bread to eat, why don't more churches and individuals work to develop a practical theology of artistic expression? What would that look like in your community?

From the Domain of Government

Though we may be growing cynical about the potential for government solutions, is it possible that God can use people in this domain to bring about community transformation that reflects kingdom values? Our Malaysian friend Richard Rajoo reminds us that *everything* is affected by politics—from policies to taxes to permits to the common good. Though we have mentioned it before, we can't ignore the powerful testimony provided by the example of English parliamentarian William Wilberforce (1759–1833), who in 1787 wrote in his diary, "God Almighty has set before me two great objects, the suppression of the slave trade and the reformation of manners."[219] Every lawmaker of each generation has a similar opportunity to put forth and vote for humane laws that are broadly reflective of the kingdom.

• • •

These are only a few examples from several domains. The reality is that in a world filled with overwhelming need, *every* person in *every* domain can be engaged in the process of kingdom transformation. We need creativity and wisdom to help people discover how their gifts, abilities, talents, and experiences can be used to engage and change the different domains of the city. Could we build spiritual movements across every domain in the city?

A couple of years ago, on a trip to China, we were talking with a Christian professor from one of China's most prestigious universities. He and several other professors were discussing which domains of society were the most influential in Chinese culture. The top three domains they identified were the government, the intellectuals (writers and artists), and the business world. Identifying these leverage points helped them to determine where they might best target their evangelistic and church-planting efforts. More recently, Pastor Dave Runyon of Foothills Community Church in Arvada shared with us that his efforts are focused primarily on establishing collaboration between just three domains— local government, local churches, and local businesses. He explained that local government provides direction, local churches provide manpower, and local businesses provide finances. These are the domains that provide the greatest opportunities for collaborative effort that will lead to transformation. We say this simply to note that some domains may be more influential than others, depending on our cities and cultures. What are the key domains of your city? Are there any domains that if transformed would influence transformation in other domains? Is business really the key domain? Or is it education? Or family? Arts and entertainment? Government or media?

Theology, Vision, Leaders, and Examples

Thinking about cities in terms of sectors and domains helps us think *specifically* about the process of transformation. But how do we initiate change itself? Where do we begin? And how do we know if we are making progress? Are there ways of measuring the impact of our efforts?

We recommend that you begin with the Scriptures, studying them for yourself to discover what God says about each domain of a city. We need to develop a theology that can serve as a biblical foundation for our efforts, one that reflects the heart of God in each domain. If we are working with families, have we developed a *theology* that informs what a healthy family structure looks like (including one for blended or single-parent families)? Do we have a theology for the arts or a theology of education? Do we have a theology of government that can inform our work with government leaders? Do they know and understand that they are put into positions of power to assist the weak, the afflicted, and the needy (Psalm 72)?

> Are there any domains that if transformed would influence transformation in other domains?

Let's take a practical example of this from the domain of business. Does God have anything to say about business? Is there a theology that can govern our actions, goals, and choices in the private sector? Is it possible for a business to reflect the heart of God and further his purposes in the world? The word translated as "business" is used some seventeen times in the Bible (NIV). While this is hardly an overwhelming number, the scriptural principles these verses contain inform topics like long-term planning, decision making, goal setting, mission, vision, values, leadership, just compensation, sowing and reaping, training, profit, and the fair treatment of partners and employees. We can begin by studying these passages, examining the context in which they are written, and distilling them into principles that can inform our vision and our decision making.

VISION

After a solid, biblical theology has been established, we need a vision of what a particular domain would look like if it operated on these kingdom principles. We want to create a compelling and attractive picture of the future, giving people a vision that leads them to say, "Please let me be a part of this!" Tim Keller helps us flesh out what this might look like for the domain of business:

> What would happen to a company that was operated on the principle of being a "sign of the kingdom"? One of the signs of the kingdom is helping the company's broader community and neighborhood flourish. Another is promoting kingdom character such as integrity and love. Another is promoting the whole welfare of its workers so they flourish not only professionally but personally. What if these things were ends and not means? And what if making a profit was the means not the end? (In other words, we must make a profit in order to promote the welfare of our community and our workers—creating jobs, producing products for customers that really help them and make their world more civilized, helping people grow.)[220]

What would happen in your city if an increasing number of business leaders began to run their businesses as *kingdom* businesses?

WHAT IS OUR VISION?

As a church, we are pretty good at telling our communities what we are *against*, so good that they are often left wondering what we stand for. Vision is a picture of what could be if this domain were under the reign of God. What vision does the church have for the community? What is our "better (kingdom) story," the life that we are inviting our neighbors to be a part of? It is easy to deconstruct and criticize the work of others, but what are we doing to cast a vision that would benefit all? As followers of the King and workers in his kingdom, we need to be dreaming and thinking creatively, inviting others into what could be. What would a community look like where everyone could read? What would

> What is our "better (kingdom) story," the life that we are inviting our neighbors to be a part of?

a community look like where people lived out the Golden Rule? What would it look like if every student graduated from high school? What would it look like if every orphaned child had a mentor? What would things look like if the kingdom came to our community?

In Atlanta, during an event led by Chip Sweney of Perimeter Church and the citywide effort Unite! church leaders cast this compelling vision of what could be:

> The approximately 150 schools in northeast Atlanta represent over two hundred thousand families — What if . . .
>
> * within two years every school in N.E. Atlanta was "adopted" by at least one church, and many schools had people from more than one church working together?
> * within three years, as Unite! spreads across the metro area, every school in metro Atlanta was "adopted" by at least one church?
> * within five years every school in Georgia was "adopted" by at least one church, and Georgia was ranked in the top ten of graduation rates instead of number forty-nine?

Rather than verbally reacting in a negative way to the problems around us, we could be the ones providing solutions and offering a holistic, comprehensive, and compelling vision. Joel Kotkin tells the story of one minister who was able to cast a vision of what could be for the city of Los Angeles:

> Before arriving in Los Angeles, [the Rev. Dana] Bartlett had ministered in St. Louis, where crowded slums and belching factories seemed to scar both souls and the landscape. With its mild climate and spectacular scenery, its clear vistas, ample land and lightly industrialized economy, Los Angeles, Bartlett hoped, could become "a place of inspiration for noble living." In his book *The Better City*, written in 1907, Bartlett laid out a vision for a planned "City Beautiful" that would offer its residents easy access to beaches, meadows, and mountains, taking advantage of the wide-open landscape, manufacturing plants would be "transferred" to the periphery, and housing for the working class would be spread out to avoid overcrowding. Rather than confined to stifling tenements, workers would live in neat, single-family homes.[221]

Although it was far from perfect, Bartlett's vision was adopted by the city leaders of Los Angeles, and single-family homes have provided a much better living experience for generations of families over the past hundred years. Did his vision make a difference? Absolutely! Do *we* have a compelling and attractive vision for others to consider?

After developing a theology and creatively discerning a vision, we need *leadership*. Leadership, in one sense, is really the first thing we need, since nothing usually happens apart from passionate leaders, and if we begin with a leader, that person can unlock the theology and shape the vision. But we include leadership in our current order because at the point of decisive action, leaders are needed to implement the theology and cast the vision. So, for sake of illustration, let's say that a leader or small cadre of leaders from the business domain are taken in by a vision, and they find themselves praying, "Lord, help me build my business to reflect you and your kingdom." The more ambitious ones may even pray, "Lord, use me to transform the way business is done in our city, that it reflects you and your purposes." Leaders are those who can create what doesn't currently exist. By definition, they always have an agenda for change. Spiritual leaders embrace their God-given mission no matter what domain they are working in. Leaders can be used by God to change a domain, an entire city, and maybe even the world. James Davison Hunter, professor of Religion, Culture, and Social Theory at the University of Virginia, has suggested that "between 150 and 3,000 people (a tiny fraction of the roughly 23 billion people living between 600 BC and 1900 AD) framed the major contours of all world civilizations."[222] If this is true, individual leaders can indeed change the world!

Kingdom-minded leaders must be able to shape their "proof of concept" in such a way that others, who need an example to follow, can learn from what these kingdom pioneers have already done. A good intermediate goal is to have at least one transformational example from each domain. Having even one example of the kingdom being lived out in each domain helps leaders to practically answer the question, "Is this actually working anywhere? Is there an example I could take a look at?"

City transformation begins with theology, develops into a vision, is enacted by godly leadership, and results in practical examples. We've created a diagram that identifies and illustrates these four areas, showing how a community can measure the progress they are making toward transformation (see fig. 18).[223]

ENGAGING EVERY DOMAIN IN TRANSFORMATION

Imagine what it would be like if we had a theology, a vision, leaders, and a concrete example of kingdom transformation operating in every domain of society in every community. What if there were spiritual and transformational movements across every domain in the city? Would that not become a catalyst for change? What if the leaders in each domain were able to work together with

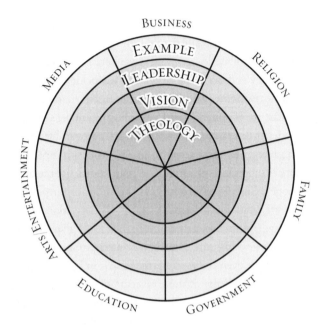

Figure 18

leaders of other domains to take on the big problems of a community? Is that even possible? The truth is that there are examples of believers all over the world who are demonstrating the values of the kingdom in their own social domains. A diagram like this acts like a map to effectively communicate to these believers the steps and the process that can lead to city transformation and where they fit into that plan. For which domains do you have a developed theology? For which do you have a vision to cast? For which do you have the right leadership? For which do you have a concrete example? We can shade in the areas that are completed while allowing the white spaces to pull us forward as we pray and look for ways to make progress in those areas. Recently I (Eric) did this very exercise with a group of cross-domain leaders from a dozen cities around the United States. Not surprisingly, the diagrams were not colored in sequentially. Some domains had a leader and an example but lacked vision and theology. Other domains had a theology and a leader but had no vision or example. This diagram was very helpful for city leaders as they tried to get a quick snapshot of their progress.

Diffusion of Innovations

How are big ideas spread? How do people begin to adopt new practices? Several years ago, Everett Rogers wrote a book titled *Diffusion of Innovations*. In this work, Rogers tells how social adaptation spreads within a given social group. Rogers defines five categories of individuals in any social system: the *innovators*, the *early adopters*, the *middle adopters*, the *late adopters*, and the *laggards*. Understanding the role that each of these individuals has in the spread of an idea is helpful as we consider the spread of transformative ideas in the various domains of the city.

- Innovators make up roughly 3 percent of a social system. They are those who come up with new ways of thinking about something and doing things that challenge and change the status quo.
- Early adopters make up roughly 13 percent of society, and though they are not themselves the innovators, they know how to recognize a good idea. They tend to be oriented toward action and usually begin to implement the new ideas without asking, "Who else is doing this?"
- Middle adopters are 34 percent of the social system. They may understand the new thing but need a bit more certainty before they can buy into it. They ask, "Where is this working? Are there models I can take a look at?"
- Late adopters are another 34 percent and generally want to know where the new idea is working successfully in a setting similar to their own. "I can see this working in Little Rock, Arkansas, but are there any places in the Northwest where this is being implemented?"
- Laggards are 16 percent of the social system and are usually the last to get on board. As Sam wryly notes, they often end up serving on boards. Why? Because boards are established to protect the status quo and the values and practices of the organization.[224]

Rogers diagrams this distribution in a bell curve that can be depicted as in figure 19.

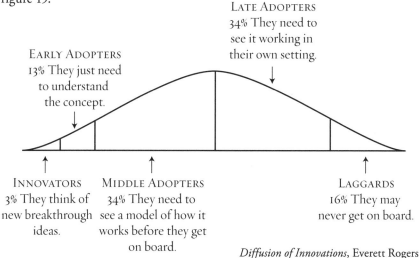

LATE ADOPTERS
34% They need to
see it working in
their own setting.

EARLY ADOPTERS
13% They just need
to understand
the concept.

INNOVATORS
3% They think of
new breakthrough
ideas.

MIDDLE ADOPTERS
34% They need to
see a model of how it
works before they get
on board.

LAGGARDS
16% They may
never get on board.

Diffusion of Innovations, Everett Rogers
Figure 19

Just a few observations we'd like to make. What this diagram shows us is that almost everyone can be persuaded to embrace a new idea — eventually. The difference is that each group needs different amounts of information and time before they are comfortable enough to adopt the new innovation. Each group is influenced *only* by the group ahead of them (to the left in the diagram). In other words, the early adopters don't look to middle adopters to inform them of what they should do or what's coming next. The only exception is the laggards, who can sometimes hold positions of power and control where they say, "That will never work!" In that case, the late adopters may tend to agree with them, and the influence reverses from right to left. When this happens, the innovators and early adopters are either marginalized or fired! There is also a critical mass that affects the speed of adoption by a given group. We often assume that we need at least 51 percent of a group to buy in before we can move forward with an idea, but this diagram suggests something different. Unless you have incredibly high social capital with those you are trying to lead, the only people who are able to immediately buy in to a new innovation are the early adopters, and possibly a few of the middle adopters. Work with the willing — the early and early-middle adopters — rather than waiting for a majority. Help these early adopters to tell their stories. They are the ones who form the critical mass that can get the ball rolling on a new idea.

How does this concept apply to our discussion of domains and our need for concrete examples? Early adopting leaders who create examples can help to form a critical mass as they answer the question that others will eventually ask: "Where is this working?" You will need people who can answer that question if you want an idea to spread. When a church leader says, "Is this working anywhere?" you can respond, "Yeah, and I've arranged lunch with the owner of a kingdom-minded company so you can see how she does it." One example becomes two examples, then three, and the movement spreads. It's the power of diffusion.

UNDERSTANDING YOUR CITY

As a city leader, seek to be an expert on your city. Are you able to drive or walk new church planters or newly elected city officials around town, pointing out where the first church building was constructed, where the first places of commerce were established, and where key historical events took place? (Think of how impressed your in-laws would be!) We should never underestimate the motivating and animating effect that good research plays in the lives of people. Recall the story of Nehemiah and how his life was changed when he asked his brother for two pieces of information: "Tell me about the city, and tell me about the people" (Neh. 1:1–2). The information his brother, Hanani, shared with him changed the course of his life and shaped the book of Nehemiah into a story of how Nehemiah rebuilt the city (chaps. 1–7) and rebuilt the people (chaps. 8–13).

Researchers talk about two types of research—quantitative research, which comes from data which can be counted and measured, and qualitative research, which comes from personal interviews and conversations. If you want to get a quick read on some basic facts about your community, there are several websites that will give you demographic information about your zip code or city, information that includes income and education levels, the number of people living under the poverty level, their ethnicity, and even the number of single parents living in your community. Quantitative information is a great place to start in understanding your city. However, remember that quantitative information deals with statistical averages, so it's best to heed the words of Mark Twain regarding the incomplete nature of statistics: "If a man has one foot in the fire and the other in a bucket of ice, statistically he should be comfortable." Statistics don't give us the full picture of what a community is really like.

QUALITATIVE RESEARCH

Quantitative research is a good place to start, but we need qualitative research as well—stories and examples of what is really happening in our cities. Jim Collins (author of *Built to Last* and *Good to Great*) reminds us of the need for both quantitative and qualitative research. Collins refers to such research as "evidence." He writes, "What matters is that you rigorously assemble evidence—quantitative or qualitative—to track your progress. If the evidence is primarily qualitative, think like a trial lawyer assembling the combined body of evidence. If the evidence is primarily quantitative, then think of yourself as a laboratory scientist assembling and assessing the data."[225]

We need both hard data and stories to communicate the full story of life in our community.

Ray Bakke is a rare individual who serves as scholar, teacher, guide, and friend to those who have come under his leadership. We often refer to him as "the foremost scholar on urban missiology." He is a treasure trove of insight, and one of the things Ray does best is helping others understand cities—sometimes even their own. A friend of ours, who has ministered in New York City for nearly twenty years, took Ray's class on New York City and was surprised by the insight Ray brought to his own city.

Ray grew up in rural Washington State, but he went to Bible college at Moody Bible Institute in downtown Chicago. As a young pastor, Ray was determined to discover God's agenda for the city, so he started researching and learning more about the city he was transplanted into — Chicago. Through his quantitative research, Ray discovered that Chicago is made up of "77 communities, 228 square miles of space, and 5,200 miles of roads and streets. . . . The city's politics were Irish; its architecture, German; its ambience, Polish; its music and jazz culture, black."[226] For his qualitative research, Ray spent one year calling on the leaders of the 440 Roman Catholic parishes and Protestant churches, with a simple introduction: "Hello, my name is Ray Bakke. I'm a new pastor in the city and in need of your help. Can you tell me the most important lesson you have learned about being a pastor in this city?" Ray would often follow up with other questions, asking these leaders what was the best book he could read about the city or asking if he could drive or walk through the neighborhood with them to see the city through their eyes. This was probably the single best thing Ray could have done. Why? Because it positioned him as a learner and a student of the city and put him in relationship with people whom he still considers friends, even thirty years later. As you consider the example of Ray Bakke, what could you do to get to know your city as Ray did in Chicago?

Becoming an expert on your city also comes about through an "exegesis" of your city. Although the word *exegesis* is commonly reserved for the interpretation of text, we think it is also an appropriate word for understanding a city.

In August of 2001, I (Eric) met with Michael Mata, World Vision's director of Tools for Transformation, along with a group of twenty-seven visiting seminary students from Seoul, Korea, at the historic United Methodist Church on Olivera Street in downtown Los Angeles. Michael was teaching a one-day class titled Mailboxes, Stucco and Graffiti: Learning to Read and Assess the Story of an Urban Community. After a couple of hours of class time followed by lunch, we took a field trip into Michael's Korean/Hispanic neighborhood in LA. As we walked around the neighborhood, Michael taught us how to "read" the story of the community. What do the buildings tell us? Houses that were once single-family dwellings were now four separate apartments. We passed a Korean Presbyterian church that had originally been a Jewish synagogue. A former funeral parlor was now a ten-thousand-member Muslim mosque. Michael also asked us to look for the "scraps of life"; unattended personal items like clothes on the clothesline will tell you quite a bit about who is living there. What is left on the porch or balcony will tell you a lot about the demographics of the families living in the neighborhood. Are there bikes or rocking chairs? What do people throw away? What do they value?

We looked at signage—billboards, window ads, and even graffiti. We discovered that the marketers had already studied the neighborhood and were well positioned with culturally appropriate advertising promoting products that people could afford to buy. The Korean advertisements, written in Korean (like the Crown Whiskey billboards), typically targeted wealthier people, as the Koreans usually represented a higher economic level. The Spanish-language advertisers, on the other hand, peddled Miller Genuine Draft.[227] In poorer neighborhoods, we noted that most of the advertisements centered on alcohol, cigarettes, and health announcements. For Rent and For Sale signs told us who was leaving and who was coming in—as well as who was or was not welcome in the neighborhood. For example, a sign advertising an apartment for rent that was written in Korean would purposefully exclude any Spanish speakers. We looked at whether the neighborhood had banks, pawnshops, or check-cashing services, factors that will tell you quite a bit about the economic vitality of the community.

> We looked at whether the neighborhood had banks, pawnshops, or check-cashing services, factors that will tell you quite a bit about the economic vitality of the community.

The graffiti of a community also tells you a story. Gangs use their logos to define their territory. Taggers, kids who write their names in as many places as possible, show their bravery and cunning by making their names as ubiquitous as they can. Names of people who are killed are typically crossed out. Sometimes merchants even pay gangs to paint murals on empty walls, as one Korean-owned grocery store had done.

Michael also asked us to look for "signs of hope" in the city. Where were the churches? Were there other community-building organizations, like the YMCA? Were the children laughing and playing? This is a sign of a healthy community (Zech. 8:5).

Dr. Glenn Smith of Christian Direction, Inc.,[228] in Montreal, Canada, provides twenty specific steps leaders can take to gain a more thorough knowledge of their community, in a brief paper titled "How to Exegete a Neighborhood." The first step he lists is exploring the history of your city. A few years ago, I (Eric) began scratching the surface by studying the history of my own city of Boulder, Colorado. I discovered the location where the first white settlers camped, and read about the Arapahoe Indians who greeted them. Many times, I have stood on the corner of Broadway and Pearl Street, the starting point from which the city was plotted and the lots were subdivided. Interestingly, when farmland was being sold for a dollar an acre, these downtown city lots were selling for one thousand dollars each! I visited the spot (now Casey Middle School) where Billy Sunday built a portable tabernacle that seated four thousand people and held five weeks of meetings in September and October of 1909. The whole city showed up at the train station to say goodbye when he pulled out of town. I have sat in the stadium where Coach Bill McCartney launched the first really large Promise Keepers gathering. I know that the first sermon preached in the first church service in our city was on John 3:3–5. I know the original location where the first African American church — the Second Baptist Church of Boulder — was started in January of 1908. At that time, there were around 150 African Americans living in Boulder. They met in a carpentry shop at Twenty-fourth and Pearl Streets. The history of a city matters — and it is a sign of our commitment toward and our love for the city that we take the time to understand its history.

Still, as good as these investigative tactics are, there is probably nothing better that you can do than simply ask questions of the people who live in the city. Partnerships and collaboration are fostered when we minister "with" people and not just "to" them. This is the foundation of what is sometimes called "asset-based" community development. As you consider your city, do you see it full of *needs* or filled with *assets*? Asset-based community development seeks to unlock and unleash the potential within the community.

Kevin Lynch, in his book *The Image of the City*, gives us one additional way of understanding the city. He suggests that there are five physical elements we can use to map out (literally) any city. Each city will always have these five definable elements: paths, edges, districts, nodes, and landmarks. If you have a physical map of your city, you can draw, color, shade, or symbolize each of these elements.

1. *Paths*. "Paths are the channels along which the observer customarily, occasionally, or potentially moves. They may be streets, walkways, transit lines, canals, railroads." Paths can be used to identify locations (as in "the corner of Fifth and Main"). Paths are the primary organizing elements of a community. What are the main paths in your city? Where do people walk, drive, or bike?
2. *Edges*. "Edges are the linear elements not used or considered as paths by the observer. They are the boundaries between two phases, linear breaks in continuity: shores, railroad cuts, edges of development, walls. They are lateral references rather than coordinate axes. Such edges may be barriers, more or less penetrable, which close one region off from another; or they may be seams, lines along which two regions are related

and joined together." Boulder, Colorado, has edges at the Rocky Mountains on the west side of the city, while the other edges are open space purchased by the city over the years. The mountains and the open space help to keep Boulder a well-defined city. These geographic features are one of the elements that hold our city together and give it a sense of identity. What are the defining edges of your city?

3. *Districts.* "Districts are the medium-to-large sections of the city, conceived of as having two-dimensional extent, which the observer mentally enters 'inside of,' and which are recognizable as having some common identifying character. Always identifiable from the inside, they are also used for exterior reference if visible from the outside." Districts can define neighborhoods, subdivisions, or places of commerce. Do you know the districts of your town? What distinguishes one district from another?

4. *Nodes.* "Nodes are points, the strategic spots in a city into which an observer can enter, and which are the intensive foci to and from which he is traveling." Nodes can be the intersection of paths or the gathering spots for people—where people hang out. One of my (Eric's) favorite nodes is the city square in Cuernavaca, Mexico. This is the place where families gather in the evenings, the elderly sit on the park benches, and children run and play. It's a place of mariachi bands and street musicians. What are the nodes of your city?

5. *Landmarks.* "Landmarks are another type of point-reference, but in this case the observer does not enter within them. They are external. They are usually a rather simply defined physical object: a building, sign, store, or mountain. Their use involves the singling out of one element from a host of possibilities." We usually use landmarks to give directions or to orient ourselves. Those who live in Colorado on the front range (the east side of the Rocky Mountains) often refer to west as "toward the mountains" and east as "away from the mountains." What are the landmarks of your city? How would you depict them on a map?[229]

The simple exercise of drawing, coloring, shading, or symbolizing these five elements of your city would take you a long way toward understanding the physical layout of your city. In the summer of 2009, we were working with a group of thirty pastors from seven different cities in San Diego County. We asked each church leader to bring a copy of a map of his or her city or community. One of their activities was to identify the boundaries, paths, districts, nodes, and landmarks of their city. It was a very valuable and revealing exercise. Some pastors who knew the layout of their church facility were helpless in identifying the layout of their city, yet the majority of our missional ministry takes place in the city—not in a church building. More recently I (Eric) guided a group of pastors and Christian leaders through this same exercise in Beijing, China. Working in teams of five or six, each group of leaders was able to define the boundaries, paths, nodes, districts, and landmarks of this great city. Through this exercise, they were also able to give me a bird's-eye view of this historic city. Give this exercise a try on a map of your city. You may be surprised at what you learn!

> Some pastors who knew the layout of their church facility were helpless in identifying the layout of their city, yet the majority of our missional ministry takes place in the city — not in a church building.

City Leaders

Every city transformation movement must have leaders who are able to see the forest as well as the trees. There must be certain key individuals who are able to view the city from a strategic vantage point. Every city has strategic and tactical initiatives that are designed to impact different parts of the city. To maximize the contributions of all the players, there must be someone who thinks about the big picture. Carefully consider figure 20.

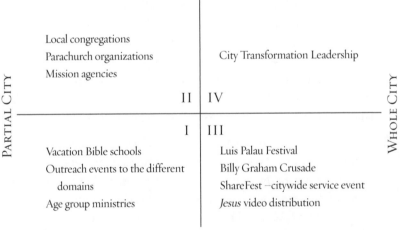

STRATEGIC INITIATIVES

PARTIAL CITY

Local congregations
Parachurch organizations
Mission agencies

II

City Transformation Leadership

IV

I

III

WHOLE CITY

Vacation Bible schools
Outreach events to the different
    domains
Age group ministries

Luis Palau Festival
Billy Graham Crusade
ShareFest –citywide service event
Jesus video distribution

TACTICAL INITIATIVES

Figure 20

THE ROLE OF THE QUADRANT IV LEADER

Ori Brafman and Rod Beckstrom, in their insightful book *The Starfish and the Spider*, write that every movement needs a champion.[230] For churches to work together, there needs to be at least one person who wakes up every day thinking about the city ... about how he or she can catalyze the churches of the city to work with leaders in other domains to transform the city. Where there is a dedicated leader—a champion—the city movement thrives. Without dedicated leaders, city movements flounder. Although leaders in every quadrant are necessary to transform a city, there are some leaders who specifically need to situate themselves in Quadrant IV, where they can always be thinking about the whole city. Quadrant IV leaders are servant-leaders who are adept at building networks, relationships, and partnerships and who always value people and have concern for "the whole." Those who are situated in Quadrant IV know how to appreciate and lift up the contributions of those living and working in Quadrants I to III, without ever feeling the need to compete with them. City transformation movements often falter because the right person(s) is not working in the Quadrant IV role or the movement is being led by a Quadrant III leader who claims to speak or lead from Quadrant IV but lacks the support of the other leaders.

A Quadrant IV leader doesn't have to be the leader of the largest church in town, but it is necessary that this leader has the gravitas to convene the pastors of the largest churches. Quadrant IV leaders don't need to come up with the best ideas themselves, but they should be able to recognize and implement the best ideas of others. Sometimes this person comes from a church that already has a vision to embrace the city. Ray Williams in Little Rock, Chip Sweney in Atlanta, Eric Marsh in Long Beach, and Andy Rittenhouse in Knoxville are examples of leaders who serve on a church staff but have been freed up to give leadership to a city movement. Other city movements, like Mission Houston or Transform Berlin, are led by parachurch leaders who serve as neutral conveners for both church and civic leaders. We think there is also room for a "patronage model," where one or more business leaders would pay the salary and expenses of leaders who work to catalyze the churches and the domains of a city. A leader or champion cannot replace a team of leaders or a guiding coalition, but it is necessary to have someone who is working full-time to see that the movement continues to move, and wakes up every day thinking about the city. He or she serves as the go-to person in the city. Could you be that person?

For Reflection and Discussion

1. How effectively have the three main sectors in your city—public, private, and social—worked together to make your community a better place to live?
2. Would you add any other significant domains to your community? What would they be?
3. How does the concept of sectors and domains help you think strategically about your city?
4. If you were to draw out a diagram of the domains of your city and shade in the areas of progress (theology, vision, leaders, and examples), how would you say you are doing? What progress are you making? What needs to happen next?
5. As a ministry leader, which of the four quadrants do you traffic in?
6. How would you rank the influence and importance of the seven domains in your city?
7. How could you engage people from every domain in transforming your city?
   - Business
   - Family
   - Education
   - Government
   - Media
   - Arts/Entertainment
   - Religion

CHAPTER EIGHT

PARTNERING WITH OTHERS WHO CARE

The primary purpose for the evangelization of culture and the social mission ... is not to protect Christians against the world or even to advance the power of Christians within human society, but rather to promote and to serve the common good.

— Keith A. Fournier, "The Common Good"

After a twenty-year pastorate in San Diego, I (Sam) moved to the San Francisco area to teach at a seminary and pastor a small church. I quickly realized that I was not in San Diego anymore. Although these two cities are only five hundred miles apart, culturally they are *worlds* apart. I knew enough to know that if our church and our ministry were going to be effective in this new city, we needed to first understand the mindset of the people we were going to reach. So we hit the streets and asked a single question: "What is your opinion of church?" I was not prepared for the answers. One man we interviewed seemed to succinctly express what the others were also telling us: "The church is a parasite. It owns the best property. Doesn't pay any taxes. And doesn't help anybody." Sadly, this response summed up the attitude of many of those we questioned. City residents did not have positive opinions about the church. During our initial debrief and review of the results, we were defensive. "We help a lot of people; we help them spiritually. It's just that no one can see it." After some time, though, we saw that there were two problems with our defensive posture. First, there *was* something wrong with the fact that we provided no visible service to people. Jesus once said, "Let your light shine before men, that they may *see* your good deeds and praise your Father in heaven" (Matt. 5:16, emphasis ours). We also realized that if only 7 percent of the people in our community were attending church at all, and a much smaller percentage of those people were attending our church, we really weren't helping all that many people, even with their spiritual needs. The man was right. Relative to the size of our community, we were helping almost no one, especially those who really needed it the most!

Properly convicted, we decided that we needed to change and become something different as a church. We wanted to let more of our light shine in the community. Since the Easter holiday was approaching, we rented an outdoor amphitheater and did some extensive advertising in our community. That morning, a crowd three times the size of our regular attendance showed up. At the point in the service where we normally received an offering, I stood before the crowd and said, "I have good news. All of our bills are paid. Our church doesn't need this offering, so we are going to give it all away. Half of it will be given to the homeless coalition here in our county. The other half will be used to send seminary students to third world countries this summer to serve the needs of others who are in desperate circumstances. So without apology, I am asking you to give generously."

> "The church is a parasite. It owns the best property. Doesn't pay any taxes. And doesn't help anybody."

And they gave. That morning, we received one of our largest offerings ever. The next day we wrote a nice-sized check to the local homeless coalition. We had not talked to them in advance about our intentions, so they had no context for receiving this check—it was a complete surprise to them. Even more surprising, though, was what happened a few days later, when the check was returned to us ... uncashed. We called the coalition leaders to ask why they had not cashed our check. "We don't know what your agenda is, but you can't buy influence here," was their response. Again we received a crash course on how the church was viewed by the community. They had assumed that we were trying to buy their support to manipulate their mission! After numerous conversations back and forth, the ministry finally came to believe that we had no agenda other than to help them help the homeless in our community. They cashed the check.

A few months later, the homeless coalition called us and let us know that there was a vacancy on their board. They asked if someone from our church would like to fill it. Good deeds apparently did create some goodwill! One of our pastors stepped up and filled the vacancy, and by serving at the shelter, he discovered that the majority of the homeless in our county—those most likely to fall through the cracks—were women and children. Because these single women have no childcare, they are unable to look for a job, and if they find work, they have no one to care for their children. However difficult life is for an adult living on the streets, it is only magnified for children and the mothers who care for them.

Our church felt called to address this problem. Working with the homeless coalition, we developed a plan, raised money, acquired a five-bedroom house in a nice neighborhood, and opened Gilead House—a place of healing for families. It was a place where five women and their children could live for up to six months. At Gilead House these women and children receive food, clothing, childcare, and job training, learn financial management, get spiritual direction, and undergo counseling. On the day we opened Gilead House, a reporter from the local paper showed up to cover the event. The following Sunday, there was a full-page story on Gilead House and our church, complete with pictures, on the front page of the local section of the paper. The reporter closed her story with a compelling statement: "This is the kind of thing all churches should be doing."

The very next day we received a phone call from a woman who had read the story in the paper. As we talked, she asked us if we had plans to open a second house anytime soon. We indicated that we would like to do that at some point, but operating one house was an expensive endeavor, and we didn't have the necessary funds available. She responded, "Would it help if I gave you a house?" This woman had a beautiful Victorian home with a guesthouse. She was willing to live in the guesthouse and let the women live in her home. We agreed to work with her, and soon this dear, dear woman began attending our church, became a follower of Christ, and eventually became the director of the Gilead House ministry. Fifteen years later, Gilead House is still providing healing for those whose lives and families have been broken.

Through this endeavor, our church discovered that we could have greater impact by working with others in the community than we could have by working alone. Soon after this, we began participating in events for the betterment of our city. The culture of our church began to change as well. Serving in the community was esteemed and applauded just as much as volunteering in the church. Each of our staff members began giving a "tithe" of their workweek to also serve in a community organization. Our church was changing, and so was our community.

It's a Lot of Work

To transform a city takes more work and resources than we can possibly imagine. Trying to change the city by ourselves, as a single congregation—or even as a unified church in the city—is an expensive exercise in futility. Rather than creating entirely new faith-based entities, why not partner with others in the city who share a common concern for the things we care about? In their book *Forces for Good*, authors Leslie Crutchfield and Heather Grant identify six key practices that characterize high-impact nonprofit organizations. Collaboration with others is not simply one of the six characteristics—it is so essential that it informs all six practices. They write, "The secret to success lies in how great organizations mobilize every sector of society—government, business, nonprofits and the public—to be a force for good. In other words, *greatness has more to do with how nonprofits work outside the boundaries of their organizations than how they manage their own internal operations....* Great organizations work *with and through* others to create more impact than they could ever achieve alone."[231]

We need to tap into the power of these cross-sector networks. The church can serve the city by initiating collaboration between the different domains of the city. James Davison Hunter tells us that all world-changing ventures are accomplished by domains working together: "Again and again we see that the impetus, energy and direction for changing the world were found where cultural, economic and often political resources overlapped; where networks of elites, who generated these various resources, come together in common purpose ... *in common purpose*—something we should never forget."[232]

In city transformation movements, we work together with other domains *in common purpose* for the welfare of the city. Peter Drucker, the recognized "father of modern management," identifies the critical role churches play in the transformational process. According to Drucker, "Social-sector institutions aim at changing the human being. The 'product' of a hospital is a cured patient. The 'product' of a church is a churchgoer whose life is being changed. The task of social-sector organizations is to create human health and well-being." Thus Drucker encourages the emergence of churches "which focus on the spiritual needs of individuals ... and then put the spiritual energies of their members to work on the social challenges and social problems of the community."[233] Drucker firmly believed that the unleveraged power was through the sectors working together.

Bounded-Set and Centered-Set Thinking

In the 1970s, missiologist Paul Hiebert from Fuller Seminary introduced church leaders to the difference between a bounded set and a centered set (see fig. 21). He suggested that each denomination (and many individual churches as well) could be illustrated by a closed circle—what he called a "bounded set." Inside that circle were the various doctrines and theological positions that distinguished one denomination from another. So one of the dots in the circle might represent a view on baptism — by immersion or sprinkling? Is it for believers or infants? Is it mandatory or optional for salvation? Or a dot could represent a view on the Lord's Supper. Do you use wine or grape juice; bread or wafers? Being within that circle of common belief was the criteria for working together in common mission. The bounded-set thinker asks the question, "Do you believe like I believe?" Unfortunately, this can become a very divisive question because it separates those who are in and those who are out, limiting the people we are allowed to work with to those who sign off on our doctrinal statement.

Another way of looking at relationships is what Heibert referred to as a "centered set." A centered set has no boundary that defines who is in and who is out. Rather it places Jesus at the center, with each person's life represented by arrows moving toward Jesus or away from him. This type of thinking was demonstrated by Promise Keepers' Bill McCartney when he welcomed stadiums full of men in the 1990s by saying, "It doesn't matter if you are Baptist or Methodist or Catholic or Pentecostal [each being bounded sets], but if you love Jesus [centered set] and want to get closer to him, then you belong here!" When McCartney would say this, thousands of men would shout and high-five each other. In centered-set thinking, direction is more determinative than distance to the center. In other words, it is better to be farther away from the Lord but moving toward Jesus than to be close to Jesus but moving away from him.

We could have inserted this diagram into our chapter on the whole church, but we prefer to mention it here as we think about who we can and cannot work

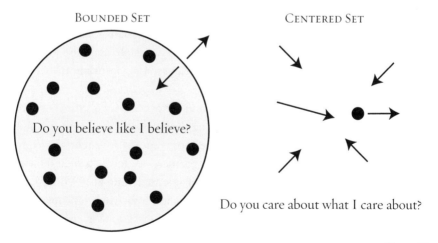

BOUNDED SET   CENTERED SET

Do you believe like I believe?

Do you care about what I care about?

Figure 21

with in our community. We would suggest that we avoid simply partnering around theological beliefs (the bounded set); instead we should rally around the things we commonly care about (the centered set). For example, we can ask the question, "Who cares about underachieving children in your community?" or "Who cares about immigrants?" or "Who cares about people dying of AIDS?" or "Who cares about single moms?" Each of these issues has organizations that care about the same things we care about, and they serve as potential partners that we can work with to solve the common problems we have in our community. Again, we don't just work with people because they believe exactly as we do; we work with them because they care about the same things we care about in the city.

> Each of these issues has organizations that care about the same things we care about, and they serve as potential partners that we can work with to solve the common problems we have in our community.

We believe that the church can effectively partner with any organization that is morally positive (for example, caring for the homeless, helping abused women, tutoring children) and spiritually neutral (they are not Christians, but they aren't actively promoting another spirituality or religious viewpoint). This allows people of good *faith* and people of good *will* to work together. What do we mean when we say this? Simply that you don't have to be a Christian to care about children who are not achieving at grade level, women who are abused, or people who are hungry — and we can work with people who share our concerns. Richard Lovelace writes, "In all these efforts [of social transformation] Evangelicals should unite with all other professing Christians wherever possible and also with non-believing persons of good will. The Clapham leaders [William Wilberforce's group] joined forces with Unitarians and agnostics in their social initiatives."[234]

What? "Joined forces with Unitarians and agnostics"? Of all the ideas presented in this book, this idea may be the hardest to swallow ... and the most counterintuitive. For most of us, it just does not seem *right*. Whenever we give a talk about partnering with these unlikely partners, we follow a slide showing the centered-set diagram with a picture of people marching at a World AIDS Day march at Cal State Fullerton. In the photo are some church people holding a sign saying "First Evangelical Free Church of Fullerton" (a church where Chuck Swindoll pastored for many years). The photo shows this group marching alongside several other people holding a sign that reads "Orange County Witches and Pagans." There are these two groups standing side by side. But here is the key: these two groups are there *not* based on a common theology or worldview but *because they both care about people who are dying of AIDS.* Keep in mind that if the church avoids this march, the march still goes on without us. We recognize that this idea requires careful discernment and may push some of us out of our comfort zone, but we would simply ask you to consider that photo once again. Think about all of the conversations that took place that day that otherwise *never would have happened* had the church been absent. How can the church be the leavening agent of transformation when we are absent from the community?

At the 2008 Portland CityFest initiated by evangelist Luis Palau, more than six hundred churches engaged more than twenty-six thousand volunteers, committing more than one hundred thousand hours of work to three hundred projects, including five large needs identified by the leaders of the city of Portland. The mayor officially declared a summerlong Season of Service, releasing resources and the cooperation of the city government. Corporate sponsors contributed their employees and their money in this cooperative effort. The Season of Service was followed by a weekend festival of concerts, family activities, youth activities, and preaching by Palau. I (Sam) was present at this festival and witnessed an attendance of over 185,000 people, with over 10,000 indicating a desire to know Christ personally. The mayor and the CEOs of major corporations stood on the stage, shoulder to shoulder with Palau. The mayor himself recognized the unusual nature of that moment, proclaiming, "Here's to odd combinations!" He then asked, "What do a liberal mayor and a conservative evangelist have in common?" His answer: "We both care about the needs of the people of Portland." Comments like this reflect centered-set thinking. The mayor recognized that this diverse group of people could work together because they all cared about the well-being of the city. In a moment of genuine enthusiasm, the mayor declared another Season of Service for the following summer, and the crowd roared its assent (although I [Sam] still think I heard a few tired believers say, "What? I thought this was a one-time event!").

A city transformation movement is really a loosely bound collection of centered sets — mini-movements, if you will — where people coalesce around different sets of common concerns but are loosely bound together by a common love for the city. We can diagram a city transformation movement as in figure 22.

Each concern or cause, represented by a dot, most often reflects something broken that God is in the business of restoring, utilizing people of good faith and people of goodwill working together for the common good. Think of a city filled

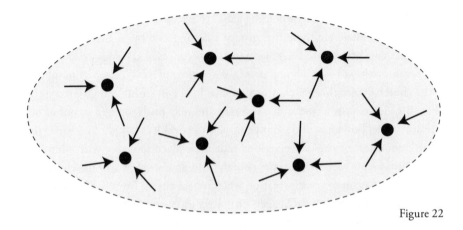

Figure 22

with these restorative movements everywhere, where everyone would know and work with someone who truly followed Jesus.

Morally Positive and Spiritually Neutral

Churches discover new opportunities when they recognize that they are free to partner with most any organization or entity that is morally positive and spiritually neutral. Again, to define our terms, we would say that *morally positive* means that the partnering organization is working to provide a just solution to a problem that God cares about. Health, hunger, the welfare of children, homelessness, and sex trafficking are all examples of issues that we would suggest are morally positive. While we, as the church, may disagree with these organizations as to the precise cause and cure, we can often agree that there is a very real problem. What this means is that if the city already has a homeless shelter, we don't need to start a *Christian* homeless shelter. If the city has a food bank, we don't need to start a *Christian* food bank. Why spend kingdom resources creating a parallel, competing organization when one already exists in the city by God's common grace? Instead we can partner with others in the city who care about the people we care about. Many churches have discovered

> Think of a city filled with these restorative movements everywhere, where everyone would know and work with someone who truly followed Jesus.

the advantages of joining what God is doing through his common grace by partnering with existing nonprofit agencies rather than creating and resourcing a new ministry of their own. What human-services organizations need is not competition from the church. They need people who will come alongside to help them accomplish their (can we say *God-given?*) mission.

The term *spiritually neutral* is a bit harder to define. Generally, this means that the partnering organization has no overt spiritual agenda that they are advocating or advancing through their programs. Most civic, community, business, and educational institutions fall into this category—they are not for or against any particular religion. This definition does not mean that we *cannot* work with those of other religions (as illustrated by our friends from Fullerton at the World AIDS Day march). Often, working alongside those who differ with us provides unique opportunities for face-to-face contact, and unlikely relationships that spawn a thousand unlikely conversations develop. In many cases, these conversations lead people to faith in Christ.

> If a group is not blatantly *against* us, we should consider them *for* us and move forward with the work of the kingdom.

Though it may be subtle, we also differentiate between *partnership* and *partnering*. We've tried to use the latter term and avoid the former. Partnership (where we have an equal stake in the risk and rewards) can suggest that we are equally yoked with others in a way that the apostle Paul warns us against (2 Cor. 6:14–18). Partnerships tend to be for the long haul. By contrast, partnering is about working together to solve problems we both care about. Partnering is usually project-based and short-term. Though it requires discernment and wisdom, we believe that we can partner with others who do not believe the same things we do about God, and do this with a clear conscience. If a group is not blatantly *against* us, we should consider them *for* us and move forward with the work of the kingdom (Mark 9:39–40).

Working Together to Solve Big Problems

Churches should also work with other domains to solve problems they commonly care about. In 2006, Denver's mayor, John Hickenlooper, announced a comprehensive ten-year plan called Denver's Road Home,[235] a plan to end homelessness in Denver, where there lived nearly four thousand homeless men, women, and children. Sixty percent of the homeless were families with children. Forty percent of the homeless were actually working a job. In this initiative, the mayor asked for help from individuals, corporations, government … and the faith community. He asked if a thousand churches would embrace a thousand homeless families with housing and faith-based mentoring. Four years into the program, 564 families and seniors have been mentored out of homelessness.[236] This is a great example of how churches can willingly join in what God is already doing through people of goodwill in the community.

Homelessness is a challenge in many communities. We earlier mentioned the work of Chip Sweney of Perimeter Church and Unite!—a network of over one hundred churches in the Atlanta area. When the Katrina disaster hit the Gulf Coast in December 2005, it forced the evacuation of many residents to Atlanta. The Unite! churches let their light shine by providing shelter and food and establishing relationships with these dispossessed people. Chip Sweney writes,

> Not too long after this, Unite! was invited to several meetings in our county to talk about a new homeless initiative. The demographics of our area are changing rapidly, and there has been a homeless challenge for a number of years. The county has no emergency shelters for the homeless. The leaders at the table were from county government, faith based and secular nonprofits, United Way, the Salvation Army, and Unite! churches. The team worked together for two years on a plan that is coming to fruition. The exciting part is that Unite! churches are funding over 50% of the costs of the first phase of this homeless initiative. All of those groups are so thankful that churches have stepped up to the plate and said, "We are with you—let's do this together." This is what we are trying to do as churches working together in a community or a city. We could never be this effective if we were all doing our own thing. This kind of partnering must happen in a city if real change and transformation is to take place![237]

More recently, the Unite! churches have come together to form their ambitious and audacious "2020 Vision." Under the common vision of churches partnering together for community transformation, these churches, working in cross-domain cooperation, are partnering around four impact areas—family, poverty, justice, and education. Each impact area has a goal and corresponding measurement for their citywide initiative. For example, under education, the 2020 goal is that "all students have the opportunity to graduate." This goal will be measured successful if they reach a 95 percent high school graduation rate and all third graders are reading at a third-grade level. The citywide initiative to accomplish this is an Adopt-a-School program where churches adopt schools by starting personal-tutoring and mentoring programs and working to bring the goals to fruition.

Can We Work with Others Who Are Not Spiritually Neutral?

For most of us, it is not too difficult to consider partnering with non-Christians or secular organizations (schools, government, business leaders), since this shoulder-to-shoulder service creates opportunities for us to build community and possibly enter into spiritual conversations with those we partner with. But what about those of other faiths or religious views who want to join in the work? Inevitably, once churches begin to unite around service, they will find other folks who want to join them. These groups will also want to join in the work—and benefit from the results! Don't be surprised if you are approached by these groups. It may be helpful to remember the lessons of Nehemiah when this happens. As the noble work of God was happening and they were rebuilding the wall (and rebuilding the people), other folks tried to slip their own agenda into the hustle and bustle that accompanies transformation. Eliashib the priest rented out a room in the storehouse to Tobiah—the chief antagonist of the rebuilding project (Neh. 4:1–4; 13:4–5). There were those who saw the Sabbath as an extra day to get some work done, so they were out "treading winepresses ... bringing in grain and loading it on donkeys, together with wine, grapes, figs and all other kinds of loads" (13:15). "Men ... were bringing in fish and all kinds of merchandise and selling them in Jerusalem on the Sabbath to the people of Judah" (13:16). As Nehemiah went about the work of God, there were others who wanted to join in, some with impure, selfish motives.

Remember the three intersecting circles we diagrammed, with "Service" sitting in that sweet spot where the circles intersect. Whoever occupies this spot, Christian or not, will have the hearing of the community. Such is the universal power and attraction of service. So how should we respond? Volunteer guru Don Simmons suggests that the organizers of events such as ShareFest, CareFest, and Serve Day can start by *clearly defining the purpose of the event* and training participants around that purpose. There are four different but equally valid approaches we can take when organizing service events:

1. *Single church serves alone.* The benefit of serving alone is that you can control the message and the response. There is little chance for you to be misinterpreted or misunderstood. A few friends and neighbors who do not attend your church may join you in serving, but it will be clear that

one church is serving. Your training should include how to engage in spiritual conversations with those who receive or observe your service.

2. *Closed affiliated group of churches serve together.* This can be a group of churches or a denomination that has previously formed and is committed to a common doctrinal statement or shares common geography or a similar missional approach. The membership does not include all Christian churches or even every evangelical church — only those churches that are part of this particularly defined group. If other churches or religious groups ask to join you, you can simply say, "I'm sorry, this is limited to our Lutheran Synod churches" or "I'm sorry, but this is the servant component of City Fellowship and is limited to those participating churches." Again, the advantage of working with other churches is that you now have a larger workforce, yet you can still manage the message and the impression you will have on the community. We would recommend that you avoid a public website where people can sign up. Again, your training should include how to engage in spiritual conversations with recipients, sponsors, or observers of your service.

3. *All churches in the city serve.* Be prepared when those of other faiths and religious traditions ask to sign up to serve. Training in your church should include how to have meaningful conversations with those who work *alongside* you, as well as with those you are serving. Once we understand the purpose of the event, we can train volunteers around that purpose. On the plus side, the more people involved, the greater the opportunities to make a difference in the community. The downside is that Christians will not be able to fully control the message or the impressions that are created by this event. It could, however, be a rich environment for spiritual conversations with others who are serving. Be warned, though: this type of approach may *not* necessarily yield a larger turnout than the second or even the first approach, since many people are cautious about these types of events and may even have theological concerns.

4. *All in the community serve, in an event like Make a Difference Day, Family Volunteer Day, or Volunteer Day.* The principles, the expectations, and the training for these types of events will be similar to those of the third approach. The purpose of this event is very simple — working together with others to make the community a better place. There is no explicit evangelistic training for these events.

Leveraging Common Grace

To understand and take advantage of what currently exists in your community, we use the four-quadrant diagram in figure 23 to explain to churches that they do not have to spend precious kingdom resources duplicating services. Of the four quadrants of ministry, we firmly believe that the biggest opportunity for impact is also the least utilized quadrant, the lower right—churches participating in ministries that other churches or nonprofit organizations have already begun. If our goal is to maximize our resources and make the most of our effort, then the best opportunities are found outside the walls of the church, where someone else is organizing the effort and paying the light bills.

> If our goal is to maximize our resources and make the most of our effort, then the best opportunities are found outside the walls of the church, where someone else is organizing the effort and paying the light bills.

The Fresno Model

How can differing domains work together to transform their city? A healthy model for community transformation was developed in the early nineties by

OWNERSHIP

| | INTERNALLY FOCUSED | | EXTERNALLY FOCUSED |

Ministries inside your church that originated with your church

Ministries outside your church that originated with your church

Ministries inside your church that others have begun that you are participating in

Ministires / Nonprofits outside your church that others have begun and you are participating in

PARTNERSHIP

Figure 23

neighborhood leaders in Fresno, California. Their thinking about cities differs from most church strategies. As we discussed earlier, most church-based transformational initiatives begin with the different domains of society on the periphery and place the church at the center. Our friends in Fresno realized that transforming the community required more resources than the church had to offer. Instead they placed their families, schools, and neighborhoods at the center while relegating the church to the periphery along with the other domains in the community. The church then took a *catalytic responsibility* for connecting and harnessing the energy, resources, and horsepower of the other domains to tackle the problems of neighborhoods, schools (elementary schools are often used to define a neighborhood), and families — the smallest individual unit in a neighborhood. The brilliance of diagramming their strategy this way is that it allows them, in humility, to share this vision with leaders in the other domains, and it doesn't appear to be a church-centered program. Still, since there are usually believers within each domain of society, although the church is no longer in the central

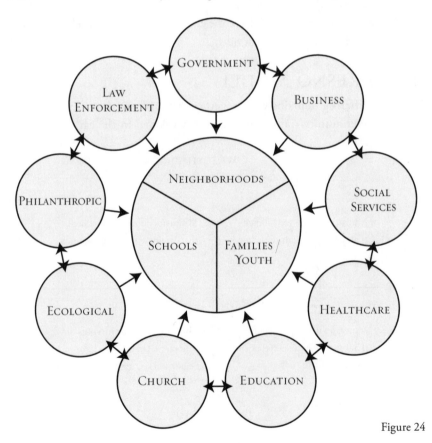

Figure 24

position of influence, individual church members have a presence everywhere in the city. The Fresno model can be diagramed as in figure 24.

Notice how the church is just one of the players here. The power of this approach is in recognizing that transformation begins by transforming the relationships between the church and the other domains of the community — from those of suspicion and skepticism to relationships of trust.

> God has dropped the breadcrumbs that lead us into relationships. We simply need to follow them.

The church in the city, even when working from the periphery, is in the best position to be the catalyst for change. We are the ones who call the party together! Of all the social and economic institutions that exist, it is the schools and churches that have the most sustaining permanence in a city. Businesses may come and go, but local churches last an average of seventy years! Schools don't often have the political will to lead the community, but the church can connect these disparate domains — not to control them but to serve as a catalyst for change. We can even apply this approach to our international efforts. What if the church initiated a partnership with a struggling but developing city in Africa? Churches could partner with local churches in that city, but the church could also invite businesses to partner with businesses in that city, and schools to partner with schools in that city, and artists and musicians to partner with artists and musicians in that city. What would it be like if every elementary school in your city had a partnership with an elementary school in a city in Africa, ensuring that each child had a pair of shoes and school supplies? What would that do for the kids in Africa, much less the children in your community? In this example, we are simply placing something else at the center — a city in Africa — but the church still serves as the catalyst to get others involved.

INFLUENCE AUDIT

Churches often overestimate their power but underestimate their influence in a community. By taking an "influence audit," churches can discover who they know in positions of influence. Often we will learn that we are at most only one or two relationships removed from leaders in every domain of society. Gaining awareness of this social network is helpful, not to get our land rezoned but to help form coalitions for change. The church can be the greatest connector in a community. God has dropped the breadcrumbs that lead us into relationships. We simply need to follow them.

Social Capital

Not only do cities and communities need a healthy church to transform the sectors of society, but also churches are of inestimable value in building what is known as "social capital." Harvard professor Robert D. Putman (author of *Bowling Alone* and *Better Together*) defines social capital as "social networks, norms of reciprocity, mutual assistance and trustworthiness."[238] Like many others, he is convinced that social capital is just as important, or perhaps even more important, than physical, financial, and human capital. In an essay titled "The Prosperous Community," he quotes Scottish philosopher David Hume (1711 – 1776) regarding the consequences of life without social capital: "Your corn is ripe today; mine will be so tomorrow. 'Tis profitable for us both, that I should labor with you today, and that you should aid me tomorrow. I have no kindness for you, and know you have as little for me. I will not, therefore, take any pains upon your account; and should I labor with you upon my own account, in expectation of a return, I know I should be disappointed, and that I should in vain depend upon your gratitude. Here then I leave you to labor alone; you treat me in the same manner. The seasons change; and both of us lose our harvests for want of mutual confidence and security."[239]

Social capital is the sense of mutuality that we feel for one another that expresses itself in trust and care. It is your good being bound together with my good. Unlike financial and human capital that can be infused very quickly into a city or community, social capital is built over time ... and only over time. It accrues from time spent together in bowling leagues and soccer clubs, Scouting and PTA meetings—even the local barbershop. The influence of social capital is felt through neighborhood watch programs or when you pick up a neighbor's kid from school. It's about neighbors and friends looking out for one another and recognizing that my good is somehow wrapped up in your good. We're in this together!

The Importance of Social Capital

Social capital is essential to building healthy communities. In *Better Together*, Putnam writes, "The more neighbors who know one another by name, the fewer crimes a neighborhood as a whole will suffer. A child born in a state whose residents volunteer, vote, and spend time with friends is less likely to be born underweight, less likely to drop out of school, and less likely to kill or be killed than the same child—no richer or poorer—born in another state whose residents do not."[240]

Do you know the names of your neighbors? In response to Putnam's research, our friend Dave, who is leading the city transformation movement in northwest Denver, is helping people from participating churches map their neighborhoods and host block parties as part of a neighboring initiative.

Robert Putnam points out there are two types of social capital. The first is what he calls "bonding" social capital. Bonding capital is the strength of the relationships between the members of a group of people—a family, affinity group, ethnic group, club, or church. Bonding capital is what Putnam calls the "Super Glue" of society. It's what holds us together. It is measured by the number of neighbors who know each other by name; by how many people vote or volunteer or bring meals to their neighbors or shovel a neighbor's walk. It is the social capital displayed in the Old Testament in passages like Judges 1:3: "Then the men of Judah said to the Simeonites their brothers, 'Come up with us into the territory allotted to us, to fight against the Canaanites. We in turn will go with you into yours.'" You help us with harvesting our corn today, and we will help you harvest your corn tomorrow. Social capital is seen in the willingness to share resources with others.

> Do you know the names of your neighbors?

A church is an ideal place to build this bonded capital. It is a community of belonging. It is a place where people feel they are part of a family. A church provides what Ray Oldenburg, in *The Great Good Place*, describes as a "third place"—a place that is neither work nor home, where people can spend time together in "happily anticipated gatherings of individuals beyond the realms of home and work."[241] The church provides opportunities for relationships and connections—a place to build organizational leadership skills. The church is a place where people can be restored to health in the context of a caring community. But even this bonding social capital is not enough to effect transformation.

A second type of social capital is what Putnam calls "bridging" social capital. Whereas bonding capital is the strength *within* a social segment of society, bridging capital is the strength *between* the segments of society. He writes, "If you get sick, the people who bring you chicken soup are likely to represent your bonding social capital. On the other hand, a society that has only bonding social capital will look like Belfast or Bosnia—segregated into mutually hostile camps. So a pluralist democracy requires lots of bridging social capital, not just the bonding variety."[242] Bridging capital is harder to build than bonding capital, since people normally prefer to hang out with people most like them. But bridging capital is necessary for diverse groups to work together, for genuine reconciliation to occur, and for relationships between groups to heal.

Turning Bonded Capital into Bridging Capital

This brings us to the real value of externally focused churches and how they can effectively transform our cities. Churches, perhaps more than any other institutions, are in a unique position. They can turn the strength of their bonded capital into the power of bridging capital. Externally focused churches are internally strong (which builds bonded capital) but outwardly focused (which builds bridging capital). They measure their effectiveness not merely by the number of people who attend but also by the transformational effect they are having on their communities. Externally focused churches have the capacity to be the conduit to the people and the various domains within the community. They don't need to control any domain but can be a servant to all domains by playing this bridge-building role. As churches partner with people in neighborhoods, schools, human-services agencies, businesses, and government agencies, they are creating bridging capital within the community, not just by linking the domains of the community to the church but also by helping to link the domains to one another. It is the church's care and love that builds bridges through running tutoring programs, ministering to the battered women in the safe house, hosting job fairs, and opening daycare facilities. As churches seek to be agents of community transformation, they should not ignore the advantage they have, bringing social capital to a community and building community bonds and bridges. Putnam agrees: "In any comprehensive strategy for improving the plight of America's communities, rebuilding social capital is as important as investing in human and physical capital."[243] Whether you realize it or not, your church is in a great position to improve your community through building social capital.

Changing the Scorecard

For churches to really engage in community, they must first change the metrics of effectiveness. Churches have been great at counting noses and nickels, but that may not be what God is most concerned with. It's not just our Sunday morning attendance that matters. It's not just about having activities in our church—it's about people actively serving in the community. It's not about the money we receive; it's about the money we give away. How many suffering people have no one to comfort them? How many children are alone in the streets of our community? Maybe we need to change our scorecard so that it matches God's and begin measuring success by the right standards—kingdom standards.

For Reflection and Discussion

1. What are the problems you most care about in your city?
2. Who else cares about the same thing(s) you care about?
3. How can you work together with other organizations that are morally positive and spiritually neutral? How would you go about discerning who to work with?
4. Why is social capital important in a community?
5. How might your church take a more catalytic leadership position in your community in building social capital?

CHAPTER NINE

WHAT'S NEXT?

Now to him who is able to do immeasurably more than all we ask
or imagine ...

—Ephesians 3:20

This book is far from being a conclusive or comprehensive resource on city transformation. We recognize that we do not adequately address the role of prayer, the topic of asset-based community development, or the deeper theological issues associated with social justice. We have not examined the crucial transformational role of leaders like John Perkins and the Christian Community Development Association (CCDA). We have not introduced you to many of the outstanding women leaders, who in every society play a transformational role in that society. We think of meeting with Ruth Callanta from the Philippines, who, through her Center for Community Transformation, had 125,000 women in her Bible study chain. In each Bible study, they practiced what she called the "Four Ws": welcome, worship, word, and work. Work consisted of what women were doing to get out of debt, save money, or start a business. We haven't introduced you to those who labor tirelessly in urban ministry or those investing in the next generation of children and youth. Instead, this book is intended to serve as more of a primer on current, contemporary models of ministry to cities, written with the understanding that people don't usually get involved in these issues of justice until they have tried to be ministers of mercy.[244] People don't usually probe the systems that cause the symptoms until they have first attempted to address the symptoms. Perhaps you've tried to make a difference in your community. We've written to help you think more holistically and strategically about your own work at city transformation. Tactics, programs, and various approaches will need to change, be abandoned or refined over time, but everything we learn about our communities will help to form a bigger and more comprehensive picture of what God is doing in our cities. The paradigmatic shifts we have outlined in this book—from church to city, congregation to kingdom—will hopefully start you thinking differently about your own ministry. We hope that your world and your heart for the world increase. Remember: we can never expect *too much* from God, and we can never ask him for more than he is willing to give—so dream big!

> The paradigmatic shifts we have outlined in this book—from church to city, congregation to kingdom—will hopefully start you thinking differently about your own ministry.

So what comes next? We'd like to suggest six practical things you can do to get started.

1. Recognize that loving, serving, and ministering to our communities—getting the church outside the walls—is something God is already doing. God wants our churches to be salt, light, and leaven—all agents of transformation that work by direct contact and not at a distance. Wherever we travel, we meet leaders who tell us that God is up to something amazing in their city. We see a growing desire for unity among the body of Christ. Many church leaders are finding that this unity is best found as they work together in partnership and share a common commitment to the good of their city. The influential book *Experiencing God* by Henry Blackaby reminds us that much of effective ministry is simply looking at where God is working and joining him in that work. We want to encourage you and let you know that God is already at work in the city. God is getting people out of the pews and into the streets. As difficult as it is to learn to surf, it is much easier to catch a wave than to cause a wave. Externally focused churches are engaging their communities with the good news of Jesus and are doing good deeds. They are riding a wave that God has initiated. Will you get on the wave?

2. Understand that we cannot get different results from just doing more or trying harder at the same things we've done in the past. To create a different future, we need to think differently, be different, and do things differently. If we really were getting great results from our current approaches to city ministry, we could simply accelerate those efforts. Unfortunately, that is not the case in most communities. The world has changed. More people live in cities than in rural areas now, and as we mentioned before, that is an irreversible trend. We need to learn what it means to think strategically about our cities. In the past, the church has acted alone. Today the best opportunities come through cross-domain collaboration—uncommon partners who can achieve uncommon results by working together.

3. Learn all you can about your city. In chapter 7, we wrote about the power of information and how we can really understand our cities. To this body of information, we'd like to add the insights of Dr. Glenn Smith of Christian Direction, Inc., in Montreal, Canada. Glenn suggests twenty specific steps to help you to exegete your city. We include fourteen of his most

> The best opportunities come through cross-domain collaboration — uncommon partners who can achieve uncommon results by working together.

relevant steps here from his article titled "How to Exegete a Neighborhood" (a fuller version is available from Glenn at *www.direction.ca*). Much of this information is best acquired through personal contact. Just walk around your city, observing and asking questions!

A. Study the history of the city, particularly its growth patterns.

B. Understand clearly the sections or zones which make up the city.

C. Study the neighborhoods: their ethnic, social, and economic composition, religious affiliations, occupational patterns, younger and older populations, concentrations of the elderly, young professionals, singles, and problem groups.

D. Determine and analyze the power centres in the city—the political figures, the police department, the religious leaders, and so on.

E. Analyze the felt needs of specific people groups within the city. You are looking for indications of receptivity and "keys" which may unlock doors to homes and hearts.

F. Examine the traffic flow of the city.

G. Seek to discover how news and opinion spread in the city, and among particular groups.

H. Examine the relationship between city dwellers and the rural, small-town communities outside the city.

I. Locate the churches in the city on a map and identify them by denomination and size and age.

J. Inquire about church planting in the past several years: who has tried it, who has planted churches, and why/where did they succeed or not succeed?

K. Learn what strategies have been tried in the past, and identify what has succeeded or failed and why.

L. Identify Christians in positions of influence among the different domains in the city.

M. List and analyze the parachurch ministries operating in and providing service to the city. How might each contribute something to the overall strategy?

N. List and evaluate the community agencies (private, religious, and civic) that are designed to meet particular needs (literacy, overnight shelter, emergency food and clothing, etc.)[245]

4. *Remember that you are a kingdom builder and not just a community volunteer.* As much as we love and respect community volunteers, volunteers become kingdom workers when they combine good deeds with the good news. Because good deeds and goodwill can never substitute for the message of God's good news, we need to constantly be thinking of new and creative ways in which we can combine compassionate service with passionate evangelism. Evangelism should never be our ulterior motive in serving and loving others, but if we fail to recognize it as our ultimate motive — the thing that makes the mission of the church unique — we have lost sight of our calling.

5. *Begin meeting with other city leaders and share your heart and vision for transformation.* We would like to give you a challenge: for the next ninety days, have lunch or coffee with at least six pastors in your city. If you are a pastor or parachurch leader, you might initiate the meeting by saying something like this: "I feel a bit embarrassed that we've been ministering in the same town for all these years and haven't yet gotten to know each other. Could I take you to lunch?" While together, you might initiate a conversation with the following questions: "Where have you seen God at work in our city?" "Where do you see the pain of the city?" "Is there anything God might have us do together that would make a bigger impact for the kingdom than what we are presently doing by ourselves?"

Then, after you have met with church leaders, for the ninety days following have lunch or coffee with six executive directors of human-services agencies in your city. You might say something like this: "Hi, this is Pastor Harvey Bland from Big Sky Community Church here in the city. I know your agency has been serving the city for decades, and as a pastor, I am aware of how little I know about what your organization does. Can I take you to lunch?" While together, ask about the mission and history of the organization and then say, "As you were talking, I realized that you care about a lot of the same things we care about in the city. Is there something we could do together? If we had twenty-five people available for four to six hours with no strings attached, how could we help you?"

Finally, in a third period of ninety days, do the same thing with some school or government officials, asking these leaders to identify the biggest needs of the schools and the city government. Again, you could take another ninety days after this and do the same with six leaders from the business domain in your city—company presidents, CEOs, or other executives. You might initiate by saying something like this: "What do you see as the biggest needs of our city?" "If you could change one thing about the future of our city, what would it be?" After listening and jotting down responses, you might say something like this: "Over the past nine months, I've been meeting with church leaders and leaders of government, schools, and nonprofits to try to identify the biggest needs of our community. Here's what we've come up with. I think we'd all agree that to solve these problems, it will take cooperation among all sectors of our community—the public sector (government), the private sector (business), and the social sector (human-services agencies and churches). How can we work together to solve some of these issues?" We think you'll find that there is a new awareness and openness in working together, not just with other churches or Christian organizations but also in cross-domain collaboration.

Dr. Glenn Barth of GoodCities, through his city consultation work, has discovered that much of this exploratory process can be shortened if the transformation effort has a committed team leading the charge. Glenn begins the exploration phase with leaders representing the seven domains. Each of these leaders recruits a team of six who will in turn each conduct five interviews with influential Christians in their respective domain. Two questions that Glenn always includes in his interview are: (1) "Do you think there is anything we could accomplish more effectively if the various domains worked together rather than each one working seperately?" and (2) "If there are those from other domains interested in exploring possible areas of greater collaboration in serving our city, would you be interested in being a part of those discussions?"

The result is 210 interviews, or thirty total interviews in each domain. The results are compiled for each domain, and an overall report is produced. The result of the process is both informational and relational. The end result informs these leaders as to whether they are ready to move ahead to other stages of the transformation efforts.

6. Remember that this is a work of God, who uses yielded people of faith, prayer, and action. The world can be transformed only by those who themselves have been transformed by God's Spirit. If your own life is not a witness to this, get started today (or tomorrow, if you are reading this at night). Begin praying and seeking out like-minded, like-hearted people who want to change the world.

> The world can be transformed only by those who themselves have been transformed by God's Spirit.

Every movement of God starts with just one passionate person who says yes. We tend to overestimate what we can accomplish in a single year and underestimate what we can get done in five years. A Chinese proverb says, "The best time to plant a tree is ten years ago." But there is a corollary to this that is often left out: "The second-best time to plant a tree is today." We may not have done what we could have done or should have done in the past, but there is no time like today to begin.

• • •

Thanks for sticking with us to the end of the book. Hopefully, for you it is the beginning of a great adventure. May God bless you as you move forward to love and transform your city!

SUGGESTED RESOURCES

ONLINE RESOURCES

The following are additional online resources that can help you to engage your city in spiritual and societal transformation.

www.cityvisiontc.org. For the past several years, Dr. John Mayer, executive director of City Vision in Minneapolis, has compiled a 150-page book, *Cityview Report: Strategic Data for Effective Ministry,* on the quantitative research data on his city. John firmly believes that "to reach your community, you must know your community." His *Cityview Report* serves as a great model for a quantitative approach you could take in exegeting your own city.

www.compassioncoalition.org. No one does a better job than Andy Rittenhouse of Knoxville, Tennessee, in compiling both quantitative and qualitative research on a city. Several years ago, he and a team of talented researchers put together their first *Salt and Light Guidebook* for the city of Knoxville. This work serves not only as a great tool to inform the people of Knoxville of the specific areas of need but also as a great template that other cities can follow.

www.goodcities.net. GoodCities is led by a good friend of ours — Dr. Glenn Barth. Glenn has a great depth and breadth of knowledge related to city transformation. The website contains excellent information regarding the stages of city transformation.

www.ccda.org. Anyone interested in urban ministry would benefit by getting to know Christian Community Development Association. Begun by Rev. John Perkins more than twenty years ago, CCDA provides the basis for "asset-based community development."

http://www.urbanministry.org/fasten-homepage. The Faith and Service Technical Education Network (FASTEN) offers resources and networking opportunities to faith-based practitioners, private philanthropies, and public administrators who seek to collaborate effectively to renew urban communities. An initiative of Pew Charitable Trusts, FASTEN identifies best practices in faith-based services and multisector collaboration. It is a treasure trove of city resources.

www.simonsolutions.com. Simon Solutions provides collaborative technology tools that help people connect and partner with other entities in the city to make a huge difference in their communities. Their best tool for community transformation is CharityTracker (*www.charitytracker.com*). CharityTracker makes it easy to identify needs, mobilize resources, eliminate duplicated services, collaborate with other organizations, and measure impact. Thousands of care providers in over two hundred cities use CharityTracker.

www.urbanentry.org. Urban Entry is a series of individually packaged DVDs. Each ten-to-fifteen-minute DVD addresses a particular issue, like homelessness, gentrification, racism, and suburban poverty; features bonus video material, like teaching from Robert Lupton; and offers resources, like small group Bible studies, for those who want to learn more.

The following additional websites (all active at the time of publication) can help you as you exegete your own city.

- *www.zipskinny.com*
- *www.census.gov*
- *http://factfinder.census.gov/home/saff/main.html?_lang=en*
- *www.dataplace.org*
- *www.city-data.com*
- *www.epodunk.com*
- *http://realestate.yahoo.com/neighborhoods*
- *www.neighboroo.com*

City Books

Bakke, Raymond. *A Biblical Word for an Urban World.* Valley Forge, Pa.: Board of International Ministries, American Baptist Churches in the U.S.A, 2000.

———. *A Theology As Big As the City.* Downers Grove, Ill.: InterVarsity, 1997.

Bakke, Raymond, and Jon Sharpe. *Street Signs: A New Direction in Urban Ministry.* Birmingham: New Hope, 2006.

Barth, Glenn. *The Good City.* Tallmadge, Ohio: J. D. Myers Publishing, 2010.

Bellesi, Denny, and Leesa Bellesi. *The Kingdom Assignment.* Grand Rapids, Mich.: Zondervan, 2001.

———. *The Kingdom Assignment 2.* Grand Rapids, Mich.: Zondervan, 2002.

Bernard, Daniel. *City Impact: How to Unify, Empower and Mobilize God's People to Transform Their Communities.* Grand Rapids, Mich.: Chosen, 2004.

Bishop, Bill. *The Big Sort: Why the Clustering of Like-minded America Is Tearing Us Apart.* New York: Houghton Mifflin, 2008.

Bosch, David J. *Transforming Mission: Paradigm Shifts in Theology of Mission.* Maryknoll, N.Y.: Orbis, 1996.

Boyce, James Montgomery. *Two Cities, Two Loves: Christian Responsibility in a Crumbling Culture.* Downers Grove, Ill.: InterVarsity, 1996.

Brafman, Ori, and Rod A. Beckstrom. *The Starfish and the Spider: The Unstoppable Power of Leaderless Organizations.* London: Penguin, 2006.

Butler, Phill. *Well Connected: Releasing Power, Restoring Hope through Kingdom Partnerships.* Federal Way, Wash.: Authentic, 2006.

Cahill, Thomas. *Desire of the Everlasting Hills: The World Before and After Jesus.* New York: Random House, 2001.

Campolo, Tony. *Revolution and Renewal.* Richmond, Va.: John Knox Press, 2000.

Carle, Robert D., and Louis A. Decaro Jr., eds. *Signs of Hope in the City: Ministries of Community Renewal.* Valley Forge, Pa.: Judson Press, 1999.

Carson, D. A. *Christ and Culture Revisited.* Grand Rapids, Mich.: Eerdmans, 2008.

Collins, Jim. *Good to Great and the Social Sector: A Monograph to Accompany Good to Great.* New York: Harper Collins, 2005.

Conn, Harvie M. *Evangelism: Doing Justice and Preaching Grace.* Grand Rapids, Mich.: Zondervan, 1982.

———. *The Urban Face of Mission.* Phillipsburg, N.J.: P&R, 2002.

Crocker, David W. *Operation Inasmuch: Mobilizing Believers beyond the Walls of the Church.* Danvers, Mass.: Lake Hickory Resources, 2005.

Crouch, Andy. *Culture Making: Recovering Our Creative Calling.* Downers Grove, Ill.: InterVarsity, 2008.

Cymbala, Jim. *Fresh Wind, Fresh Fire.* Grand Rapids, Mich.: Zondervan, 1997.

Dennison, Jack. *City Reaching: On the Road to Community Transformation.* Pasadena, Calif.: William Carey Library, 1999.

Drummond, Henry. *The City without a Church.* Radford, Va.: Wilder, 2008. (From an address in 1893.)

Dudley, Carl S. *Next Steps in Community Ministry.* Herndon, Va.: Alban Institute, 1996.

Elliott, Barbara. *Street Saints: Renewing America's Cities.* Radner, Pa.: Templeton Foundation Press, 2004.

Ellul, Jacques. *The Meaning of the City.* Grand Rapids, Mich.: Eerdmans, 1970.

Emerson, Michael O., and Christian Smith. *Divided by Faith: Evangelical Religion and the Problem of Race in America.* New York: Oxford Univ. Press, 2000.

Florida, Richard. *Who's Your City? How the Creative Economy Is Making Where to Live the Most Important Decision of Your Life.* New York: Basic, 2008.

Garland, Diana S., ed. *Church Social Work: Helping the Whole Person in the Context of the Church.* Botsford, Conn.: North American Christians in Social Work, 1992.

Green, Clifford J., ed. *Churches, Cities, and Human Community: Urban Ministry in the United States 1945–1985.* Grand Rapids, Mich.: Eerdmans, 1996.

Grigg, Viv. *Companion of the Poor: Christ in the Urban Slums.* Waynesboro, Ga.: Authentic Media with World Vision, 2004.

Hall, Ron, and Denver Moore with Lynn Vincent. *Same Kind of Different As Me: A Modern-Day Slave, an International Art Dealer, and the Unlikely Woman Who Bound Them Together.* Nashville: Nelson, 2006.

Harnack, Adolf. *The Expansion of Christianity in the First Three Centuries.* Vol. 1. Eugene, Ore.: Wipf and Stock, 1998.

———. *The Expansion of Christianity in the First Three Centuries.* Vol. 2. Eugene, Ore.: Wipf and Stock, 1998.

Harper, Nile. *Urban Churches, Vital Signs: Beyond Charity towards Justice.* Grand Rapids, Mich.: Eerdmans, 1998.

Haugen, Gary A. *Good News about Injustice: A Witness of Courage in a Hurting World.* Downers Grove, Ill.: InterVarsity, 1999.

Hawthorne, Steve, and Graham Kendrick. *Prayer-Walking: Praying On Site with Insight.* Lake Mary, Fla.: Charisma House, 1993.

Hugen, Beryl, ed. *Christianity and Social Work: Readings on the Integration of Christian Faith and Social Work Practice.* Botsford, Conn.: North American Association of Christians in Social Work, 1998.

Hunter, George C. *The Celtic Way of Evangelism: How Christianity Can Reach the West … Again.* Nashville: Abingdon, 2000.

Hunter, James Davison. *To Change the World: The Irony, Tragedy, and Possibility of Christianity in the Late Modern World.* New York: Oxford Univ. Press, 2010.

Hunter, Joel C. *A New Kind of Conservative.* Ventura, Calif.: Regal, 2008.

Jacobs, Jane. *The Death and Life of Great American Cities.* New York: Modern Library, 1993.

Jacobson, Eric O. *Sidewalks in the Kingdom: New Urbanism and the Christian Faith.* Grand Rapids, Mich.: Brazos, 2003.

Jones, E. Stanley. *The Unshakable Kingdom and the Unchanging Person.* Bellingham, Wash.: McNett Press, 1995.

Keller, Timothy J. *Ministries of Mercy: The Call of the Jericho Road.* Phillipsburg, N.J.: P&R, 1997.

Kinnaman, David, and Gabe Lyons. *unChristian: What a New Generation Really Thinks about Christianity . . . and Why It Matters.* Grand Rapids, Mich.: Baker, 2007.

Kotkin, Joel. *The City: A Global History.* New York. Modern Library, 1996.

Kretzmann, John P., and John L. McKnight. *Building Communities from the Inside Out.* Chicago: ACTA, 1993.

Lewis, Robert. *The Church of Irresistible Influence.* Grand Rapids, Mich.: Zondervan, 2001.

Linthicum, Robert. *City of God, City of Satan.* Grand Rapids, Mich.: Zondervan, 1991.

————. *Transforming Power: Biblical Strategies for Making a Difference in Your Community.* Downers Grove, Ill.: InterVarsity, 2003.

Lovelace, Richard F. *Dynamics of Spiritual Life: An Evangelical Theology of Renewal.* Madison, Wis.: InterVarsity, 1979.

Lupton, Robert D. *Theirs Is the Kingdom: Celebrating the Gospel in Urban America.* Edited by Barbara R. Thompson. New York: Harper Collins, 1989.

Marsh, Charles. *The Beloved Community: How Faith Shapes Social Justice, from the Civil Rights Movement to Today.* New York: Basic, 2005.

Massaro, Thomas, S.J. *Living Justice: Catholic Social Teaching in Action.* Lanham, Md.: Rowman and Littlefield, 2000.

McKinley, Rick. *Jesus in the Margins: Finding God in the Places We Ignore.* Sisters, Ore.: Multnomah, 2005.

————. *This Beautiful Mess: Practicing the Presence of the Kingdom of God.* Sisters, Ore.: Multnomah, 2006.

McNeal, Reggie. *Missional Renaissance: Changing the Scorecard for the Church.* San Francisco: Jossey-Bass, 2009.

————. *The Present Future: Six Tough Questions for the Church.* San Francisco: Jossey-Bass, 2003.

Meeks, Wayne A. *The First Urban Christians: The Social World of the Apostle Paul.* 2nd ed. New Haven and London: Yale Univ. Press, 1983.

————. *In Search of the Early Christians.* Edited by Allen R. Hilton and H. Gregory Snyder. New Haven and London: Yale Univ. Press, 2002.

————. *The Moral World of the First Christians.* Philadelphia, Pa.: Westminster Press, 1986.

Minatrea, Milfred. *Shaped by God's Heart: The Passion and Practices of Missional Churches.* San Francisco: Jossey-Bass, 2004.

Moffitt, Bob, and Karla Tesch. *If Jesus Were Mayor*. Phoenix, Ariz.: Harvest Publishing, 2004.

Mumford, Lewis. *The City in History: Its Origins, Its Transformations, and Its Prospects*. New York: Harcourt Brace, 1961.

Myers, Bryant L. *Walking with the Poor: Principles and Practices of Transformational Development*. Maryknoll, N.Y.: Orbis, 1999.

Nathan, Rich. *Who Is My Enemy? Welcoming People the Church Rejects*. Grand Rapids, Mich.: Zondervan, 2002.

Oldenburg, Ray. *The Great Good Place: Cafés, Coffee Shops, Bookstores, Bars, Hair Salons and Other Hangouts at the Heart of a Community*. New York: Marlowe, 1999.

Perkins, John. *Beyond Charity*. Grand Rapids, Mich.: Baker, 1993.

———. *Restoring At-Risk Communities: Doing It Together and Doing It Right*. Grand Rapids, Mich.: Baker, 2000.

Pier, Mac. *Spiritual Leadership in the Global City*. Birmingham: New Hope, 2008.

Pier, Mac, and Katie Sweeting. *The Power of a City at Prayer: What Happens When Churches Unite for Renewal*. Downers Grove, Ill.: InterVarsity, 2002.

Pollock, Doug. *God Space: Naturally Creating Room for Spiritual Conversations*. Loveland, Colo.: Group, 2009.

Putnam, Robert D., and Lewis M. Feldstein. *Better Together: Restoring the American Community*. New York: Simon & Schuster, 2003.

Rizzo, Dino. *Servolution: Starting a Church Revolution through Serving*. Grand Rapids, Mich.: Zondervan, 2009.

Roberts, Bob, Jr. *Glocalization: How Followers of Jesus Engage a Flat World*. Grand Rapids, Mich.: Zondervan, 2007.

Roesel, Charles. *Meeting Needs, Sharing Christ*. Nashville: Lifeway, 1995.

Roxburgh, Alan J. *The Missionary Congregation, Leadership, and Liminality*. Harrisburg, Pa.: Trinity Press, 1997.

Roxburgh, Alan, and Fred Romanuk. *The Missional Leader: Equipping Your Church to Reach a Changing World*. San Francisco: Jossey-Bass, 2006.

Rusaw, Rick, and Eric Swanson. *The Externally Focused Church*. Loveland, Colo.: Group, 2004.

Rybczynski, Witold. *City Life*. New York: Touchstone, 1996.

Sassen, Saskia. *Global Networks, Linked Cities*. New York: Routledge, 2002.

Sherman, Amy L. *Reinvigorating Faith in Communities*. Fishers, Ind.: Hudson Institute, 2002.

———. *Restorers of Hope*. Wheaton, Ill.: Crossway, 1997.

Sider, Ronald J., Philip Olson, and Heidi Roland Unruh. *Churches That Make *a Difference: Reaching Your Community with Good News and Good Works.* Grand Rapids, Mich.: Baker, 2002.

Sider, Ronald J., John M. Perkins, Wayne L. Gordon, and F. Albert Tizon. *Linking Arms, Linking Lives: How Urban-Suburban Partnerships Can Transform Communities.* Grand Rapids, Mich.: Baker, 2008.

Sider, Ronald J., and Heidi Unruh, eds. *Hope for Children in Poverty: Profiles and Possibilities.* Valley Forge, Pa.: Judson Press, 2007.

Sjogren, Steve. *101 Ways to Reach Your Community.* Colorado Springs: NavPress, 2001.

————. *Conspiracy of Kindness.* Ventura, Calif.: Servant, 1993.

Sjogren, Steve, Dave Ping, and Doug Pollock. *Irresistible Evangelism: Natural Ways to Open Others to Jesus.* Loveland, Colo.: Group, 2003.

Skjegstad, Joy. *Starting a Nonprofit at Your Church.* Herndon, Va.: Alban Institute, 2002.

Smith, David. *Mission after Christendom.* London: Darton, Longman and Todd, 2003.

Stark, Rodney. *Cities of God: The Real Story of How Christianity Became an Urban Movement and Conquered Rome.* New York: Harper Collins, 2006.

————. *The Rise of Christianity: How the Obscure, Marginal Jesus Movement Became the Dominant Religious Force in the Western World in a Few Centuries.* San Francisco: Harper Collins, 1997.

Stringer, Doug. *Somebody Cares.* Ventura, Calif.: Regal, 2001.

Swanson, Eric, and Rick Rusaw. *The Externally Focused Quest: Becoming the Best Church for the Community.* San Francisco: Jossey-Bass, 2010.

Sweney, Chip. *A New Kind of Big: How Churches of Any Size Can Partner to Transform Communities.* Grand Rapids, Mich.: Baker, 2011.

Unruh, Heidi. *Community Study Guide: Connecting with Your Church's Context for Ministry.* Available at *http://www.compassioncoalition.org/wp-content/uploads/2010/02/Community-Study-Guide-and-Tools.doc.*

Van Engen, Charles, and Jude Tiersma, eds. *God So Loves the City: Seeking a Theology for Urban Mission.* Monrovia, Calif.: Marc, 1994.

White, Randy. *Encounter God in the City: Onramps to Personal and Community Transformation.* Downers Grove, Ill.: InterVarsity, 2006.

————. *Journey to the Center of the City: Making a Difference in an Urban Neighborhood.* Downers Grove, Ill.: InterVarsity, 1996.

White, Tom. *City-wide Prayer Movements: One Church, Many Congregations.* Ann Arbor, Mich.: Vine, 2001.

Woodson, Robert L. *The Triumphs of Joseph: How Today's Community Healers Are Reviving Our Streets and Neighborhoods.* New York: Free Press, 1998.

Wright, N. T. *Simply Christian: Why Christianity Makes Sense.* San Francisco: Harper One, 2010.

————. *Surprised by Hope: Rethinking Heaven, the Resurrection, and the Mission of the Church.* San Francisco: Harper One, 2008.

NOTES

1. Robert Lewis, *The Church of Irresistible Influence* (Grand Rapids, Mich.: Zondervan, 2001).
2. Denny Bellesi and Leesa Bellesi, *The Kingdom Assignment* (Grand Rapids, Mich.: Zondervan, 2001).
3. Although this character and this setting are fictitious, the facts of the story fit the circumstances that happened that day. "Working with United Nations estimates that predict the world will be 51.3 percent urban by 2010, the researchers projected the May 23, 2007, transition day based on the average daily rural and urban population increases from 2005 to 2010. On that day, a predicted global urban population of 3,303,992,253 will exceed that of 3,303,866,404 rural people." *http://news.ncsu.edu/releases/2007/may/104.html* (accessed July 26, 2008).
4. British urbanologist David Clark names a population of fifty thousand people or less a *town* or a *village*. On the other hand, *cities* are agglomerations that have up to two hundred thousand residents. A *metropolitan area* has more than two million people, but a *megalopolis* is an urban area of over five million people. Glenn Smith, "Community Development in Canada: What Overarching System? What Type of Sustainability?" (unpublished paper), 10.
5. Spiro Kostof, *The City Shaped: Urban Patterns and Meaning through History* (New York: Bullfinch Press, 1991), 37.
6. Richard Sennett, *The Fall of Public Man* (New York: Norton, 1992), 39.
7. Ibid.
8. To learn more about the Q conference, visit *www.qideas.org.*
9. Joel Kotkin, *The City: A Global History* (New York: Modern Library, 2005), xvi.
10. We use the term *innovation* here to distinguish from *invention*, as innovations are the economic applications of inventions.
11. Eric O. Jacobsen, *Sidewalks in the Kingdom: New Urbanism and the Christian Faith* (Grand Rapids, Mich.: Brazos, 2004), 170.
12. Witold Rybczynski, *City Life* (New York: Touchstone, 1996), 42–46.
13. Ibid., 43–44.
14. Tim Keller (address, Q conference, New York City, April 10, 2008).
15. Wayne A. Meeks, *The First Urban Christians: The Social World of the Apostle Paul*, 2nd ed. (New Haven and London: Yale Univ. Press, 2003), 14, quoting Ramsey MacMullen, *Roman Social Relations* (New Haven and London: Yale Univ. Press, 1974), 15, 27.
16. Henry Drummond, *The City without a Church* (Redford, Va.: Wilder, 2008), 14–15.
17. Ibid., 41.
18. Ray Bakke and Jon Sharpe, *Street Signs: A New Direction in Urban Ministry* (Birmingham: New Hope, 2006), 84.
19. Kotkin, *The City*, xx.
20. Ibid., 21.
21. Richard Florida, *Who's Your City? How the Creative Economy Is Making Where to Live the Most Important Decision of Your Life* (New York: Basic, 2008), 61.
22. Ibid., 118–19.
23. Tim Keller, "A New Kind of Urban Christian," *Christianity Today*, May 2006, *www.christianity today.com/ct/2006/may/1.36.html* (accessed August 21, 2009).

24. Keller (Q conference, New York, 2008).

25. Lewis Mumford, *The City in History: Its Origins, Its Transformations, and Its Prospects* (New York and London: Harcourt, 1961), 109.

26. The Indian film industry produces more films and sells more tickets than any other country, but most of its influence remains in the Hindi-speaking part of the world. *http://en.wikipedia.org/wiki/Bollywood* (accessed August 21, 2009).

27. Kotkin, *The City*, 95.

28. Geoffrey B. West, "Innovation and Growth: Size Matters," *Harvard Business Review* (February 2007), 35.

29. Fareed Zakaria, *The Post-American World* (New York: Norton, 2008), 93.

30. Matt Power, "A/C Is OK," *Wired* (June 2008), 158. Power also notes in the same article that each of the nation's forty million lawn mowers spews eleven cars' worth of pollutants per hour.

31. Bakke and Sharpe, *Street Signs*, 37.

32. Rodney Stark, *Cities of God: The Real Story of How Christianity Became an Urban Movement and Conquered Rome* (New York: Harper Collins, 2006), 2.

33. Ibid., 25.

34. The process of the middle and upper classes moving back to the city is commonly referred to as "gentrification." The downside of gentrification in America is the relocation of the poor from the city centers (where most resources and public transportation are available) to the suburbs, where the poor can experience even more isolation.

35. Tim Keller, "Ministry in the New Global Culture of Major City-Centers," *The Movement* (e-newsletter of the Redeemer Church Planting Center), Spring 2006, *www.redeemer2.com/themovement/issues/2006/spring/ministry_in_globalculture_IV.html* (accessed December 4, 2008).

36. Ted Fishman, *China Inc.* (New York: Simon and Schuster, 2005), 7.

37. It is important to recognize that although millions of people choose to live in large cities because of stated reasons, many of the world's poor migrate to cities out of desperate poverty and the need to survive.

38. Fishman, *China Inc.*, 7.

39. C. K. Praalad, *The Fortune at the Bottom of the Pyramid* (Upper Saddle River, N.J.: Wharton School Publishing, 2006), 12.

40. Bakke and Sharpe, *Street Signs*, 83.

41. From an email written to Eric March 23, 2010.

42. Philip Jenkins, *The Next Christendom: The Coming of Global Christianity* (New York: Oxford Univ. Press, 2002), 93.

43. Ibid., 97.

44. Ibid.

45. Larry E. Christensen, in the foreword to a reprint of Tony Carnes, "New York's Hope," *Christianity Today* (December 2004), 33.

46. Beryl Hugen, ed., *Christianity and Social Work: Readings on the Integration of Christian Faith and Social Work Practice* (Botsford, Conn.: North American Association of Christians in Social Work, 1998), 29.

47. Ibid., 27.

48. Ibid., 30.

49. Clarence L. Barnhart and Robert K. Barnhart, eds., *The World Book Dictionary* (Chicago: World Book, 1987), 2:2221.

50. Ibid., 2:1756.

51. James McGregor Burns, *Transforming Leadership* (New York: Atlantic Monthly Press, 2003), 24.

52. Jonathan Sharpe, PowerPoint presentation emailed to author (Eric Swanson), January 17, 2005.

53. Gary Edmonds, conversation with author (Eric Swanson) at gathering of city leaders in Charlottesville, Va., sponsored by Andy Rittenhouse and Compassion Coalition, September 6–7, 2006.

54. Jack Dennison, "The Next 25 Years," PowerPoint presentation emailed to author (Eric Swanson), November 17, 2005.

55. Chennai Transformation Network, *www.ctn.org.in/* (accessed November 4, 2008).

56. Robert Moffitt, "Transformation: Dream or Reality?" *Harvest Foundation*, Evangelical Mission Quarterly, October 2005, *www.harvestfoundation.org/* (accessed November 6, 2008).

57. Francis Schaeffer, "A Christian Manifesto," *Boundless* webzine, *http://www.boundless.org/2005/articles/a0001588.cfm* (October 4, 2007). (Accessed March 14, 2010.)

58. Jim Wallace, *The Great Awakening: Reviving Faith and Politics in a Post–Religious Right America* (New York: HarperOne, 2008), 12.

59. This diagram is based on a concept by Sam Chand in an email received December 12, 2010.

60. For a more complete definition of these kinds of churches, see Rick Rusaw and Eric Swanson, *The Externally Focused Church* (Loveland, Colo.: Group, 2004).

61. Robert D. Carle and Louis A. Decaro Jr., eds., *Signs of Hope in the City: Ministries of Community Renewal* (Valley Forge, Pa.: Judson Press, 1999), 21.

62. For a further and deeper explanation, please see Rick Rusaw and Eric Swanson, *Living a Life on Loan* (Loveland, Colo.: Group, 2004), 53–69.

63. After reading this chapter, Pastor Bob Roberts of NorthWood Church in Keller, Texas, gave us a healthy pushback regarding the order of transformation. Bob's comments are so insightful that we wanted to include them here. Bob writes, "The common idea is that you see an individual transformed, then a church transformed, and then a city transformed. I disagree with that. That is exactly what the church has been all trying to do the past few decades, and I don't know where those churches are. I haven't heard that story yet, even though we keep saying that's how it happens. I see individuals transformed who wind up going to church and get stuck inside the church thinking that is where they are to live out their faith. I believe we focus on individuals being transformed—or made disciples (a disciple is the lowest common denominator of the church)—then we help them engage with society or the city to see transformation. The city is the grid on which the disciple operates, not the church. When that happens, the church emerges, and the church that emerges out of that is a church [that] has a radically different DNA. Evangelism and engagement are what that church does, not what it strives to do. It's the story of Antioch and the pattern of Acts. They didn't start churches to do evangelism or engage the city; they made disciples that transformed cities and churches emerged. Most conferences today focus on redefining the church—wrong conversation; dead-end conversation. Make disciples who engage society and you'll have one world-changing church!" (From an email from Bob March 17, 2010.)

64. David Kinnaman and Gabe Lyons, *Unchristian: What a New Generation Really Thinks about Christianity ... and Why It Matters* (Grand Rapids, Mich.: Baker, 2007), 48.

65. David Hollenbach, S.J., *The Global Face of Public Faith: Politics, Human Rights, and Christian Ethic* (Washington, D.C.: Georgetown Univ. Press, 2003), 92.

66. Christine Wicker, "Dumbfounded by Divorce," *Dallas Morning News*, 2000, *www.adherents.com/largecom/baptist_divorce.html* (accessed July 26, 2008).

67. "U.S. Abortion Statistics," *www.abort73.com/HTML/II-A-abortion_statistics.html* (accessed July 26, 2008).

68. Rich Nathan, *Who Is My Enemy?* (Grand Rapids, Mich.: Zondervan, 2002), 239, quoting *Chicago Tribune* article dated August 12, 1996. The 250,000 figure is based on the statistic that one in five women who had abortions in 1990 claimed to be born-again.

69. Ibid., 22.

70. Paul Weston, *Lesslie Newbigin: Missionary Theologian: A Reader* (Grand Rapids, Mich.: Eerdmans, 2006), 214.

71. Cal Thomas, "Religious Right, R.I.P.," *Jewish World Review*, November 6, 2008, *www.jewish worldreview.com/cols/thomas110608.php3* (accessed December 12, 2008).

72. Ben Ecklu (comments, Campus Crusade city leaders meeting in Montserrat Monastery, Barcelona, Spain, May 29, 2008).

73. I (Eric) got this wonderful expression "compassionate deeds and passionate proclamation" from Chip Scivicque of Campus Crusade for Christ in a phone conversation on November 3, 2006.

74. Amy Sherman, *Restorers of Hope* (Wheaton, Ill.: Good News/Crossway, 1997), 58.

75. This story is recorded on Joe Cross's blog, *www.crosschronicles.com/2006_10_01_archive.html* (accessed July 31, 2008).

76. Glenn Smith, Atul Aghamkar, Ashley Barker, Scott Bessenecker, John Bond, Airhart Cameron, Samuel Devemesam, et al., "Towards the Transformation of Our Cities/Regions," Lausanne Occasional Paper 37 (2004), 15 – 16, *http://www.lausanne.org/documents/2004forum/LOP37_IG8.pdf* (accessed March 26, 2010). You may also find the following websites to be helpful in defining success measures for community transformation and engagement:
    www.successmeasures.com
    www.sustainablemeasures.com
    www.urban.org/center/cnp/projects/outcomeindicators.cfm
    www.uwex.edu/ces/pdande/evaluation/evallogicmodel.html

77. It is interesting to note that the passage George Washington quoted frequently was from Micah 4, including these verses: "But they shall sit every man under his vine and under his fig tree; and none shall make them afraid: for the mouth of the Lord of hosts hath spoken it. For all people will walk every one in the name of his god, and we will walk in the name of the Lord our God for ever and ever" (vv. 4 – 5 KJV). America from the beginning was broad enough to include people of other faith traditions. "George Washington and the Old Testament," Claude Mariottini blog, May 8, 2009, *www.claudemariottini.com/blog/2009/05/george-washington-and-old-testament.html* (accessed May 10, 2009).

78. Ronald J. Sider, *Good News and Good Works: A Theology for the Whole Gospel* (Grand Rapids, Mich.: Baker, 1993), 179.

79. Robert Linthicum, *Transforming Power: Biblical Strategies for Making a Difference in Your Community* (Downers Grove, Ill.: InterVarsity Press, 2003), 75.

80. Steven Garber, "Making Peace with Proximate Justice," *Comment*, December 2007, *www.washingtoninst.org/sites/www.washingtoninst.org/files/webfm/Proximate_Justice_Comment.pdf* (accessed December 28, 2009).

81. Frank L. Lambert, "The Second Law of Thermodynamics," Occidental College, Los Angeles, *http://secondlaw.oxy.edu/two.html* (accessed August 21, 2009).

82. Rodney Stark, *The Rise of Christianity: How the Obscure, Marginal Jesus Movement Became the Dominant Religious Force in the Western World in a Few Centuries* (San Francisco: Harper Collins, 1997), 161.

83. Michael Frost and Alan Hirsh, *The Shaping of Things to Come: Innovation and Mission for the 21st-Century Church* (Peabody, Mass.: Hendrickson, 2003), 33.

84. Andy Crouch, *Culture Making: Recovering Our Creative Calling* (Madison, Wis.: InterVarsity Press, 2008), 66 – 68.

85. This is not to imply that Catholics cannot be true followers of Christ, any more than we would imply that everyone claiming the name *evangelical* is a true follower of Jesus.

86. Darrow Miller and Scott Allen, "The Power of Worldview to Shape a Nation" (unpublished paper). To explore the impact of worldview on cultural transformation in greater depth, we recommend the following: Darrow Miller with Stan Guthrie, *Discipling Nations: The Power of Truth to Transform Culture* (Seattle: YWAM, 1998), and Scott Allen, Darrow Miller, and Bob Moffitt, *The Worldview of the Kingdom of God* (Seattle: YWAM, 2005).

87. Tim Keller, *Gospel Christianity Course 1, Unit 7: What Is Jesus' Mission?* (New York: Redeemer Presbyterian Church, 2003), 4.

88. Gregory A. Boyd, *The Myth of a Christian Nation: How the Quest for Political Power Is Destroying the Church* (Grand Rapids, Mich.: Zondervan, 2005), 11.

89. Merrill F. Unger, *Unger's Bible Handbook* (Chicago: Moody Press, 1967), 383.

90. Ellie Crystal, "Roman Empire," *www.crystalinks.com/romanempire.html* (accessed August 22, 2009).

91. Arias Mortimer, *Evangelization and the Subversive Memory of Jesus: Announcing the Reign of God* (Philadelphia: Fortress, 1984), 8, quoted in Ronald J. Sider, *Good News and Good Works: A Theology for the Whole Gospel* (Grand Rapids, Mich.: Baker, 1993), 51.

92. Thomas Cahill, *Desire of the Everlasting Hills: The World Before and After Jesus* (New York: Random House, 2001), 8 – 9.

93. Ibid., 304 – 5.

94. Rodney Stark, *The Rise of Christianity: How the Obscure, Marginal Jesus Movement Became the Dominant Religious Force in the Western World in a Few Centuries* (San Francisco: Harper Collins, 1997), 6.

95. Philip Schaff, ed., *Epistle of Mathetes to Diognetus, www.ccel.org/ccel/schaff/anf01.iii.ii.v.html* (accessed January 14, 2007).

96. Adolf Harnack, *The Expansion of Christianity in the First Three Centuries* (Eugene, Ore.: Wipf and Stock, 1998), 1:189.

97. Stark, *Rise of Christianity*, 87.

98. Ibid.

99. Ibid., 6.

100. Ibid., 76 – 77.

101. Ibid., 82.

102. Ibid., 83.

103. Ibid., 84.

104. Ibid.

105. Ibid., 88.

106. Ibid., 214.

107. David Bosch, *Transforming Mission* (Maryknoll, N.Y.: Orbis, 1991), 218.

108. Cahill, *Desire of the Everlasting Hills*, 304 – 5.

109. Thomas Cahill, *How the Irish Saved Civilization* (New York: Doubleday, 1995), notes that it was the Irish who saved and preserved thousands of biblical, historical, and classic manuscripts which were used to re-educate and re-evangelize Europe after the libraries of Europe were pillaged and destroyed.

110. Mike Aquilina, "Light on the Dark Ages," *http://fathersofthechurch.com/2006/04/27/light-on-the-dark-ages/* (accessed March 12, 2007).

111. Bosch, *Transforming Mission*, 230.

112. Ibid., 232.

113. George C. Hunter, *The Celtic Way of Evangelism: How Christianity Can Reach the West . . . Again* (Nashville: Abingdon, 2000), 60.

114. Cahill, *How the Irish Saved Civilization*, 110, quoted in Hunter, *Celtic Way of Evangelism*, 23.

115. Hunter, *Celtic Way of Evangelism*, 36.

116. James J. Walsh, *The Thirteenth, Greatest of Centuries: City Hospitals — Organized Charity* (New York: Catholic Summer School Press, 1907), *www2.nd.edu/Departments/Maritain/etext/walsh-u.htm* (accessed March 12, 2007).

117. James J. Walsh, "The Middle Ages," *www.churchinhistory.org/pages/middleages/middleages.htm* (accessed March 12, 2007).

118. Thomas Massaro, S.J., *Living Justice: Catholic Social Teaching in Action* (Lanham, Md.: Rowman and Littlefield, 2000), 14–15.

119. Beryl Hugen, ed., *Christianity and Social Work: Readings on the Integration of Christian Faith and Social Work Practice* (Botsford, Conn.: North American Association of Christians in Social Work, 1998), 151.

120. James J. Walsh, *The Thirteenth, Greatest of Centuries: Francis the Saint — the Father of the Renaissance* (New York: Catholic Summer School Press, 1907), *www2.nd.edu/Departments/Maritain/etext/walsh-p.htm* (accessed March 12, 2007).

121. Bosch, *Transforming Mission*, 245.

122. David W. Hall, ed., "Earlier Paradigms for Welfare Reform: The Reformation Period," in *Welfare Reformed: A Compassionate Approach* (Phillipsburg, N.J.: Presbyterian and Reformed Publishing; Franklin, Tenn.: Legacy Communications, 1994), quoted in Bob Moffit with Karla Tesch, *If Jesus Were Mayor* (Oxford: Monarch House, 2006), 44.

123. Bosch, *Transforming Mission*, 258.

124. Ibid., 256.

125. "August Hermann Francke," *Wikipedia: http://en.wikipedia.org/wiki/August_Hermann_Francke* (accessed December 9, 2008).

126. Richard F. Lovelace, *Dynamics of Spiritual Life: An Evangelical Theology of Renewal* (Madison, Wis.: InterVarsity Press, 1979), 362.

127. Ibid., 367.

128. Chris Lowney, *Heroic Leadership: Best Practices from a 450-Year-Old Company That Changed the World*, reprint ed. (Chicago: Loyola Press, 2005), 7.

129. Ibid., 212.

130. Ibid., 247.

131. Ibid., 96.

132. Stephen Uhalley Jr. and Xiaoxin Wu, eds., *China and Christianity: Burdened Past, Hopeful Future* (Armonk, N.Y.: Sharpe, 2000), 46.

133. *www.christianhistorytimeline.com/DAILYF/2001/10/daily–10–06–2001.shtml* (December 28, 2009).

134. Uhalley and Wu, *China and Christianity*, 53.

135. Ibid.

136. Michael D. Henderson, *John Wesley's Class Meetings* (Nappanee, Ind.: Evangel, 1997), 35.

137. Ibid., 48.

138. Ibid., 50.

139. Ibid., 19.

140. Ibid., 20.

141. Ibid., 23.

142. Ibid., 71.

143. Ibid., 48.

144. Ibid., 50.

145. Lovett H. Weems, *John Wesley's Message Today* (Nashville: Abingdon, 1992), 62.

146. John Telford, "The Life of John Wesley," *http://wesley.nnu.edu/wesleyan_theology/telford/telford_ch20.htm* (accessed May 24, 2007).

147. Lovelace, *Dynamics of Spiritual Life*, 381.

148. John Wesley, "Letter to William Wilberforce," *http://gbgm-umc.org/umw/wesley/wilber.stm* (accessed May 24, 2007).

149. Bosch, *Transforming Mission*, 281.

150. Cahill, *Desire of the Everlasting Hills*, 304.

151. D. A. Carson, *Christ and Culture Revisited* (Grand Rapids, Mich.: Eerdmans, 2008), 152.

152. Jim Wallis, "A Generation Comes of Age," *Sojourners*, June 2008, *www.sojo.net/index .cfm?action=magazine.article&issue=soj0806&article=080651* (accessed August 11, 2008).

153. Ram Cnaan, Robert J. Wineburg, and Stephanie C. Boddie, *The Newer Deal: Social Work and Religion in Partnership* (New York: Columbia Univ. Press, 1999), 119.

154. C. Eric Lincoln and Lawrence H. Mamiya, *The Black Church in the African American Experience* (Durham, N.C.: Duke Univ. Press, 1996), 396.

155. Charles Marsh, *The Beloved Community: How Faith Shapes Social Justice, from the Civil Rights Movement to Today* (New York: Basic, 2005), 2.

156. Ibid., 2.

157. To be fair to Moody, we will reference a blog posting at *www.dashhouse.com/darryl/2007/10/ evangelicals_and_social_action.htm.* "Moody saw social activism just as he saw theological debate: as a distraction from evangelism. Moody cared for the poor early in his ministry. Later on, he grew frustrated that people seemed more interested in having their physical needs met. 'If I had a Bible in one hand and a loaf of bread in the other,' he wrote, 'the people always looked first at the loaf; and that was just the contrary of the order laid down in the Gospel.' Moody still cared for the poor, but he believed that evangelism was the most effective way to address social concerns."

158. Bosch, *Transforming Mission*, 318.

159. Ibid., 2.

160. *www.lausanne.org/covenant* (accessed December 28, 2009).

161. Jim Herrington (comments, GoodCities meeting with Eric Swanson, Florence, Alabama, January 8, 2009).

162. David Bosch, *Transforming Mission* (Maryknoll, N.Y.: Orbis, 1991), 248.

163. Phill Butler, "Fifteen Key Principles for Success in Kingdom Collaboration" (unpublished paper). Used with permission.

164. We are grateful to Andy and Natalie Swanson for these insights regarding John 17:20 – 23.

165. A. W. Tozer, *The Pursuit of God* (Camp Hill, Pa.: Christian, 1994), 63.

166. Jack Dennison, *City Reaching* (Pasadena: William Carey Library, 1999), 61.

167. In the summer of 2006, Leadership Network sent out surveys to approximately sixty churches who were engaged in externally focused ministry. Out of twenty-four respondents, 24 percent answered that a service project triggered collaboration with other churches, and 24 percent answered that prayer triggered their collaboration. For more details of this survey, see Krista Petty's paper "Church to Church Collaborations on the Rise," *www.leadnet.org/DownloadFile .asp* (accessed August 22, 2009).

168. Timothy C. Morgan, "After the Aloha Shirts," interview with Rick Warren, *Christianity Today* (October 2008), 44.

169. *Leadership* (Fall 2008), 25 – 26.

170. Dennison, *City Reaching*, 64.

171. Mickey Connolly and Richard Rianoshek, *The Communication Catalyst* (Chicago: Dearborne, 2002), 151.

172. Jim Tomberlin is founder, president, and senior strategist for MultiSite Solutions, which works in transformational city movements around the country.

173. Their website, *www.palau.org*, provides more details and stories of the Season of Service/Festival strategy.

174. Mark Visvasam (conversation with Eric Swanson at Montserrat Monastery, Barcelona, Spain, May 19, 2008).

175. Jaan Heinmets (comments, Montserrat Monastery, Barcelona, Spain, May 19, 2008).

176. Available at *www.ihadboulder.org/joomla/index.php?option=com_content&task=category&sectioni d=4&id=76&Itemid=108* (accessed January 15, 2010).

177. "I Have a Dream" Foundation of Boulder County, Annual Report 2008 – 9, 8.

178. Ronald J. Sider and Heidi Unruh, eds., *Hope for Children in Poverty: Profiles and Possibilities* (Valley Forge, Pa.: Judson Press, 2007), x–xi.

179. Graphic based on a similar graphic by Dr. Raymond Bakke, "Spiritual Resources for Transformational Leadership," from a class offered by Bakke Graduate University on June 10, 2002. Used with permission.

180. From an interview with Jim Tomberlin titled, "Northern Suburbs Declare 'One Church; Many Congregations,'" *http://onegreatcityblog.blogspot.com/search?updated-min=2006–01–01T00%3A00%3A00–06%3A00&updated-max=2007–01–01T00%3A00% 3A00–06%3A00&max-results=50* (accessed March 31, 2010).

181. Jim Tomberlin (email to Ray Williams, March 24, 2009).

182. N. T. Wright, *Surprised by Hope: Rethinking Heaven, the Resurrection, and the Mission of the Church* (New York: HarperCollins, 2008), 26.

183. Richard F. Lovelace, *Dynamics of Spiritual Life: An Evangelical Theology of Renewal* (Madison, Wis.: InterVarsity Press, 1979), 386.

184. Rick Rusaw and Eric Swanson, *The Externally Focused Church* (Loveland, Colo.: Group, 2004), 125.

185. For a more complete explanation, please see ibid.

186. "Religion: German Martyrs," *Time*, December 23, 1940, *http://www.time.com/time/magazine/ article/0,9171,765103,00.html* (accessed April 14, 2010). A personal letter from Albert Einstein, dated 1943, in which he comments on this quotation in *Time* was appraised in Las Vegas on August 18, 2007, on PBS's *Antiques Roadshow*, hour 2, episode 1217, which originally aired May 19, 2008, *www.pbs.org/wgbh/roadshow/archive/200706A19.html* (accessed September 9, 2008).

187. Reggie McNeal, *The Present Future: Six Tough Questions for the Church* (San Francisco: Jossey-Bass, 2003), 38.

188. Timothy Keller, *Ministries of Mercy* (Phillipsburg, N.J.: Presbyterian and Reformed, 1997), 212.

189. Viv Grigg, *Companion to the Poor: Christ in the Urban Slums* (Federal Way, Wash.: Authentic Media, 2004), 5.

190. Ibid., 154–55.

191. Ibid., 80.

192. Ibid.

193. Reggie McNeal, *Missional Renaissance: Changing the Scorecard for the Church* (San Francisco: Jossey-Bass, 2009), 24.

194. "Gray's the Color of Life: Understanding the Gray Matrix," *http://guide.gospelcom.net/resources/ gray-matrix.php* (accessed August 20, 2008).

195. For a complementary explanation of this diagram, please see Rusaw and Swanson, *Externally Focused Church*, 59.

196. Martin Luther King Jr., quoted by Jim Wallace (comments, Q conference, New York City, April 10, 2008).

197. Steve Sjogren, *Conspiracy of Kindness* (Ann Arbor, Mich.: Servant, 1993), 32.

198. David Hollenbach, S.J., *The Global Face of Public Faith: Politics, Human Rights, and Christian Ethic* (Washington, D.C.: Georgetown Univ. Press, 2003), 14.

199. Joel Kotkin, *The City: A Global History* (New York: Modern Library, 2005), xvi.

200. Timothy C. Morgan, "After the Aloha Shirts," interview with Rick Warren, *Christianity Today* (October 2008), 43.

201. Diana Wang with Talene Lee, "City Transformation in China: A Starting Point" (unpublished paper commissioned by ChinaSource).

202. This conversation was reflected in a paper available at *http://ywamcity.org/resource.asp?id=17* (accessed November 12, 2009).

203. Bob Roberts, "Power of the 'Glocal' Church," *Rev!* (September–October 2008), 138–39.

204. Rodney Stark, *Cities of God: The Real Story of How Christianity Became an Urban Movement and Conquered Rome* (New York: Harper Collins, 2006), 13.

205. To learn more about Meixia, visit *www.meixia.com/index.htm.*

206. Bruce Einhorn and Chi-Chu Tschang, "Praying for Success in Shanghai," *Business Week*, July 3, 2008, *www.businessweek.com/magazine/content/08_28/b4092087099280.htm* (accessed August 2, 2008).

207. For more information on the Power Group, see *www.powergrp.co.za/images/Press%20Releases/IHSA%20Eastern%20Cape%20Award.pdf* (accessed October 3, 2009).

208. *www.powergrp.co.za/group/group_powerways.htm* (accessed October 3, 2009).

209. *www.powergrp.co.za/group/group_charitable.htm* (accessed October 3, 2009).

210. Nathan McIntire, "Capetonians Join 500 Million People in Prayer," *Cape Times*, June 5, 2006, *www.iol.co.za/index.php?set_id=1&click_id=13&art_id=vn20060605014346318C214694* (accessed August 22, 2009).

211. *http://en.wikipedia.org/wiki/Josiah_Wedgwood* (accessed December 4, 2009).

212. *www.spartacus.schoolnet.co.uk/REwedgwood.htm* (accessed December 8, 2008).

213. Available at *www.pbs.org/now/shows/601/index.html* (accessed January 2, 2010).

214. Steven Garber, "Making Peace with Proximate Justice," *Comment*, December 2007, *www.washingtoninst.org/sites/www.washingtoninst.org/files/webfm/Proximate_Justice_Comment.pdf* (accessed January 14, 2010).

215. Steven Garber (presentation, Campus Crusade's Global Cities Leadership gathering in Mexico City, September 24, 2009).

216. Jens Erik Gould, "Venezuela Youths Transformed by Music," *BBC News*, November 28, 2005, *http://news.bbc.co.uk/2/hi/americas/4457278.stm* (accessed December 8, 2008).

217. Ibid.

218. Ibid.

219. Richard F. Lovelace, *Dynamics of Spiritual Life: An Evangelical Theology of Renewal* (Madison, Wis.: InterVarsity Press, 1979), 370.

220. Tim Keller, *Gospel Christianity Course 1, Unit 7: What Is Jesus' Mission?* (New York: Redeemer Presbyterian Church, 2003).

221. Joel Kotkin, *The City: A Global History* (New York: Modern Library, 2005), 111.

222. James Davison Hunter, "To Change the World" (speech, Denver, Colorado, June 2002), *www.ttf.org/index/findings/detail/to-change-the-world/* (accessed September 22, 2006).

223. I (Eric) am grateful for Viv Grigg's insights on the sectors of society, from a diagram titled "Transformative Revival: Generating Kingdom Movements in Society," which I found to be very perceptive.

224. Everett M. Rogers, *Diffusion of Innovations*, 4th ed. (New York: The Free Press, 1995), 261–66.6

225. Jim Collins, *Good to Great and the Social Sectors: A Monograph to Accompany Good to Great* (New York: Harper Collins, 2005), 7.

226. Ray Bakke and Jon Sharpe, *Street Signs: A New Direction in Urban Ministry* (Birmingham, Ala.: New Hope, 2006), 36. I first heard this information from Ray on June 10, 2002, at First Presbyterian Church in Seattle, in a class titled Spiritual Resources for Transformational Leadership.

227. Ray Bakke observes that walking into a grocery store will tell you as much about the people living in a community as most any other single observation. The ethnic foods, the language of the signage, the hours of operation are all informative about the neighborhood. In contrast, he says, most churches in the neighborhood have a sign out front in English that reads, "Sunday School at 9:30 and Worship at 11:00."

228. To learn more about Christian Direction, Inc., see *www.direction.ca.*

229. Kevin Lynch, *The Image of the City* (Cambridge, Mass.: MIT Press, first printing 1960; twelfth printing 1974), 47–48.

230. Ori Brafman and Rod A. Beckstrom, *The Starfish and the Spider: The Unstoppable Power of Leaderless Organizations* (London: Penguin, 2006), 98–101.

231. Leslie R. Crutchfield and Heather McLeod Grant, *Forces for Good: The Six Practices of High-Impact Nonprofits* (San Francisco: Jossey-Bass, 2008), 19.

232. Ibid., 19.

233. *www.theatlantic.com/politics/ecbig/soctrans.htm* (accessed October 12, 2009).

234. Richard F. Lovelace, *Dynamics of Spiritual Life: An Evangelical Theology of Renewal* (Madison, Wis.: InterVarsity Press, 1979), 395.

235. To learn more about Denver's Road Home, see *www.DenversRoadHome.org*.

236. *www.DenversRoadHome.org* (accessed December 29, 2009).

237. Chip Sweney (email to Eric Swanson, September 2008).

238. Robert D. Putnam and Lewis M. Feldstein, *Better Together: Restoring the American Community* (New York: Simon and Schuster, 2003), 2.

239. Robert D. Putman, "The Prosperous Community: Social Capital and Public Life," March 21, 1993, *The American Prospect: www.prospect.org/cs/articles?article=the_prosperous_community* (accessed February 4, 2006).

240. Putnam and Feldstein, *Better Together*, 269.

241. Ray Oldenburg, *The Great Good Place: Cafés, Coffee Shops, Bookstores, Bars, Hair Salons and Other Hangouts at the Heart of a Community* (New York: Marlowe, 1996), 16.

242. Putnam and Feldstein, *Better Together*, 2–3.

243. Robert D. Putnam, "The Prosperous Community: Social Capital and Public Life," *The American Prospect*, no. 13 (Spring 1993): 9.

244. At Willow Creek's 2006 Leadership Summit, U2's Bono told about raising $250 million in the first Live Aid concert to relieve hunger in Africa. This was mercy. He was compelled, however, to find out more … to dig a little deeper. He then discovered that poor African nations paid $250 million per day(!) to G8 nations in interest payments. This propelled him to ask the G8 nations to forgive billions in African debt. This was beyond mercy.

245. Available upon request from Dr. Glenn Smith at *www.direction.ca*.

Share Your Thoughts

With the Author: Your comments will be forwarded to the author when you send them to *zauthor@zondervan.com*.

With Zondervan: Submit your review of this book by writing to *zreview@zondervan.com*.

Free Online Resources at
www.zondervan.com

Zondervan AuthorTracker: Be notified whenever your favorite authors publish new books, go on tour, or post an update about what's happening in their lives at www.zondervan.com/authortracker.

Daily Bible Verses and Devotions: Enrich your life with daily Bible verses or devotions that help you start every morning focused on God. Visit www.zondervan.com/newsletters.

Free Email Publications: Sign up for newsletters on Christian living, academic resources, church ministry, fiction, children's resources, and more. Visit www.zondervan.com/newsletters.

Zondervan Bible Search: Find and compare Bible passages in a variety of translations at www.zondervanbiblesearch.com.

Other Benefits: Register yourself to receive online benefits like coupons and special offers, or to participate in research.

ZONDERVAN®

ZONDERVAN.com/
AUTHORTRACKER
follow your favorite authors